COLORADO:
A NEWCOMER'S AND
RESIDENT'S MANUAL

GW00670460

SCHOOLS, BUSINESSES, ORGANIZATIONS
This book is available at quantity discounts with bulk purchase for educational, business or sales promotional use. Contact the Publisher at:

Bradford Publishing Company
1743 Wazee Street
Denver, CO 80202
303-292-2500
marketing@bradfordpub.com
www.bradfordpub.com

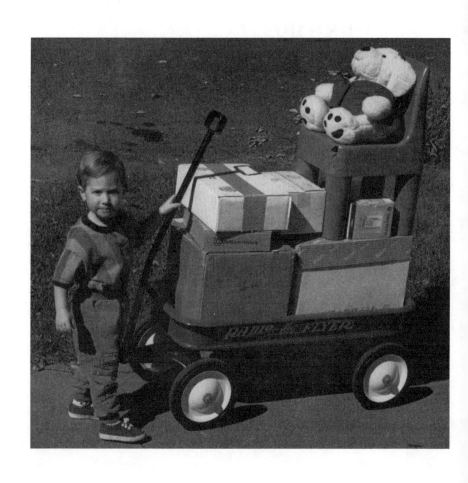

"O.K. Mom, let's head for Colorado!"

COLORADO:
A NEWCOMER'S AND RESIDENT'S MANUAL
Everything You Need to Know About
Living in Colorado

By T.J. Walker

Second Edition

Bradford Publishing Company
Denver, Colorado

COLORADO: A NEWCOMER'S AND RESIDENT'S MANUAL
Everything You Need to Know About Living in Colorado

By T.J. Walker

Published by Bradford Publishing Company, Denver, CO, U.S.A.

Copyright © 1998 by Bradford Publishing Company

Cover Design by Vango Graphics, Denver, Colorado
Edited by Rebecca Walker

Second Edition
ISBN 1-883726-11-5
Library of Congress Catalog Card Number: 95-79220

Printed and bound in the United States by Gilliland Printing

Publisher's Cataloging in Publication
(Prepared by Quality Books Inc.)

Walker, T.J., 1956-
    Colorado : a newcomer's and resident's manual : everything you need to know about living in Colorado / by T.J. Walker. -- 2st ed.
    p. cm.
    Includes bibliographical references and index.
    ISBN 1-883726-11-5

    1. Colorado--Guidebooks. 2. Colorado--Miscellanea. I. Title.

F774.3.W35 1995   978.8'033
                       QBI95-20491

ACKNOWLEDGMENTS

To my wife. For her patience, support, and encouragement.

To my sister. The first edition of this book was an incredible undertaking. Mounds of data were collected, compiled, edited, validated and typeset into a useable format. While I was the sole author of the first edition, I can not take credit for the daunting task of updating all the data for this second edition. For that, I am eternally grateful to my sister, Rebecca. She is solely responsible for the entire updating of the 200 plus pages of facts, figures, statistics, and phone numbers contained in this edition. This second edition would have never come to be without her invaluable efforts.

The information in this book was compiled from over 100 separate government, business and private resources. In every case, someone had to respond to my request for data. To list them all would require more space than is available. My thanks go to everyone who contributed and cooperated with this endeavor.

Cover Design by Vango Graphics
Edited by Rebecca Walker

Warning—Disclaimer

This book is designed to provide information about the subject matter covered. It is sold with the understanding that the publisher and author are not engaged in rendering legal, accounting or other professional services. If legal or other expert assistance is required, the services of a competent professional should be sought.

It is not the purpose of this book to reprint all the information that is otherwise available. For additional information, see the many references throughout each chapter and in Appendix A.

Every effort has been made to make this book as complete and accurate as possible. **However, there may be mistakes both typographical and in content**. This text should be used only as a general guide and not as the ultimate source of information on the subject matter covered.

The author(s) and publisher assume no responsibility for errors, inaccuracies, omissions or any other inconsistency herein. Neither shall the author(s) or publisher assume any liability to any person or entity with respect to any loss or damage caused, or alleged to be caused, directly or indirectly by the information contained in this book.

What Others Are Saying About This Book

Welcome Home Magazine

"This book can save you countless hours of frustration . . . perfect for every resident of Colorado . . . Highly recommended!"

The Denver Post

"The book ought to be part of any home reference library . . . For someone just moving here with kids, the list of all of the state school systems—public, private, college—is particularly useful. There's also advice on how to live at high altitude, the ins-and-outs of car registration, driver's licenses, insurance and emissions."

The Denver Business Journal

"Looking for answers? [This] new book has plenty! ...a reference guide for residents . . . new residents, and even natives, can experience the best of Colorado."

The Four Corners Business Journal

"T.J. Walker's compilation of lists and figures of things people need to know about living in Colorado, possibly one of the most comprehensive of its kind, can be a great resource of information for potential, recent or life-long residents."

The Ten Mile Times, Frisco, CO

"I was impressed . . . a concise, comprehensive and easy to get around book . . . The section on schools and libraries is superb. You'll be guaranteed a good time if you take off with a copy of Chapter Nine [State-Wide Recreation & Entertainment] under your arm . . . Good times are all around you and Walker can help you find them."

What Others Are Saying About This Book
(Continued from previous page)

The Loveland Reporter-Herald, Loveland, CO

". . . unsure about new homes, schools, recreation . . . What could be better than a manual that helps you deal with a new environment?"

The Cortez Sentinel

". . . an impressive amount of basic information on many aspects of our state. . . a valuable reference book for anyone living in this state—not only new immigrants."

The Crestone Eagle

". . . a timely compendium of facts and figures about the state . . . an excellent reference . . . a lot of interesting things within the covers. . . makes this state simple and easy to understand . . . it's a good investment."

The Glenwood Post, Glenwood Springs, CO

". . . a book full of helpful hints to help with just about every question a new resident could have. In fact, this useful little book will probably come in handy even for those who have called Colorado home for a number of years."

TABLE OF CONTENTS

CHAPTER ONE
Once Upon A Time In The West (Dire Straits, 1979)
The State of Colorado

CHAPTER TWO
The Powers That Be (Roger Waters, 1987)
Colorado's Government

CHAPTER THREE
School's Out Forever (Alice Cooper, 1972)

CHAPTER FOUR
This Must Be The Place (Talking Heads, 1983)

CHAPTER FIVE
Behind The Wheel (Depeche Mode, 1987)

CHAPTER SIX
Send Lawyers, Guns, And Money (Warren Zevon, 1978)

CHAPTER SEVEN
Changes in Latitudes, Changes in attitudes
(Jimmy Buffet, 1977)

CHAPTER EIGHT
Money For Nothing (Dire Straits, 1985)

CHAPTER NINE
Get Out Of Denver (Bob Seger, 1974)

CHAPTER TEN
Eight Miles High (The Byrds, 1966)

CHAPTER ELEVEN
So Far Away (Dire Straits, 1985)

CHAPTER TWELVE
New Kid In Town (The Eagles, 1976)

CHAPTER ONE
ONCE UPON A TIME IN THE WEST

THE STATE OF COLORADO
Facts At A Glance
History
Geography/Topography
Weather

The information in this chapter was compiled from various sources including, but not limited to, government reports and publications (Federal, State, and Local); materials provided by business and civic organizations; and books produced by independent Colorado publishers including:

A Colorado History, Seventh Edition, Pruett Publishing Company
Ancient Walls, Fulcrum Publishing
Colorado, A History of the Centennial State, University Press of Colorado
Denver, Mining Camps to Metropolis, University Press of Colorado
Leadville's Ice Palace, Ice Castle Productions
The Archaeology of Colorado, Johnson Books
The Four Corners Anasazi, Johnson Books

For a complete description of the above books and related titles, please see the Publisher's listing in Appendix A.

I moved to Colorado more than a decade ago. I fell in love with the breathtaking beauty of the mountains and the easy-going manner of the people I met while visiting my sister who had moved here exactly one year before me. To this day, the new sights, sounds, smells, and discoveries the state freely offers on a seemingly unlimited basis amaze me. Also, to this day, I still have to ask my wife or sister where this town or that city is located, how to dress for mountain ventures or about the history of a pile of sawdust that used to be a mining town.

I never bothered to learn much about this state. Trying to put a limit on the number of facts, figures, data, maps, and stories I seem to constantly cram into my head, I acquired new knowledge about Colorado only on a need-to-know basis. Being a self-employed entrepreneur, I quickly learned almost everything about conducting business here. Yet, before researching the material for this book, I couldn't tell you much about Colorado's history (weren't there cowboys and Indians here?), geography (the mountains are West of Denver), weather (it can rain in December and snow in July), unique laws (you can be fined 3 times the amount of a bad check), or high-altitude living (things just don't cook the same this high up).

In fact, while gathering information for this chapter from other Colorado publishers, one asked me if I planned to include a section on the state's pre-history. My first thought was "If something is *pre*-history, how do we know anything about it?" Allowing for the non-literal meaning of the word, I soon discovered this state has a very rich and interesting *pre*-history. Moving forward from there, I found the modern, high school type of history (which previously bored me to tears) to be full of wonderment. Since completing this chapter, I can proudly say "I know about the cliff dwellings in Mesa Verde, I know the location of Montrose, I know Colorado gets an average of 300 days of sunshine a year, and I can even tell you Colorado has 35 registered motorcycles per 1,000 residents!"

All that being said, I still have this thing for learning a new subject in two stages. First, I want to see the bare-bones facts. Statistics that give me an outline understanding. Then, at my leisure, I go back and fill in the blanks with dialog, prose and explanations. In keeping with this tradition, the first section of this chapter contains some bare-bone facts about Colorado, followed by some fascinating lessons on the pre-history, modern history, geography, topography, and weather of the most beautiful state in the country.

COLORADO FACTS AT A GLANCE

Please Note: All demographic information about population is the most current available. However, Colorado's incredible growth since the 1990 census should be considered when evaluating this data.

PEOPLE OF COLORADO

POPULATION, 1990: 3,294,394; 1994: 3,655,647
PROJECTED POPULATION, YEAR 2000: 4,813,000
POPULATION DENSITY, 1990: 31.76 persons per sq mile
POPULATION, 1980-1990: +14.0% change
POPULATION OVER 18 YEARS, 1990: 2,433,128
POPULATION UNDER 18 YEARS, 1990: 861,266
POPULATION 65 YEARS OLD AND OVER: 9%

Lark Bunting

ASIAN/PACIFIC ISLANDER POPULATION, 1990: 59,862
ASIAN/PACIFIC ISLANDER POPULATION RATE: 1.82%
BLACK POPULATION, 1990: 133,146
BLACK POPULATION RATE, 1990: 4.04%
HISPANIC POPULATION, 1990: 424,302
HISPANIC POPULATION RATE, 1990: 12.88%
NATIVE AMERICAN POPULATION, 1990: 27,776
NATIVE AMERICAN POPULATION RATE, 1990: 0.84%
WHITE POPULATION, 1990: 2,905,474
WHITE POPULATION RATE, 1990: 88.19%

Bighorn Sheep

METROPOLITAN AREA POPULATION: 81.7%
METROPOLITAN AREA POPULATION, 1980-1990: 15.5% change
HOUSING UNITS, 1990: 1,477,349
HOUSEHOLDS, 1990: 1,282,000
HOUSEHOLDS, 1980-1990: 20.8% change
BIRTH RATE: 16.30 per 1,000 population
BIRTHS TO TEENAGE MOTHERS: 10.20% of total

Cutthroat Trout

BIRTHS TO UNMARRIED WOMEN: 18.9% of total
LIFE EXPECTANCY, BOTH SEXES: 75.30 years
LIFE EXPECTANCY, FEMALE: 78.80 years
LIFE EXPECTANCY, MALE: 71.78 years
DEATH RATE: 6.4 deaths per 1,000 population
MARRIAGE RATE: 9.6 marriages per 1,000 population
DIVORCE RATE: 5.7 divorces per 1,000 population
VIETNAM VETERANS: 155,000

Stegosaurus

GEOGRAPHY IN COLORADO

TOTAL AREA: 104,091 square miles

LAND AREA: 103,595 square miles
WATER AREA: 496 square miles
AVERAGE ELEVATION: 6,600 feet
HIGHEST POINT: Mt. Elbert, 14,433 feet
LOWEST POINT: Arkansas River, 3,350 feet
HIGHEST TEMPERATURE: 118 degrees Fahrenheit
LOWEST TEMPERATURE: -61 degrees Fahrenheit
NATURAL RESOURCES: Petroleum, natural gas, coal
LAND IN NATIONAL PARKS: 588,200 acres
AREA IN STATE PARKS: 5,455,000 acres
FEDERAL LANDS: 36.2% owned by federal government
HAZARDOUS WASTE SITES: 16 sites on national priority list

EDUCATION IN COLORADO

EXPENDITURES FOR PUBLIC SCHOOLS: $787 per resident
PUBLIC SCHOOL EXPENDITURES: $4,633 per pupil
PUPIL/TEACHER RATIO: 19.08 pupils per teacher
SPENDING, PUBLIC HIGHER EDUCATION: $2,780 per student
TUITION REVENUES, HIGHER EDUCATION: $1,883 per student
COLLEGE ENROLLMENT, TOTAL: 184,000 students

GOVERNMENT OF COLORADO

OFFICIAL NAME: State of Colorado
CAPITAL: Denver
ADMITTED TO UNION: Aug. 1, 1876
ORDER OF STATEHOOD: 38
ELECTORAL VOTES: 8
EXECUTIVE TERM: 4 years

State Flag

GOVERNOR: Roy Romer (D)
SENATORS: Wayne Allard (R), Ben Nighthorse Campbell (R)
NUMBER OF U.S. REPRESENTATIVES: 6
FLAG: Three alternating horizontal stripes of blue, white and blue with a large red C containing a gold disk in the center.
MOTTO: Nil Sine Numine (Nothing without providence)
SYMBOLS:
Animal: Rocky Mountain Bighorn Sheep
Bird: Lark Bunting
Flower: White and lavender columbine
Gem: Aquamarine
Song: Where the Columbines Grow
Tree: Blue Spruce

State Seal

AGE OF BUYING ALCOHOL: 21
AGE OF LEAVING SCHOOL: after age 16
AGE OF MAJORITY (FULL CIVIL RIGHTS): 18
AGE OF MARRIAGE WITH CONSENT: 16
AGE OF MARRIAGE WITHOUT CONSENT: 18
DISTRIBUTION OF FEDERAL FUNDS: $3,943 per capita
FEDERAL EMPLOYEES, CIVILIAN: 52,000
FEDERAL INCOME TAXES PAID: $1,483 per capita
FEDERAL SPENDING, DEFENSE PROGRAMS: $4,616,000,000
STATE GOVERNMENT EXPENDITURES: $1,430 per capita
STATE FUNDING FOR ART: $0.40 per capita

ECONOMY OF COLORADO
As of 1994:
INCOME PER CAPITA: $23,961
GROSS STATE PRODUCT, TOTAL: $ 82,463,000,000
GROSS STATE PRODUCT, AGRICULTURAL: $1,660,000,000
GROSS STATE PRODUCT, CONSTRUCTION: $3,787,000,000
GROSS STATE PRODUCT, FINANCE: $13,957,000,000
GROSS STATE PRODUCT, GOVERNMENT: $ 11,89,000,000
GROSS STATE PRODUCT, MANUFACTURING: $10,318,000,000
GROSS STATE PRODUCT, MINING: $1,185,000,000
GROSS STATE PRODUCT, RETAIL TRADE: $8,472,000,000
GROSS STATE PRODUCT, SERVICES: $17,634,000,000
GROSS STATE PRODUCT, TRANSPORTATION: $8,330,000,000
GROSS STATE PRODUCT, WHOLESALE TRADE: $5,214,000,000

COMMUNICATIONS IN COLORADO

COMMERCIAL TELEVISION STATIONS: 13
EDUCATIONAL TELEVISION STATIONS: 3
COMMERCIAL AM RADIO STATIONS: 77
COMMERCIAL FM RADIO STATIONS: 68
EDUCATIONAL FM RADIO STATIONS: 20
DAILY NEWSPAPERS: 26

Columbine

TRAVEL IN COLORADO

INTERSTATE HIGHWAYS: 942 miles
REGISTERED AUTOMOBILES: 675 per 1,000 population
REGISTERED MOTORCYCLES: 35 per 1,000 population

PRE-HISTORY OF COLORADO

In the beginning was the Word, or maybe the Big-Bang, or perhaps both (maybe the sound of the Big-Bang was the Word). Regardless, we can jump ahead a few billion years to only 300 million years ago. This was the time of the Ancestral Rockies, a vast mountain range which was eventually washed away and became part of a great ocean. Fossil evidence of this can be found near the town of Lyons in deposits of sandstone that provided material for Denver's sidewalks as the city grew. Shells of billions of sea creatures turned into the Colorado limestone used to produce concrete for many of the state's highways and buildings.

Between the Ancestral Rockies and the beginnings of the modern Rockies (about 70 million years ago), what would become Colorado was home to such dinosaurs as the bony-backed stegosaurus, the three-horned triceratops, and the 85-foot long diplodocus. In fact, Colorado has produced some of the richest fossil finds in the country. Also, during this time period, much of this region was swampland, leaving behind debris that would eventually become vast deposits of coal and natural gas. Volcanoes were not uncommon and their lava flows created many geological features of Colorado including the Table Mountains near Golden.

Skipping ahead to more recent pre-history, we can look at the nomadic tribes of the first Americans who lived here for more than 10,000 years before the first frontier city was built.

At one site, 40 miles north of Denver, artifacts have been carbon-dated to at least 11,250 years ago. Artifacts dating back over 10,000 years have also been found in another site 25 miles southeast of Denver. The origin of the first humans in the southwest is still debated; however, it is generally agreed that some 15-20 thousand years ago, nomadic hunters followed herds of prey across a temporary land bridge which is now the Bering Strait between Alaska and Siberia. Dependent on traveling with their food source, these Asian visitors eventually migrated south. As these tribes evolved from nomadic hunters into agricultural farmers, they laid down roots in places such as Mesa Verde, Colorado, some 2,000 years ago.

Mesa Verde is located in Four Corners, the place where Arizona, Colorado, New Mexico, and Utah meet. This entire area was home to early tribes collectively known as the Anasazi. During the thirteenth century the Anasazi numbered more than 50,000. Yet a half-century later there were none. They didn't die out, their descendants still live in New Mexico and Arizona. For some unknown reason, they simply abandoned the area. We are not talking about leaving some tents or caves here. By the thirteenth century, Mesa Verde was filled with over 500 cliff dwellings, from one-room houses to large

6

communal structures three or four stories high containing more than 200 rooms.

Between the 14th and 19th centuries, other more familiar tribes including the Ute, Comanche, Navajo, Apache, Kiowa and Shoshoni inhabited Colorado. Numerous wars and slaughters took place between various tribes, the Spanish, French and finally "American" pioneers. This really becoming reminiscent of high school history class so I believe it's time to move on. For those closet archaeologists, great delight will be found in several of the books mentioned at the beginning of this chapter. A couple are coffee table books, full of fantastic full-color photos of ancient ruins and, while the others may not be able to compete with a rainbow, they are loaded with B/W photos and unlimited details about every major archaeological site in Colorado. See Appendix A for details.

MODERN HISTORY

After the end of the Mexican/American War in 1848, farmers from New Mexico settled large portions of Colorado. This slow migration and settlement increased dramatically with the discovery of gold. Virtually all the older towns and cities of Colorado have their origins in mining and prospecting. In 1858, the Green-Russel party found gold along Little Dry Creek near the junction of the South Platte River and Cherry Creek. Exaggerated accounts of the discovery spread eastward, causing the Pikes Peak Gold Rush of 1859. Thousands of fortune hunters hurried across the plains on foot, on horseback, and in wagons. Most of these failed to find any gold and trudged wearily back home. But they had founded several little clusters of huts, known as Montana City, St. Charles, Auraria, and Denver City (named after General James W. Denver, territorial governor of Kansas); and these gradually grew into the capital city of Colorado.

On May 6, 1859, John H. Gregory discovered the Gregory Lode, a vein of gold-bearing quartz, near present-day Central City. Mines were quickly developed on the branches of Clear Creek, in South Park, and across the Continental Divide on the branches of the Blue River.

In 1859 the land that later became Colorado was within the territories of Kansas, Nebraska, Utah, and New Mexico. But the pioneers felt they should have a government of their own, so they created the Jefferson Territory, containing all of present-day Colorado and liberal strips of what is now Utah and Wyoming. Many of the miners ignored the authority of this territorial government and established local laws of their own, electing officials to enforce them.

On February 28, 1861, a law was signed creating the Colorado Territory. William Gilpin, appointed by President Lincoln, was the first governor. The territory was named for the river that rises in Grand Lake and flows through rugged chasms and fertile valleys to the great depths of the Grand Canyon and finally to the Pacific Ocean. (Other rivers rising in Colorado are the Rio Grande, Gunnison, Yampa, White, San Juan, Dolores, Arkansas, Republican, South Platte, and North Platte).

During the first decade following the Pikes Peak gold rush, Colorado's development was slow. Refractory ore (difficult to extract, process, and transport) was encountered in the mines. The Civil War claimed citizens for soldiers, and Indian resistance threatened the existence of the territory.

After surviving the ordeals of early years, Colorado made rapid progress in her second decade as a territory. Railways were completed to Colorado in 1870, narrow-gauge rail lines in the mountains tapped the mining regions, colony towns were founded, agriculture was extended, new mines were opened in the San Juan region and immigration escalated.

In 1864, Congress passed an Enabling Act to permit Colorado to become a state. However, the people voted against it because they did not want to pay the taxes needed to support a state government. Finally, more than ten years later, Colorado entered the Union as the 38th state on August 1, 1876, and was called the "Centennial State" in honor of the 100th anniversary of the Declaration of Independence.

During the 1880s progress continued on a grand scale. Mineral wealth poured forth from Aspen and other mining centers such as Leadville. Many other towns flourished, colleges and opera houses were built, and brownstone mansions rather than log cabins became representative of the times. Agriculture expanded with the construction of irrigation systems and the introduction of dry farming. The range livestock industry prospered. Wood production soared. Smelters were erected for the reduction of ores. Although the Panic of 1893 (which followed a devaluation of silver) was a severe blow to the mining industry, Colorado rallied. The great gold camp at Cripple Creek aided revival. Farming continued to expand, and new crops such as sugar beets created new wealth. By 1890, Colorado claimed a population exceeding 413,000.

The city of Leadville, mentioned above, was also home to one of the most unique human-made structures. Built in 1895, Leadville's Ice Palace was constructed by approximately 300 craftsmen in less than 60 days. The main building materials were 8,000 tons of ice and 307,000 board feet of lumber. When completed, this crystal castle housed a skating rink, ballroom, banquet room, riding gallery, lounges, a kitchen and more. It covered over 5 acres, was electrically lit and heated by coal burning stoves. If you are fond of quirky little pieces of history, get a copy of *Leadville's Ice Palace* by Ice Castle Productions. Weighing in at 391 pages, this fascinating book is the definitive work on the bizarre project one city used in an attempt to boost its economy (maybe another book is due about Denver International Airport?). See Appendix A for more information on *Leadville's Ice Palace* and also a book entitled *Tales, Trails and Tommyknockers* by Johnson Books. The latter is a great Colorado history book for children.

This brings us up to the beginning of the 20th century. Since the turn of the century, historically significant events have been multiplying in geometric proportions. The great depression, World Wars I & II, the Korean War, the civil rights movement, more wars, on and on. To describe Colorado's involvement in all these events would take much more space than can be allotted in this book. If you are interested in more recent history, please check the Additional Resources section of this chapter or the books listed in Appendix A.

COLORADO'S GEOGRAPHY/TOPOGRAPHY

Colorado is the eighth largest state in the nation, with an area of 104,247 square miles and with over 35% of this area owned by the federal government. The state is rectangular, extending 387 miles east to west and 276 miles north to south.

The main feature of the state's geography is the Continental Divide, extending Northeast to Southwest and roughly bisecting Colorado into the Eastern and Western Slopes. Waters west of the Divide flow into the Pacific, east of the Divide into the Atlantic. The major rivers are the Arkansas, Platte, Rio Grande and Colorado. The state's largest natural lake is Grand Lake which human enterprise has outdone with projects like the John Martin Reservoir on the Arkansas River and Blue Mesa Reservoir on the Gunnison River.

Colorado contains 75% of all the area in the United States over 10,000' high. It contains 53 peaks of more than 14,000' with the highest being Mt. Elbert at 14,433', and over one thousand peaks two miles high. In fact, the mountainous area of Colorado is six times that of Switzerland. Three of the nation's highest highways are in Colorado. The roads to the summits of both Pikes Peak and Mt. Evans are over 14,000' above sea-level and Trail Ridge Road, which crosses through Rocky Mountain National Park and over the Continental Divided at 12,183', is the nation's highest continuous paved highway. The principal mountain ranges are the eastern Front Range, the central Sawatch Range, the Park range in the north, the southern Sangre de Cristo Mountains and the San Juan Mountains in the southwest.

Plateaus, mesas, and canyons make up the western 25% of the state with high plains bordering Wyoming, Nebraska, Kansas, Oklahoma and New Mexico being 40% of the state to the east. Sloping upward from Kansas, Colorado's central plains gently rise approximately 2,000' from 3,386' to 5,200' above sea-level.

Colorado has two national parks, six national monuments, 12 national forests, 43 state parks, three national recreation areas, and 16 hazardous waste sites on the national priority list.

Colorado's 63 counties are divided into five informal sub-state regions (see map in Appendix B):

Front Range	Adams, Arapahoe, Boulder, Denver, Douglas, El Paso, Jefferson, Larimer, Pueblo, Weld
Western Slope	Archuleta, Delta, Dolores, Eagle, Garfield, Grand, Gunnison, Hinsdale, Jackson, La Plata, Mesa, Moffat, Montezuma, Montrose, Ouray, Pitkin, Rio Blanco, Routt, San Juan, San Miguel, Summit
Eastern Plains	Baca, Bent, Cheyenne, Crowley, Elbert, Kiowa, Kit Carson, Lincoln, Logan, Morgan, Otero, Phillips, Prowers, Sedgwick, Washington, Yuma
San Luis Valley	Alamosa, Conejos, Costilla, Mineral, Rio Grande, Saguache
Eastern Mountains	Chaffee, Clear Creek, Custer, Fremont, Gilpin, Huerfano, Lake, Las Animas, Park, Teller

COLORADO'S WEATHER

Unpredictable, unbelievable, unanticipated calm, chaotic, implausible, improbable, beautiful, nasty, wonderful, violent, serene, ominous, threatening, and blissful are a few of the ways I can describe Colorado's weather.

Having grown-up in Florida, I experienced my share of violent thunderstorms and hurricanes. However, not until I moved to Colorado did I experience a real-life use of the Emergency Broadcast System. I was driving around Denver, listening to one of my favorite songs, when that nasty, high-pitched tone did its job and startled me back into reality. The clouds had been looking ominous but I had not seen any rain, lightening or thunder. The tone was followed by reports of three tornadoes over the area with one touching down and ripping a path along one of Denver's parkways less than a mile from my location. Being a closet thrill-seeker, I stopped my van and climbed on top to watch the show until I realized one mile is not exactly a safe distance from a fast moving, totally unpredictable tornado.

On another occasion, during a morning hike outside of Breckenridge, I experienced bright sunshine, sleet, rain, snow, and more sunshine followed by a heavy misty fog, all before lunch! Fortunately, I had been in Colorado long enough to know to pack the right clothes.

The reason I share these stories is that although I will cover the "for the tourist" descriptions of our weather, such descriptions don't relay the whole story. They consist of basic highs, lows, and averages but don't convey the extreme changes. Every year there are news stories of inexperienced hikers being rescued from snow storms dressed in shorts and T-shirts. After all, it was 90 degrees in the city when they left for the mountains. If you look in a guide or tour book or break open an encyclopedia, this is basically what you will find about Colorado's weather.

Colorado enjoys an average of nearly 300 days of sunshine per year, with an average humidity of 33%. Precipitation varies with respect to elevation and location of a given area. This can range from 60" per year on the western slopes to 16" or less on the Great Plains and the Colorado Plateau. Rainfall is concentrated in the spring and summer and the plains are subject to heavy winter snowfalls. The annual average temperature (Fahrenheit) ranges from about 51° on the plains to less than 36° in the mountains. The state's recorded high was 118° in 1888 while in 1985 the lowest recorded temperature was -61°. During cold months, Colorado's front range occasionally experiences Chinooks—fast moving (up to 100 mph), warm winds—which can cause local temperatures to rise as much as 50° in a matter of hours. First snows may occur as early as September with the last as late as July or August. At lower elevations, winters are fairly mild and snow seldom stays on the ground more than a few days under the warm, bright sun.

WEATHER/POLLUTION INFORMATION NUMBERS

Clean Air Hotline	(303) 758-4848
Wood Burning Hotline	(303) 692-3280
Smoking Vehicle Hotline	(303) 777-0517
Public Transit	(303) 299-6000
Air Quality Information	(303) 782-0211
Carpools	(303) 458-7665

For a more rounded, complete picture of Colorado's weather; see the section on high-altitude gardening in chapter ten. What follows is a month-by-month account of interesting weather facts provided by Mike Nelson of KUSA 9News and Nolan J. Doesken of the Department of Atmospheric Science, Colordo State University.

January: Colorado's coldest New Year's day occurred in 1979. A morning temperature of -60° was reported at Maybell.

February: A remarkable "Fog Storm," February 5-15, 1978 covered much of eastern Colorado. Rime ice several inches thick broke miles of power lines across the region.

March: A massive blizzard over northeast Colorado, March 10-11, 1977. Snow piled into 25' high drifts, killed thousands of cattle and resulted in the deaths of nine people.

April: A remarkably strong cold front crossed Colorado on Easter Sunday, April 19, 1987. Afternoon temperatures along the Front Range were in the 80's. By evening it was snowing with Denver receiving 3".

May: A late spring snowstorm dumped 27.8" of snow in Fort Collins within a two day period. Comparable amounts fell in Boulder with larger totals in the foothills.

June: June is Colorado's severe weather month with an average of 15 tornadoes and 46 damaging hailstorms. On June 6, 1990, a tornado ripped through the town of Limon. Good warnings prevented loss of life although the town itself was almost wiped out.

July: A brutal hailstorm ravaged an area from Estes Park to Colorado Springs on July 11, 1990. In 3 hours, the storm caused more than $600 million in damages to cars and homes.

August: Denver's all time record high reached 105° on August 8, 1878. Denver's high temperature on August 10, 1968 only reached 58°.

September: An early Front Range snowstorm September 16-18, 1971 dropped 1-2' of snow from Fort Collins to Pueblo. Millions of dollars of damage occurred from broken tree branches. In repeat performance, another early snowstorm hit the Front Range on September 20, 1995. Over 80% of all the trees in Denver were damaged.

October: Following a very mild autumn, a severe cold wave killed thousands of trees over eastern Colorado. Denver's high temperature on October 30, 1991 was only 21°.

November: A snowstorm that deposited 20-50" of snow over most of eastern Colorado from November 2-6, 1946 was responsible for at 13 deaths

December: The worst and most widespread heavy snow to hit the Colorado Front Range occurred between December 1-5, 1913. 46" of snow fell in Denver and 86" at Georgetown. Many roofs collapsed and locomotives were stranded.

CHAPTER TWO
THE POWERS THAT BE

COLORADO'S GOVERNMENT

Colorado's Political Process
State Government Departments and Agencies

The information in this chapter was compiled from various sources including, but not limited to, government reports and publications (Federal, State, and Local); materials provided by business and civic organizations; and books produced by independent Colorado publishers including:

Colorado: The State We're In, Revised Edition 1995, League of Women
    Voters of Colorado
The Colorado General Assembly, University Press of Colorado
For a complete description of the above books and related titles, please see the Publisher's listing in Appendix A.

As a citizen of Colorado you are guaranteed the right of access to your government. The State's constitution reads "All elections shall be free and open; and no power, civil or military, shall at any time interfere to prevent the right of suffrage." Of course, this is tempered by the old saying "You can't fight city hall." Either way, you have pre-defined rights and responsibilities as a citizen. This chapter is designed to give you a better understanding of how the state government functions and, more important, who is responsible for what and how to contact them.

COLORADO'S POLITICAL PROCESS
THE VOTING PROCESS
VOTER REGISTRATION
The qualifications to become a registered voter in Colorado are:

- 18 years of age by Election Day

- United States citizenship

- Address of residence within a given precinct for 30 days by Election Day. A citizen who will reach 18 or become a U.S. Citizen during the 30 days prior to the election must register before the 30 days in order to vote

A yearly function, voter registration is the responsibility of the election commission or county clerk. Both operate during normal business hours and can designate additional sites for registration (shopping malls, grocery stores, etc.) during the weeks preceding an election. If qualified, you can register up to, and including 30 days before an election. If you have moved or changed your legal address since the last election, you must register the change at any location where voter registrations are completed.

In 1984, Colorado voters passed an initiative known as the Motor Voter which allows you to register at all offices where driver's licenses are issued. In addition, in 1992, a law was passed which allows a registrar at each high school to register qualified high school students.

EARLY VOTING
You may vote in person at a place designated by the county clerk up to 24 days before any election and no later than the Friday prior to the election. Every county must provide a polling place for Early Voting.

MAIL-IN VOTING
After January 1 of any election year, you may obtain an application for a mail-in ballot. This option is available the entire year up to the Friday immediately preceding the election.

ELECTION DAY
This section explains what elections are held in what years. Don't worry if it seems terribly confusing—television, radio, and printed ads provide more than enough information about the issues prior to any election.

General Elections are held on the Tuesday succeeding the first Monday of November in even-numbered years. National and state offices are decided by this election and there may also be ballot issues. Since 1993, initiatives or

14

referenda concerning fiscal matters may be on the ballots of the Statewide Election held in November in odd-numbered years.

The November General Election is held every fourth year and coincides with the Presidential Election. Colorado's Presidential Election is held on the first Tuesday of March during Presidential Primary Election years. Voters choose their candidates for president and vice-president in the party in which they are affiliated. They also select a slate of delegates to their party's national convention who are committed to support the candidates who win the Presidential Primary Election.

The Regular State Primary Election is on the second Tuesday of August in even-numbered years. Those who have party affiliation decide contested races within the party. This is the final nomination of the candidate who will represent the party. Only those who have declared a choice of party may vote in the Primary Election. However, any unaffiliated voter may declare a party affiliation at the polling place.

THE VOTING PROCESS ON ELECTION DAY

Each precinct has its own polling place, usually located in public places such as schools, fire stations, churches, or other buildings open to the public. To insure each voter has complete information or to offer assistance, election judges staff each polling place.

The polls are open from 7 a.m. to 7 p.m. The polls are not declared closed until all that were in line at 7 p.m. have voted. Precinct results are reported to the county clerk or the election commission and the final report is sent to the Secretary of State.

The League of Women Voters provides nonpartisan information for the public to encourage all that have registered to be informed voters. In addition, a 1994 law requires the nonpartisan research staff of the General Assembly to prepare a ballot information booklet on any initiated or referred constitutional amendment or legislation. This booklet includes the text and title of each measure and a fair and impartial analysis of each measure that includes a summary and the major pros and cons of each issue. The booklet is distributed at no charge to registered voters statewide at least 30 days before the election.

INITIATIVES AND REFERENDUMS

In 1910, Colorado adopted the process of direct legislation by Initiative and Referendum to amend either the state constitution or the Colorado Revised Statutes. These types of ballot proposals have two different forms.

Initiative is the process by which a proposal by citizens who have circulated petitions and gathered the required number of signatures (five percent of the number of votes cast for the secretary of state in the previous election) is placed on the General Election ballot.

A referendum is a proposal passed by a two-thirds of the General Assembly, and then placed on the ballot for popular vote. Citizens may initiate a referendum to repeal a law passed by the General Assembly.

INITIATIVES

There are seven steps that must be complete before an initiative can be placed on the ballot.

- The proponents must prepare a proposal or statement of the issue.

- The Legislative Council and the Office of Legislative Legal Services must review the proposal. A public meeting must follow and the proposal can be resubmitted after any changes.

- Representatives of the Secretary of State, Attorney General and the Office of Legislative Legal Services must conduct a Title Setting Hearing. This hearing is open to the public with testimony by both proponents and opponents allowed. Challenges must be made within seven days.

- The complete text of the proposal must be made available to the media and the public.

- The proponents are provided an approved petition format that they use to have petitions printed and circulated for signatures.

- The circulators of such petitions must be registered voters who may be paid for their work. The number of valid signatures required is covered above and has been approximately 50,000 for the past several years. A 6-month window is granted for the circulation and all petitions must be returned to the secretary of state at least three months before the election.

- The Secretary of State has a verification and challenge period of 30 days after the deadline to verify if a sufficient number of the signatures are valid. A fifteen days cure period is granted the proponents if the number of signatures is ruled insufficient. However, the entire process must be complete no later than three months before the election.

If approved by the Secretary of State, the proposal is given a ballot issue number and appears on the ballot for the November election. The ballot issue must receive a majority of votes in order to be approved.

THE BRANCHES OF GOVERNMENT

The U.S. Constitution established three branches of Federal Government with a balance of power. Colorado went a step further when they provided for a vote of the people on issues referred by the General Assembly. Although described only briefly herein, a complete understanding of the General Assembly's functions and history can be found in the book *The Colorado General Assembly* mentioned at the beginning of this chapter. Below is a brief description and breakdown of the three branches of Colorado's State Government.

THE EXECUTIVE BRANCH

The Executive Branch encompasses the offices of state elected officials and administrative departments that conduct state business. In 1970, the state constitution was amended to limit the number of executive departments to 20.

THE GOVERNOR OF COLORADO

(Roy Romer, Democrat, re-elected in 1994)

The Governor is the head of the Executive Branch. The voters elect the Governor, Lieutenant Governor, Secretary of State, Treasurer, and Attorney General for terms of four years each. Article IV, Section 2 of the state constitution gives the Governor supreme executive power to take care that the laws be faithfully executed.

One of the major powers of this office is the right to appoint approximately 400 judges, heads of departments, board members and commissioners. The Governor also has the power to veto bills passed by the General Assembly and has line item veto of items in the state budget. Also under the control of the Governor's Office are the Office of State Planning and Budgeting, the Office of Energy Conservation, the Office of Business Development, the International Trade Office and the Colorado Office of Space Advocacy.

The Governor's Cabinet consists of the four other elected officials mentioned above and the heads of the state departments. Included by invitation at cabinet meetings are the commissioners of Education and Higher Education.

THE LIEUTENANT GOVERNOR

(Gail Schoettler, Democrat, elected 1994)

The Lieutenant Governor is always elected as a package deal with the Governor and would automatically become Governor should the office be vacated.

The Commission on Indian Affairs falls under the control of this office and provides services and coordinates relations between the Tribal Governments and the State.

THE SECRETARY OF STATE—THE DEPARTMENT OF STATE

(Victoria Buckley, Republican, elected 1994)

The Secretary of State administers and enforces the laws and codes concerning elections, registration of licenses and incorporation, and also reports political campaign funding.

Additional offices under the Department of State include the Corporations Division, Licensing Division, Administrative Division, and the Elections Division.

THE STATE TREASURER—THE DEPARTMENT OF THE TREASURY

(Bill Owen, Republican, elected 1994)

This office has three main divisions. The Accounting Division reviews all state bank accounts. The Investment Division is responsible for the safe and profitable investment of state moneys. The Unclaimed Property Program attempts to locate owners of dormant funds. If the owners cannot be found, the moneys go into the state general fund.

THE ATTORNEY GENERAL—THE DEPARTMENT OF LAW

(Gail Norton, Republican, elected 1994)

Charged with protecting the people by enforcing laws concerned with consumer fraud, anti-trust, and consumer credit, the Attorney General acts as the state's lawyer. The Department of Law is the administrative arm of the Attorney General who acts as its executive director. State agencies and the General Assembly receive legal services from Assistant Attorneys General. They also represent the state in liability cases, review state contracts, and prepare legal opinions. The Attorney General represents the state's interest in state and federal courts.

THE JUDICIAL BRANCH

The Judicial Branch was created to ensure the balance between individual rights and the powers of the state government. Its major function is to protect the rights of individuals as it interprets and applies the laws.

THE FUNCTION OF THE COURTS

Colorado courts are empowered to resolve conflicts in both criminal and civil matters. Civil cases can include disputes over wills, contracts, personal injuries or family law matters. The Colorado Criminal Code and the Colorado Rules of Procedure govern procedures in a criminal case. A district attorney files criminal charges. A grand jury can hand down an indictment based on probable cause, but this procedure is seldom used in a criminal case.

SMALL CLAIMS COURT

The Small Claims Court is a division of the County Court. Civil matters involving no more than $5,000.00 are argued in this court without attorneys. Both day and evening sessions are available. *Winning Big in Colorado Small Claims Court* by Charles Brackney is an excellent resource about using the small claims court.

MUNICIPAL COURTS

Municipal Courts handle violations of city laws committed within city limits. This includes offenses of traffic laws, shoplifting (under $300), disturbing the peace, and other petty violations. Any decision of a Municipal Court can be appealed to a State Court. A defendant has the right to a jury trial in this court.

COUNTY COURTS

These courts handle traffic violations, minor criminal offenses and civil actions involving no more than $10,000. Denver is somewhat different because it is both a city and a county (one of a kind in Colorado). The County Court functions as a municipal as well as a County Court and is funded entirely by Denver taxes and fines paid by offenders. Denver also has the only separate Juvenile Court and a separate Probate Court. These types of cases are handled by the district courts in the rest of the state.

DISTRICT COURTS

District courts are organized into 22 judicial districts. There may be more than one district judge who may serve more than one county in their district. A district court decision may be appealed to the Colorado Court of Appeals or the Colorado Supreme Court.

WATER COURT

This is a division of the District Court. A district judge from within the water district is appointed by the State Supreme Court to preside over cases concerning water rights or the uses of water resources. There are no juries in this court but decisions can be appealed to the Colorado Supreme Court.

THE COURT OF APPEALS

The Court of Appeals serves to hear appeals to decisions in civil and criminal cases. There are 16 judges and their decisions are final unless the Colorado Supreme Court agrees to review a case.

THE COLORADO SUPREME COURT

A decision by this court is final and case reviews are not guaranteed. This court is headed by the Chief Justice who is selected by the seven judges of the court from its own membership. The Chief Justice also serves as the executive head of the Judicial Branch of the state government.

Duties of the Chief Justice include the supervision of all other State Courts and the attorneys who practice law in Colorado. There are four committees that handle the administrative duties of the Colorado Supreme Court.

The State Board of Law Examiners reviews the educational, professional, ethical, and moral qualifications of people who apply for licenses to practice law in Colorado.

The Grievance Committee, composed of 15 attorneys and 4 civilians, investigates all complaints about attorneys. The committee has the power to recommend an attorney be censured or suspended, or that his or her license be revoked.

The Public Defender Commission appoints the state Public Defender, who then appoints assistants in regional offices to serve all the state courts. In mental health cases, a Public Defender may be appointed as *guardian ad litem* to represent the person in a single lawsuit.

The State Court Administrator is responsible for managing court personnel, finances, data processing, research and other responsibilities under the supervision of the Chief Justice.

BECOMING A JUDGE

In 1966, the voters of Colorado approved an initiative that allows state judges to be appointed rather than elected. When a vacancy in any state court occurs, a judicial nominating commission interviews applicants and recommends several to the governor for consideration. The governor appoints the judge for a provisional term of two years.

Judges retained by the voters serve the remaining years of the term to which they have been appointed. Upon completion of their term, they may submit their names for retention in the General Election. In this manner, voters have the opportunity to decide whether or not the performance of a judge merits continuation on the bench. Terms of judges are different for each jurisdiction. A county judge serves for four years, a district judge for six years, an appeals court judge for eight years, and a Supreme Court justice for ten years. The only exception to this is Denver. Again, being the only city-county, a vacancy is filled by appointment of the mayor from a list of three candidates recommended by the Denver County Court Nominating Commission. The mayor of Denver also has the authority to dismiss a judge when there is sufficient cause.

JURIES

Every citizen of Colorado is subject to summons for jury duty if they meet the following qualifications:

- Citizen of the United States
- At least 18 years of age

- Resident of the county
- Able to read, speak and understand the English Language
- Not currently imprisoned for a felony conviction

Jury summonses are issued at random from a database of the names of registered voters and those who hold a Colorado driver's license. Jurors in Colorado now serve for only one day or one trial in any calendar year. Employers must pay employed jurors their regular wages for the first three days of a trial and then the state pays $50 per day thereafter. Being summoned to jury duty does not necessarily mean you will serve. However, in the city and county of Denver you can plan on spending the entire day waiting around to find out if you're needed or not.

THE LEGISLATIVE BRANCH

The General Assembly, with its Senate and House of Representatives, is the heart of the Legislative Branch. The organizational structure, functions, responsibilities, and level of funding for the Executive Branch are determined by the General Assembly. In conjunction with the Executive Branch, the Joint Budget Committee develops the state budget which, after modifications, is approved by the General Assembly. Laws passed by the General Assembly also define the responsibilities of the judicial system.

THE LEGISLATORS

The General Assembly has 100 legislators, 35 in the Senate and 65 in the House. Voters in each legislative district elect their representatives to the General Assembly in the General Election. Representatives serve two-year terms and senators serve four-year terms with half up for re-election at each General Election. Members of the General Assembly are given immunity from arrest except for treason or a felony.

THE LEGISLATIVE COUNCIL

The council is responsible for computerized legislative research and establishes a data bank on state resources, programs, and expenditures. The council is headed by the majority leader of the Senate and the Speaker of the House who serve *ex officio,* with eight senators and eight representatives serving as the council. The council staffs reference, interim, and statutory committees which include economists who forecast state revenue and costs and prepare fiscal notes estimating the cost of legislation.

THE LEGISLATIVE COMMITTEES

COMMITTEE ON LEGAL SERVICES

This committee includes the chairs of House and Senate Committees on Judiciary, four members of the House, two from each major political party, and four members from the Senate, two from each party. This committee supervises the operation of the Office of Legislative Legal Services, which consists of lawyers, technical experts, and clerical personnel who are responsible for drafting all bills, resolutions, and memorials introduced in the General Assembly.

LEGISLATIVE AUDIT COMMITTEE

Members of the General Assembly vote on the selection of a State Auditor who must be a Certified Public Accountant. This official is appointed for a five-year term. The eight-member committee oversees the review of audits of financial transactions and accounts, performance audits, and management studies of all state agencies. The committee consists of two senators from each party and two representatives from each party.

CAPITAL DEVELOPMENT COMMITTEE

This committee was created in 1985 to deal with long-range planning to meet the capital requirements of the state government. It studies capital construction needs and the maintenance requests of state agencies. It also holds public hearings, determines priorities for proposals and makes recommendations to the General Assembly.

SUNRISE AND SUNSET REVIEW COMMITTEE

The House and Senate Majority leadership appoints six or more legislators to serve on the Sunrise and Sunset Review Committee, which conducts studies of state boards and commissions and may recommend their termination.

The Sunset Law provides that agencies that no longer serve a purpose shall be terminated. When an occupational group requests state regulation, such as licensing, the committee may recommend it be provided—a sunrise.

THE JOINT BUDGET COMMITTEE

This committee reviews the fiscal needs and management of all state agencies and institutions, holds hearings on budget requests, estimates tax revenues, reviews the state's fiscal structure, and prepares the annual budget.

COMMITTEES OF REFERENCE

These committees have been formed to review proposed legislation and make recommendations to the entire legislative body. A Legislative Council member who prepares a report of the discussions and decisions is on the staff of each committee. These reports are available to the public. The Senate and House have ten separate committees of reference.

As bills are introduced, they are given a number. Bills introduced to the Senate begin each session with the number SB1. In the House they begin with HB 1001. A prefix is added to identify the year of introduction, such as HB 97-1001. These committees also handle concurrent resolutions, joint resolutions, memorials and tributes.

STATE DEPARTMENTS AND AGENCIES

This section provides information about the responsibilities and points of contact for every department and agency of the state government.

COLORADO STATE GOVERNMENT

GENERAL INFORMATION: (303) 866-5000

GOVERNOR'S OFFICE

200 E. Colfax, Room 136, Denver, CO 80203-1792
ADVOCATE CONTACT: (303) 866-2885   FAX: (303) 866-4824
MAIN OFFICE: (303) 866-2471   FAX: (303) 866-2003

DEPARTMENT OF AGRICULTURE

700 Kipling St., No. 4000, Lakewood. CO 80215-5894
MAIN OFFICE: (303) 239-4100   FAX: (303) 239-4125
RESPONSIBILITIES:
- Pesticide use (agricultural and residential)
- Livestock brand inspection
- Weights and measures certification
- Animal welfare (neglect and cruelty), rodent and predator control

DEPARTMENT OF CORRECTIONS

2862 S. Circle Drive, No. 400, Colorado Springs, CO 80906
MAIN OFFICE: (719) 579-9580
RESPONSIBILITIES:
- Prisons and parole supervision
- Transitional community correction
- Victim Notification Program

OTHER NUMBERS:
Parole Board: (719) 546-0141   FAX: (719) 540-0363

DEPARTMENT OF EDUCATION

201 E. Colfax Avenue, Denver, CO 80203
MAIN OFFICE: (303) 866-6600   FAX: (303) 830-0793
RESPONSIBILITIES:
- K-12 standards and assessments
- State Board of Education
- Teacher and administrator licensing
- School for the Deaf and the Blind
- State library services and Charter schools

OTHER NUMBERS:
Educator licensing: (303) 866-6628

Special Services Office: (303) 866-6782
Colorado School for the Deaf and Blind: (303) 534-7386
Colorado State Library: (303) 866-6900

DEPARTMENT OF HEALTH CARE

POLICY AND FINANCING
State Social Services Building, 1575 Sherman St., Denver, CO 80203
MAIN OFFICE: (303) 866-2993   FAX: (303) 866-4411
RESPONSIBILITIES:
* Health Care Reform and Medicaid
* Health Data Commission

DEPARTMENT OF HIGHER EDUCATION

First contact the individual college or university.
If the problem is not resolved, contact the Department of Higher Education.
Colorado History Museum Building
1300 Broadway, Second Floor, Denver, CO 80203
MAIN OFFICE: (303) 866-2723   FAX: (303) 860-9750

DEPARTMENT OF HUMAN SERVICES

(Formerly Departments of Social Services and Institutions)
State Social Services Building, 1575 Sherman St., Denver, CO 80203-1714
MAIN OFFICE: (303) 866-5700   FAX: (303) 866-4740
RESPONSIBILITIES:
* Public assistance (AFDC, Food Stamps, AND, OAP, LEAP)
* Medicaid eligibility and services for the elderly
* Protection of dependent adults
* Vocational rehabilitation services
* Child protection, social services to families and foster care
* Child care assistance
* Child support enforcement
* State mental institutions/mental health
* Developmentally disabled services
* Juvenile delinquency
* Alcohol and drug abuse services

OTHER NUMBERS:
Low-Income Energy Assistance (LEAP): (303) 866-5970
Governor's Council on Housing and the Homeless: (303) 762-4457
Division of Youth Corrections: (303) 762-4695
Child Support Enforcement: (303) 866-5994
Division of Child Care: (303) 866-5958
Mental Health Services: (303) 762-4088
Alcohol and Drug Abuse: (303) 692-2930

DEPARTMENT OF LABOR AND EMPLOYMENT

1515 Arapahoe Street, Denver, CO 80202
MAIN OFFICE: (303) 620-4718 FAX: (303) 620-4714
RESPONSIBILITIES:
* Labor standards
* Unemployment insurance
* Workers' compensation
* Job services

DEPARTMENT OF LOCAL AFFAIRS

Centennial Building, 1313 Sherman St., Room 323, Denver, CO 80203
MAIN OFFICE: (303) 866-2771 FAX: (303)866-251
RESPONSIBILITIES:
* Property tax administration/appeals
* Financial and technical assistance to local governments
* Rural job training
* Disaster response
* State housing development programs

OTHER NUMBERS:
Division of Property Taxation: (303) 866-4000
Motion Picture & Television Commission: (303) 620-4500

DEPARTMENT OF MILITARY AFFAIRS

6848 S. Revere Parkway, Englewood, CO 80112
MAIN OFFICE: (303) 397-3000 FAX: (303) 397-3003
RESPONSIBILITIES:
* Army and Air National Guard, Civil Air Patrol

DEPARTMENT OF NATURAL RESOURCES

Centennial Building, 1313 Sherman St., No. 718, Denver, CO 80203
MAIN OFFICE: (303) 866-3311 FAX: 9303) 866-2115
RESPONSIBILITIES:
* Mining, energy development and geology
* Parks and recreation, wildlife management
* Water supply, storage and management
* Soil and water conservation, state land management

OTHER NUMBERS:
Division of Wildlife: (303) 297-1192

DEPARTMENT OF PERSONNEL

Centennial Building, 1313 Sherman St.. No. 122, Denver, CO 80203
MAIN OFFICE: (303) 866-2321

RESPONSIBILITIES:
- State employment, testing and recruitment
- Classification and pay, including Fair Labor
- Standards Act for state employment
- Equal Employment Opportunity/Affirmative
- Action for state employment
- State employee benefits

DEPARTMENT OF PUBLIC HEALTH AND ENVIRONMENT

(Formerly Department of Health)
4300 Cherry Creek Drive S., Denver, CO 80222-1530
ADVOCATE CONTACT: (303) 692-2035
MAIN OFFICE: (303) 692-2000   FAX: (303) 782-0095
RESPONSIBILITIES:
- Environmental permits and regulations
- Water supply safety
- Air quality and landfill monitoring
- Food sanitation and product safety
- Disease monitoring
- Women, infant and children (WIC) nutrition program
- Family planning and prenatal care
- Immunizations and home health care
- Programs for children with special needs
- Emergency medical services/trauma

OTHER NUMBERS:
Vital Records: (303) 756-4464
Air Pollution Control Division: (303) 692-3100
Consumer Protection Division: (303) 692-3620
Disease Control: (303) 692-2700
Emergency Medical Services: (303) 692-2980
Hazardous Materials/Waste Management: (303) 692-3300

DEPARTMENT OF PUBLIC SAFETY

700 Kipling St, Lakewood. CO 80215
MAIN OFFICE: (303) 239-4400   FAX: (303) 239-4506
OTHER NUMBERS:
State Patrol: (303) 239-4500
Division of Fire Safety: (303) 239-4463
Division of Criminal Justice: (303) 239-4442

DEPARTMENT OF REGULATORY AGENCIES (DORA)

Civic Center Plaza, 1560 Broadway, No. 1550, Denver, CO 80202
MAIN OFFICE: (303) 894-7854   FAX: (303) 894-7885

RESPONSIBILITIES:
- Licensed occupations (doctors, dentists, plumbers, etc.)
- Insurance issues
- Real estate and investment issues
- Discrimination issues

For a complete breakdown of this department and all Regulatory Agencies and responsibilities, see the DORA section that follows.

DEPARTMENT OF REVENUE

State Capitol Annex, 1375 Sherman St., No. 404, Denver, CO 80261
MAIN OFFICE: (303) 866-3091   FAX: (303) 866-2400
*TDD NUMBER: (303) 866-4353
RESPONSIBILITIES:
- State Sales Tax and Income Tax
- Driver's Licensing
- Colorado Lottery
- Limited Stakes Gaming and Regulation
- Horse and Dog Racing Regulation
- Liquor License Enforcement

OTHER NUMBERS:
Income Tax Information: (303) 232-2446
Income Tax Forms: (303) 232-2414
Trade Name Registration Information: (303) 232-2434
Income Tax Refund Inquiries: (303) 232-2438
Liquor Enforcement Division: (303) 205-2300
Motor Vehicle Division: (303) 205-5652
Driver Licensing: (303) 534-1230
Emissions: (303) 205-5603
Gaming Division: (303) 205-1300
Sales Tax and Estate Tax Information: (303) 232-2416

DEPARTMENT OF TRANSPORTATION

4201 E. Arkansas Ave., No. 277, Denver, CO 80222
MAIN OFFICE: (303) 757-9011
*TDD NUMBER: (303) 757-9087
RESPONSIBILITIES:
- Construction and maintenance of state highways
- Long and short range planning for state transportation
- Coordination and implementation of transportation safety programs, including combating drunken driving
- Support aviation interests, safety, and maintenance needs of airports
- Assisting with alternate modes of transportation, such as public transit in rural areas, bicycle and pedestrian safety programs

OTHER NUMBERS:
Statewide highway conditions: (303) 639-1234
Metro highway conditions (within 2 driving hours of Denver): (303) 639-1111
Metro Denver road and highway construction information: (303) 573-7623

DORA

The Colorado Department of Regulatory Agencies (DORA) consists of nine different divisions and several support offices. The major purpose of DORA is to regulate businesses and individuals when the state legislature believes such regulation is necessary for the protection of Colorado citizens. Below is a brief description of the support offices, divisions and the boards that regulate professions and occupations that require licensing.

OFFICE OF THE EXECUTIVE DIRECTOR

1560 Broadway, Suite 1550, Denver, CO 80202, (303) 894-7850
The Executive Director is responsible for the overall management of the Department and its divisions. The Executive Director appoints Division Directors (with the exception of Insurance and Public Utilities Commissioners who are appointed by the Governor). The Governor makes appointments to boards and commissions and the Executive Director plays a significant role in recommending the names of people for those appointments. The Executive Director presents the Department budget to the Joint Budget Committee, and initiates and recommends legislation affecting the Department.

The Executive Director gives advice to the general assembly and the general public on questions relating to the role of the state in regulating professions and occupations.

OFFICE OF CONSUMER COUNSEL

1580 Logan Street, Suite 610, Denver, CO 80203, (303) 894-2121
The Office of Consumer Counsel (OCC) represents the interests of residential, small business and agricultural consumers before the Public Utilities Commission, certain federal agencies (such as the FCC), and in the courts on appeal. The OCC is Colorado's consumer advocate in electric, gas and telecommunications utility-rate and rule-making matters. The office represents consumers by participating in complex utility cases. The OCC examines the technical evidence filed by the utility, provides expert testimony on consumers' behalf, cross-examines other witnesses, makes legal arguments, and represents consumers in settlement negotiations. Approximately 40 other states have utility consumer advocate offices similar to the OCC.

The OCC has a staff of technical and administrative personnel as well as legal representation through the Department of Law. In addition, a statutorily authorized board appointed by the governor gives policy guidance to the OCC.

The eleven-member board is appointed to represent the public interest and, specifically, the interests of residential, small business, and agricultural utility consumers. Board members come from all geographic areas of the state.

The office is funded by an assessment on the state's regulated utilities. Since utility companies pass this cost on to their customers, ratepayers fund the office. Each Colorado consumer pays about five cents per month in combined utility bills to fund the OCC. The Office of Consumer Counsel helps consumers by lowering or eliminating utility rate increases and by ensuring that utility rates, regulations and policies are more equitable for residential, small business and agricultural consumers. The OCC is charged with representing the small consumer before the PUC, but is prohibited by statute from representing individuals in complaints with utilities. Instead, the PUC is staffed to resolve individual complaints. The OCC is interested in individual complaints when they show a pattern of rate or service problems the office believes should be addressed.

OFFICE OF POLICY AND RESEARCH

1560 Broadway, Suite 1550, Denver, CO 80202, (303) 894-7848
OPR is the research arm of the Executive Director of DORA. It prepares 'sunrise' and 'sunset' reports. DORA is required to evaluate both the need for regulation of different occupational groups seeking state regulation and the need for and effectiveness of existing regulatory agencies and functions which are scheduled for termination. The director of OPR coordinates the research and evaluation effort and the Executive Director submits DORA's findings and recommendations to the Legislature. Final reports are on file in the Executive Director's office and are available to the public. Interested members of the public who wish to provide input on agencies subject to sunset or sunrise evaluations should contact the director.

OFFICE OF REGULATORY REFORM

1560 Broadway, Suite 1530, Denver, CO 80202, (303) 894-7839
The Office of Regulatory Reform (ORR), established by the legislature in 1981, is the only state office in Colorado offering one-stop information on all federal, state and local permit, license and regulatory requirements for starting a new business or expanding an existing business. ORR holds public hearings throughout the state to receive comments from business owners about regulations and to help identify areas of duplicative, burdensome and unnecessary requirements. ORR administers the Regulatory Flexibility Act and reviews proposed state agency rules to be certain they do not adversely affect small business.

In 1992, ORR was designated to serve as the Ombudsman for small businesses as part of the Colorado Clean Air Act. ORR is responsible for representing

29

small business interests in the formulation of rules and regulations, investigating and facilitating resolution of complaints and disputes concerning the permit process and encouraging the participation of small businesses in the regulatory process.

An advisory council advises ORR on small business issues. The council members are recommended by small business organizations and chambers of commerce and are appointed by the director of ORR.

Free publications available from ORR include:

Colorado Business Start-Up Kit, containing application forms for state sales tax license, trade name registration, workers' compensation, and state and federal withholding accounts along with information about how to start a business.

Small Business Information Guide, explaining the functions of ORR.

How to Do Business with the State of Colorado, explaining the state's purchasing process.

Small Business News, a quarterly publication explaining state programs regulating or assisting small businesses.

Minority and Women Business Enterprise Certification, a pamphlet explaining the certification process and answering basic questions.

Disadvantaged Business Certification (DBE): ORR also offers the Disadvantaged Business Enterprise (DBE) certification program. The office of Certification conducts certifications for the Colorado Department of Transportation, Regional Transportation District and the Denver Board of Water Commissions. A business must be owned and controlled by women and minorities to be certified.

DIVISION OF ADMINISTRATIVE SERVICES

1560 Broadway, Suite 1550, Denver, CO 80202, (303) 894-7855

The Division of Administrative Services provides services to the department in the areas of planning, budget and fiscal management, payroll and data processing and personnel. The Division provides centralized support in the above areas to all divisions in the Department and also coordinates record management and space planning for the Department. The Division also completes special projects as assigned by the Executive Director, and is responsible for implementation of the Americans with Disabilities Act.

The personnel section serves as a liaison between employees in the Department and the State Department of Personnel. The staff addresses employee questions and concerns about personnel policies and procedures, and advises employees about job advancement and job enhancement opportunities in state government.

The Division serves as the liaison between the Department and the State Controller, State Archives, State Treasurer, State Department of Personnel, the Office of State Planning and Budgeting, and the Joint Budget Committee staff.

DIVISION OF BANKING

1560 Broadway, Suite 1175, Denver, CO 80202, (303) 894-7575
The Division of Banking is responsible for the regulation of state-chartered commercial banks, trust companies, and industrial banks and of money order companies and debt management companies. The Division holds charter and license application hearings and issues rules and regulations affecting institutions and licenses. The Division works closely with the Federal Reserve Bank and the FDIC in the regulation of commercial banks and industrial banks and certain federally insured trust companies.

Activities include chartering and licensing financial institutions, performing examinations, supervising operations, and closing state chartered banks, industrial banks, and trust companies when necessary. Also, the Division is responsible for the enforcement of the Public Deposit Protection Act, to protect public entity deposits held by state and national banks.

There is an eight-member banking board that is the policy and rule making authority for the Division. The board conducts monthly meetings and the public is encouraged to attend these meetings. Board members are appointed for four-year terms.

DIVISION OF CIVIL RIGHTS

1560 Broadway, Suite 1050, Denver, CO 80202, (303) 894-2997
The Civil Rights Division is a state agency established in 1957 to administer and enforce Colorado civil rights laws in employment, housing and public accommodations. The Division works with federal agencies, such as the Equal Employment Opportunity Commission (EEOC) and the Department of Housing and Urban Development (HUD), and with local human rights agencies. Colorado civil rights laws prohibit discrimination in employment, housing, and public accommodations on the basis of race, sex, national origin, ancestry, physical or mental handicap, creed, color or marital status (housing and public accommodations only). Discrimination based on age and marriage to a coworker in employment is also prohibited.

The Colorado Civil Rights Commission is a seven member bipartisan panel appointed by the Governor. The Commission members are selected from across the State to serve four-year terms. Two members represent the business community, two represent state or local government entities, and three are from the community at large. At least four commissioners must be from groups who have been or might be discriminated against because of handicap, race, creed, color, sex, national origin or ancestry, marital status, religion or age. The Commission meets monthly to formulate policy and to hear appeals in discrimination cases. The public may attend such meetings.

DIVISION OF FINANCIAL SERVICES

1560 Broadway, Suite 1520, Denver, CO 80202, (303) 894-2336

The Division of Financial Services regulates state-chartered savings and loan associations, credit unions, life care institutions, and small business development credit corporations. It also administers the public deposit protection program that covers all uninsured governmental unit deposits in state and federal savings and loan associations.

The Division operates under the policy-making and rule-making authority of the Financial Services Board. The Financial Services Board issues rules and regulations governing the industries regulated by the Division, may delegate many of its authorities to the Commissioner, and hears appeals of actions taken by the Commissioner under delegated authority.

The Division is empowered to approve applications to incorporate new state-chartered savings and loan associations, approve branch office applications for existing associations, approve mergers between associations, and approve changes of ownership.

State-chartered credit unions operate under the supervision of the Division. The Division is empowered to approve applications to incorporate new state credit unions and to approve mergers between credit unions. State credit unions are subject to periodic examination by the Division staff.

The Division regulates certain financial activities of life care institutions, which provide long-term residence and care for the elderly. The Division may initiate enforcement action against violations of the law by life care providers.

The Division is empowered to consider applications for licensure of, grant licenses to, and periodically examine small business development credit corporations, which are designed to provide a variety of financing options to small businesses.

The Division also handles consumer complaints and information requests regarding the industries it regulates and has available, at a nominal cost, the annual *"Financial Report on Colorado State Chartered Savings and Loan Associations and Credit Unions"* as well as copies of the statute and regulations for the industries it regulates.

DIVISION OF INSURANCE

1560 Broadway, Suite 850, Denver, CO 80202, (303) 894-7499

The Division of Insurance has responsibility for the regulation of approximately 1800 insurance companies doing business in Colorado. Entities regulated by the Division include traditional insurance companies such as auto, health and workers' compensation carriers, as well as pre-need funeral companies, bail bond companies, fraternal benefit societies, captive organizations and self-insurance pools.

The Division's consumer protection mission includes:
- Resolving consumer complaints against insurers
- Monitoring companies for financial solvency and law compliance
- Licensing agents and brokers
- Investigating illegal activities.

PUBLIC UTILITIES COMMISSION

1580 Logan Street, Office Level 2, Denver, CO 80203, (303) 894-2000
The Public Utilities Commission achieves a regulatory environment that provides safe and reliable utility services to all on just and reliable terms. The Commission strives to assure that the public receives utility services at affordable prices. It also assures that utilities have the opportunity to receive a reasonable return on their investments. This return on investments allows Colorado utilities to obtain the necessary funds to build new facilities or to upgrade existing ones.

The Commission regulates investor-owned electric, gas, telephone, and water utilities, transportation companies, and some electric cooperatives. Municipal utilities are not regulated except for wholesale activities. Over the past few years, some types of telecommunications services and products and some types of transportation carriers have been deregulated.

The Commission holds public hearings to consider rate change requests by large public utilities such as Public Service Company and US West Communications, as well as rate change requests by smaller utility companies.

The Commission has established safety regulations and permit requirements for common and contract carriers, and has established safety regulations for the transportation of hazardous materials.

Commission consumer affairs specialists work to resolve complaints against regulated utilities and provide general information about utilities and the Commission. The Commission publishes many consumer brochures that are available to the public free of charge.

DIVISION OF REAL ESTATE

1776 Logan Street, 4th Floor, Denver, CO 80203 (303) 894-2166
The Division of Real Estate regulates real estate salespersons and brokers through licensure and discipline. Licensees must comply with established educational and experience requirements, and pass a test prior to licensure. The Division regulates earnest money deposits and escrow and trust funds.

The Division administers the real estate recovery fund, which can be used by persons to recover sums lost because of the actions of a licensee. Persons who obtain a final judgment against a broker or salespersons can regain their actual loss suffered in a transaction up to $15,000 per claimant and up to $50,000 in the aggregate against any one licensee.

The Division regulates all time-share projects sold in Colorado, and regulates developers of subdivisions consisting of 10 or more residential sites, tracts or lots.

A five-member Commission meets monthly to conduct rule making hearings, make policy decisions, consider licensing matters, review complaints and take disciplinary action against licensees. Commission members serve three-year terms, and members are appointed as follows: three real estate brokers, one person with expertise in subdivision development, and one public member.

The Division also regulates real estate appraisers pursuant to the requirements of the federal Real Estate Appraisal Reform Amendments of the Financial Institutions Reform, Recovery, and Enforcement Act of 1989. The Board of Real Estate appraisers consists of seven members appointed by the Governor: four licensed or certified appraisers, one of whom must have expertise in eminent domain, a county assessor, an officer or employee of a commercial bank experienced in real estate lending, and one public member.

DIVISION OF REGISTRATIONS

1560 Broadway, Suite 1300, Denver, CO 80202, (303) 894-7690
The Division of Registrations includes most of the professional and occupational licensing boards in Colorado. These boards have been created by the Colorado legislature to protect the public from unqualified and incompetent practitioners. Boards typically are empowered to determine the qualifications necessary to obtain a license; regulate the standards of conduct for the profession; review complaints against licensees; and take disciplinary action as they determine necessary. Boards can suspend or revoke licenses, but they cannot order a licensed individual to refund money or perform repairs.

Most of the boards in the Division meet on a monthly basis, and the public is invited to attend board meetings. For information on the time and location of a particular board meeting, contact the administrator for that board at the telephone number listed.

Although each board handles the disciplinary proceedings against its licensees, the Division has established a centralized complaint process for all the boards. When complaints are received, they are ordinarily assigned to an investigator who notifies the licensee that a complaint has been filed against him and asks him to respond by letter, stating his side of the story. An investigation is then initiated to try to determine the facts of the situation. Staff of the Complaints and Investigations Section (894-7690) can answer general questions about the investigative process or specific questions about the status of the case.

The Division has available a brochure entitled *"A Guide for Filing Consumer Complaints Against Licensed Professions and Occupations."* It also publishes a brochure for licensees entitled *"Questions and Answers Concerning the Complaint Against Your License."*

BOARD OF ACCOUNTANCY

(303) 894-7800

The Board regulates the profession of certified public accountants, both individuals and public accounting firms. The practice of public accounting includes issuance of reports on financial statements, management advisory or consulting services, preparation of tax returns, and furnishing advice on tax matters.

ACUPUNCTURISTS REGISTRATION

(303) 894-2440

The Division registers individuals providing acupuncture services, described as the insertion of needles into the human body by piercing the skin of the body at specific locations based on traditional oriental concepts of evaluation and treatment. The Division also registers individuals in training who are under the direct supervision of a registered acupuncturist.

BOARD OF EXAMINERS OF ARCHITECTS

(303) 894-7800

The Board licenses persons to practice architecture which means the planning and design of buildings, preparation of construction contract documents, observation of construction as agreed upon, and administration of construction contracts for the construction, but not the performance, of buildings.

BOARD OF BARBERS AND COSMETOLOGISTS

(303) 894-7772

The Board licenses barbers, cosmetologists, cosmeticians, and manicurists. The Board also registers locations at which any of the above professional services are provided. The Board investigates, upon written consumer complaint, all suspected or alleged violations relating to its area of responsibility.

BOARD OF CHIROPRACTIC EXAMINERS

(303) 894-7759

The Board licenses chiropractors. Chiropractors who wish to practice electrotherapy or acupuncture must provide the Board with proof of additional education in that area. The Board sets standards for unlicensed personnel who operate an x-ray machine or administer radiation for diagnostic purposes.

BOARD OF DENTAL EXAMINERS

(303) 894-7759

The Board licenses dentists and dental hygienists, and specifies the tasks that unlicensed dental auxiliaries may perform. Additionally, the Board administers a dentist peer assistance program.

STATE ELECTRICAL BOARD

(303) 894-2300

The Board licenses journeymen electricians, master electricians, electrical contractors and residential wiremen. Electrical apprentices are required to register with the Board. The Board also performs electrical inspections on new and remodeled facilities throughout the state in its areas of jurisdiction. The standard used by the Board is the National Electrical Code as may be amended.

BOARD OF REGISTRATION FOR PROFESSIONAL ENGINEERS AND PROFESSIONAL LAND SURVEYORS

(303) 894-7788

The Board licenses engineers and land surveyors, and certifies engineers-in-training and surveyors-in-training. The Board enforces minimum survey standards as set by law. Land surveyors are required to file monument records with the Board.

GRIEVANCE BOARD

(303) 894-7766

The Board hears disciplinary matters and can bring injunctive actions relating to licensed psychologists, clinical social workers, marriage and family therapists, and licensed professional counselors, and also relating to certified school psychologists and unlicensed psychotherapists. The Board maintains a database for licensed and unlicensed psychotherapists which includes information about their methods of practice and years of experience. For this information call 894-7771.

BOARD OF MARRIAGE AND FAMILY THERAPISTS EXAMINERS

(303) 894-7766

The Board licenses persons who practice psychotherapy and who are marriage and family therapists. Disciplinary matters are referred to the Grievance Board.

BOARD OF MEDICAL EXAMINERS

(303) 894-7690
The Board licenses qualified physicians and physician assistants. In addition, the Board reviews complaints in order to determine whether action is necessary to protect patients. The Board administers a physician's peer health assistance program.

MIDWIVES' REGISTRATION

(303) 894-2440
Effective July 1, 1993, the Division implemented a program to register direct-entry midwives, also known as "lay" midwives. Direct-entry midwifery means the advising, attending, or assisting of a woman during pregnancy, labor and natural childbirth at home, and during the postpartum period. This program administers examinations to graduates of educational programs that meet the standards established by the Division. The Division also establishes standards of practice and has authority to investigate complaints and take disciplinary action if necessary.

BOARD OF NURSING

(303) 894-2430
The Board licenses Registered Nurses, Licensed Practical Nurses, Psychiatric Technicians, and Certified Nurse Aides. The Board approves educational programs for all types of licenses. The Nurse Aide Advisory Committee assists the Board in their duties. Additionally, the Board administers a nursing peer health assistance diversion program to assist licensees experiencing impaired practice.

BOARD OF EXAMINERS OF NURSING HOME ADMINISTRATORS

(303) 894-7759
The Board licenses nursing home administrators in an effort to ensure quality administration and sound management of nursing homes. Nursing home administrators are individuals who are responsible for planning, organizing, directing, and controlling the operations of a nursing home. The Board administers a nursing home administrator-in-training program.

BOARD OF OPTOMETRY EXAMINERS

(303) 894-7750
The Board licenses optometrists and authorizes optometrists to prescribe and administer certain pharmaceutical agents upon meeting minimum educational and practical requirements.

OFFICE OF OUTFITTERS REGISTRATIONS

(303) 894-7772

The Office regulates outfitters who provide services for the purpose of hunting or fishing by requiring insurance, bonding and proficiency in first aid, and setting standards for operation. The Office works cooperatively with the Division of Wildlife, the Bureau of Land Management, the U.S. Forest Service, various District Attorneys throughout the state, and other state and federal game and land management agencies.

PASSENGER TRAMWAY SAFETY BOARD

(303) 894-7788

The Board regulates aerial tramways, surface lifts, and tows used for recreational purposes in Colorado. While the focus is ski-related equipment, the Board also licenses other types of tramways. The Board promulgates design, operation, and maintenance standards, reviews requests for variance from the rules, and investigates accidents related to the operation of tramways. Each licensed tramway is inspected at least twice annually.

BOARD OF PHARMACY

(303) 894-7750

The Board licenses pharmacists and pharmacy interns. Prescription and other drug outlets must be registered with the Board. The Board is responsible for the control and regulation of drugs, and administers the Controlled Substances Act with the Department of Health. It cooperates extensively with other state and federal agencies. Additionally, the Board's inspectors perform routine inspections of pharmacies and conduct special investigations.

PHYSICAL THERAPY REGISTRATION

(303) 894-2440

All persons practicing physical therapy or physiotherapy must register with the Division. An advisory committee appointed by the Director assists in registration. The rules also specify supervisory requirements for physical therapist assistants.

EXAMINING BOARD OF PLUMBERS

(303) 894-2319

The Board is responsible for the licensing of residential plumbers, journeyman plumbers and master plumbers. Plumbing apprentices who work for a plumbing contractor must register with the Board. The Board employs inspectors responsible for performing inspections in designated areas of the state. The Board establishes and administers the Colorado plumbing code, which represents the minimum standards for installation, alteration, and repair of plumbing equipment and systems.

PODIATRY BOARD

(303) 894-2440
The Board licenses qualified podiatrists and reviews complaints in order to determine whether action is necessary to protect patients.

BOARD OF LICENSED PROFESSIONAL COUNSELOR EXAMINERS

(303) 894-7766
The Board licenses persons who practice psychotherapy and who are professional counselors. Disciplinary matters are referred to the Grievance Board.

BOARD OF PSYCHOLOGIST EXAMINERS

(303) 894-7766
The Board licenses persons who practice psychotherapy and who are psychologists. Disciplinary matters are referred to the Grievance Board.

BOARD OF SOCIAL WORK EXAMINERS

(303) 894-7766
The Board licenses persons who practice psychotherapy and who are clinical social workers. Disciplinary matters are referred to the Grievance Board.

BOARD OF VETERINARY MEDICINE

(303) 894-7750
The Board licenses veterinarians and specifies what tasks veterinary students may perform under the direct supervision of a licensed veterinarian. Veterinary medicine includes surgery, obstetrics, dentistry, and all other branches or specialties of animal medicine.

DIVISION OF SECURITIES

1580 Lincoln, Suite 420, Denver, CO 80203, (303) 894-2320
The Division registers securities and licenses people who distribute securities. The Division investigates complaints and monitors broker-dealer activities and sales promotions. The thrust of the Colorado regulation is to bring actions against fraudulent conduct; the Division enforcement staff works with local. state and federal law enforcement authorities. The Division performs broker-dealer field examinations of intrastate and NASD member firms.

The Division also administers and enforces the Colorado Commodity Code, enacted in 1989 to protect investors and to prevent and prosecute illegal and fraudulent schemes involving precious metals and other off-exchange commodities.

In addition, the Division regulates and monitors the issuance of certain kinds of municipal bonds in Colorado, and local government investment pool trust funds.

The Division has a publication available that lists the most common areas of investment schemes and the types of solicitation techniques used by promoters. Entitled *How to protect your Savings against Con Artist Hypnosis*, the brochure is free of charge. The Division also has available a videotape cassette entitled *Calling for Your Dollars*, a consumer protection program about boiler rooms and a series of publications called *Investor Alert*, quarterly warnings to investors produced in cooperation with the Council of Better Business Bureaus.

CHAPTER THREE
SCHOOL'S OUT FOREVER

STATE SCHOOL SYSTEMS
Public, Private, Higher Education, Libraries

The information in this chapter was compiled from various sources including, but not limited to, government reports and publications (Federal, State, and Local); business and civic organizations; and other books produced by independent Colorado publishers including:

The Guide to Metro Denver Public Schools, 1997-98 Edition, and *Colorado Private and Elementary and Secondary Schools, 1997-98,* both by Magnolia Street Press

For a complete description of the above books and related titles, please see the Publisher's listing in Appendix A.

AN OVERVIEW OF PUBLIC SCHOOLS

School Districts: In 1957, there were 239 non-operating districts in the state and 203 one-room school districts. Through the voluntary process of the School District Reorganization Act, the number of school districts was reduced to 176. Today 20 counties have only one school district, 17 counties have two school districts, and 12 counties have no more than three districts. County superintendents have been abolished.

The 176 school districts are not necessarily coterminous with any other political boundaries. Most districts maintain elementary, middle/junior high schools, and senior high schools.

Many elementary schools include kindergarten classes. A local board may establish and maintain a kindergarten; law does not mandate it. Kindergartens may be paid for from the general school fund.

Entrance Age to School: Entrance age to school is determined by local board policy. The School Attendance Law entitles state residents between the ages of 6 and 21 to a free education, and requires persons between the ages of 7 and 16 to attend school. The Constitution entitles the legislature to require by law that children of sufficient physical and mental ability attend school during at least a three-year period between the ages of 6 and 18 years unless educated by other means.

The Exceptional Children's Educational Act defines a handicapped child as one between the ages of 5 and 21, and requires that administrative units serve every handicapped child. Thus, a handicapped child may enter school at age five. There are some programs for younger children. Over half of Colorado's school districts offer programs for 3-to-5-year-olds that are handicapped or "at risk".

Enrollment Requirements: Enrollment requirements (including entrance age for school) vary from district to district, but usually include legal proof of age (preferably a birth certificate) and various immunizations. Transfer students register in the district of prospective residence. Registration requirements and grade placement vary among school districts, but transcripts of the student's records from the school previously attended are usually required. In general, school authorities will send for transcripts.

Local Control of Instruction: The Constitution of the State of Colorado, Article IX, Section 15, states: "School districts—boards of education. The general assembly shall, by law, provide for organization of school districts of convenient size, in each of which shall be established a board of education . . . Said directors shall have control of instruction in the public schools of their respective districts." In 1993, the Colorado General Assembly enacted legislation aimed at bringing about coordinated improvement in the performance and accountability of the state's K-12 education system. House Bill 93-1313 requires local school districts to redesign curriculum, instruction, testing and teacher development around academic standards that spell out what students should know and be able to do, at various stages in their schooling, in 11 areas: math, science, reading, writing, history, geography, civics, art, music, physical education, and foreign language. The new system is to be fully in place statewide by 1999.

The law now requires that history and civil government of Colorado, as well as the history and civil government of the United States (incorporating history, culture, and contributions of minorities, including but not limited to Spanish-Americans and African-Americans) be taught in the public schools of the state. The federal Constitution is also to be taught, as well as the honor and use of the flag. In addition, students must be given information on the effect of use of alcohol and controlled substances.

Textbooks: In addition to curriculum, our Constitution states: "Textbooks in public schools: Neither the general assembly nor the state board of education shall have power to prescribe textbooks to be used in the public schools." We do not have statewide approved/mandated/adopted textbooks.

Local Boards of Education: Colorado Revised Statutes 22-32-109 and 110 enumerate local boards' powers and duties. Their curricula normally include general, college preparatory, business, and vocational-technical courses. Their high school graduation requirements usually include one or more units of English, math, social studies, science, and physical education.

Meetings of local boards of education are open to the public, however they may go into executive session.

Discipline: Local boards of education are required by law to adopt discipline codes as well as written policies, rules, and regulations which relate to the study, discipline, conduct, safety, and welfare of all pupils.

Accreditation: The Colorado Department of Education accredits school districts; additionally, the North Central Association accredits some schools. Districts are not ranked or rated as to which is best.

Home Study and Nonpublic Schools: The School Attendance Law distinguishes between non-public schools and home study. Home study is permitted in Colorado under this law. Non-public schools are required to provide a basic academic education, but are protected from untoward interference by any board of education, state or local.

SCHOOL CHOICES IN COLORADO

We know when it comes to education, one size does not fit all. Children learn in different ways and have different learning strengths and interests. Students are more excited about learning and learn more when they are in educational programs that suit their learning styles and special strengths, needs, and interests. To take the best advantage of public school opportunities now available, you need to know about the choices available to you:

Open Enrollment: Legislation enacted in 1994 creates open enrollment throughout Colorado. This means you may enroll your children in any public school in the state, assuming there is space available, without paying extra money.

Charter Schools: Colorado has 50 charter schools and more are under development. Charter schools are public schools created by groups of parents, teachers, or community members to reflect different educational approaches or philosophies. These schools are self-governing, enjoy some independence from the local school district, and have a clear plan for how and what students should learn. They are open to all interested students on a space-available basis.

Magnet Schools: Many districts offer magnet schools—also called "focus" or "alternative" schools—that have specific educational approaches or philosophies. Examples include special emphasis schools in science or performing arts, as well as Montessori or Waldorf schools that reflect a particular educational philosophy. They range from highly structured schools to open schools. These schools are open to all interested students on a space-available basis. Admission is usually done by lottery.

College Classes: High school students have the opportunity to take college courses or to earn college credit for certain high school classes. These opportunities serve two important purposes: They provide challenging academic experiences for students and they can help reduce the length and expense of college.

Finally, it's important to note you don't necessarily need to look outside your neighborhood school to have an impact on your children's educational program. You can discuss your child's learning style and special interests with his or her teacher. You can help set the direction for the educational approach in your child's school by getting involved in school committees that help make educational decisions. You also can have an impact on the educational philosophy of the district by voting in school board elections. You can attend and participate in school board meetings and share your ideas and concerns with teachers, principals, and school board members. There are many ways to make your neighborhood school your school of choice.

Excerpted *from A Parent's Guide to Colorado Public Schools,* published 1994 by Governor Romer's Office.

SELECTING THE RIGHT SCHOOL

When it comes time to select a school for your child or children, the responsibility for doing so falls squarely on your shoulders! Don't assume anything! Don't accept as fact any reputation a school may or may not have. Don't expect your realtor or local school administrator to "fill you in" on the downside to any given school. Visit all prospective schools and check them out for yourself.

This chapter contains the basic information for you to do the necessary research. First and foremost, you must determine what is important to your child's education. Use the Parent Inventory of Educational Preferences below to clarify exactly what you are looking for in a school. Keeping in mind the various options available to Colorado residents, find the appropriate point of contact for your school district and start with some phone calls. After you get a feel for what's offered by the schools in your area, plan on spending an entire day making personal visits to your top choices. If you live in the greater Denver Metro area, I highly suggest you obtain a copy of *The Guide to Metro Denver Public Schools* published by Magnolia Street Press. If you are considering a private school anywhere in Colorado, the book you need is *Colorado Private Elementary and Secondary Schools,* also available from Magnolia Street Press. Both these books contain complete, accurate and up-to-date information on a school-by-school basis. See the publisher's listing in Appendix A for details.

While visiting the schools, make sure all your questions are answered by the administrators and if school is in session, stroll around and note the teacher/student ratio, the general atmosphere of the classrooms and things of special interest to you or your child. Many school systems have cut back or eliminated special classes like fine arts, music, etc., due to budget cuts. If you see temporary classrooms on the grounds, you can assume this means overcrowding. Many counties in Colorado are growing at such an explosive rate an adequate number of new school facilities may be years in the making. Check with the school district about future plans and budgets.

Finally, for the best possible inside information, visit with the parents of other children currently enrolled in the schools. The easiest way to do this is in front of the schools during normal drop-off/pick-up times or at designated bus stops.

Time spent doing this properly now can save you a lot of regrets years later.

The form below was taken from *The Guide to Metro Denver Public Schools* by Magnolia Street Press.

PARENT INVENTORY OF EDUCATIONAL PREFERENCES

What is important to you in a school for your children? Rank the following list of criteria or pick a few of greatest importance.

___Specific philosophy, curriculum or educational strategy_____
_____

___Structured/unstructured environment (circle one)
___Small teacher/student ratio (state ideal number) _____
___College-preparatory/vocational emphasis of curriculum (circle one)
___School's capability to meet special needs_____

__Enrichment for gifted/talented children
__Enrichment for all children
__Handicap access
__High level of teacher experience and training
__Neighborhood school, close to home, walking distance
__On-site before-and after-school day care
__Other services such as transportation, lunch program, or boarding
__New building, modern facilities
__Older building, historical awareness
__Non-traditional school building and/or environment
__State-of-the-art technology and emphasis in curriculum
__High standardized test scores of other students
__No tuition or low tuition
__Religious instruction and environment
__Cultural, racial, ethnic, and/or economic diversity of students
__Small school enrollment (state ideal number) _____
__High level of involvement and input by parents or community
__Specific athletic offerings_____
__Specific extracurricular offerings_____

What educational goals do you have for your children? _____

What special needs do your children have which may require services beyond the "regular" classroom? _____

What expectations or desires do your children have for school programs in addition to or differing from yours? _____

INDEX OF CITIES AND SCHOOL DISTRICTS

CITY	DISTRICT	PHONE
AGATE	AGATE 300	719-764-2741
AGUILAR	AGUILAR REORGANIZED 6	719-941-4614
AKRON	AKRON R-1	970-345-2268
ALAMOSA	ALAMOSA RE-11J	719-589-6634
ANTON	ARICKAREE R-2	970-383-2202
ANTONITO	SOUTH CONEJOS RE-10	719-376-5512
ARVADA	JEFFERSON COUNTY R-1	303-982-6500
ARVADA	WESTMINSTER 50	303-428-3511
ASPEN	ASPEN 1	970-925-3460
AULT	AULT-HIGHLAND RE-9	970-834-1345
AURORA	ADAMS-ARAPAHOE 28J	303-344-8060

AURORA	CHERRY CREEK 5	303-773-1184
AVON	EAGLE COUNTY RE 50	970-328-6321
AVONDALE	PUEBLO COUNTY RURAL 70	719-542-0220
BAILEY	JEFFERSON COUNTY R-1	303-982-6500
BAILEY	PLATT CANYON 1	303-838-7666
BASALT	ROARING FORK RE-1	970-945-6558
BAYFIELD	BAYFIELD 10 JT-R	970-884-2496
BELLVUE	POUDRE R-1	970-482-7420
BENNETT	BENNETT 29J	303-644-3234
BERTHOUD	THOMPSON R-2J	970-669-3940
BETHUNE	BETHUNE R-5	719-346-7513
BEULAH	PUEBLO COUNTY RURAL 70	719-542-0220
BLACK HAWK	GILPIN COUNTY RE-1	303-582-0625
BLANCA	SIERRA GRANDE R-30	719-379-3259
BOULDER	BOULDER VALLEY RE-2	303-447-1010
BRANSON	BRANSON REORGANIZED 82	719-946-5531
BRECKENRIDGE	SUMMIT RE-1	970-668-3011
BRIGGSDALE	BRIGGSDALE RE-10	970-656-3417
BRIGHTON	BRIGHTON 27J	303-659-4820
BRIGHTON	NORTHGLENN-THORNTON 12	303-451-1561
BROOMFIELD	BOULDER VALLEY RE-2	303-447-1010
BROOMFIELD	JEFFERSON COUNTY R-1	303-982-6500
BROOMFIELD	NORTHGLENN-THORNTON 12	303-451-1561
BRUSH	BRUSH RE-2(J)	970-842-5176
BUENA VISTA	BUENA VISTA R-31	719-395-8656
BURLINGTON	BURLINGTON RE-6J	719-346-8737
BYERS	BYERS 32J	303-822-5292
CALHAN	CALHAN RJ-1	719-347-2766
CALHAN	ELLICOTT 22	719-683-2700
CAMPO	CAMPO RE-6	719-787-2226
CANON CITY	CANON CITY RE-1	719-269-6400
CARBONDALE	ROARING FORK RE-1	970-945-6558
CASTLE ROCK	DOUGLAS COUNTY RE 1	303-688-3195
CEDAREDGE	DELTA COUNTY 50(J)	970-874-4438
CENTER	CENTER 26 JT	719-754-3442
CHERAW	CHERAW 31	719-853-6655
CHEYENNE WELLS	CHEYENNE COUNTY RE-5	719-767-5866
CHIPITA PARK	MANITOU SPRINGS 14	719-685-1235
CLIFTON	MESA COUNTY 51	970-245-2422
COLLBRAN	PLATEAU VALLEY 50	970-487-3547
COLORADO CITY	PUEBLO COUNTY RURAL 70	719-542-0220
COLORADO SPRINGS	ACADEMY 20	719-598-2566
COLORADO SPRINGS	CHEYENNE MOUNTAIN 12	719-475-6100
COLORADO SPRINGS	COLORADO SPRINGS 11	719-520-2000
COLORADO SPRINGS	FALCON 49	719-495-3601
COLORADO SPRINGS	HANOVER 28	719-683-2247
COLORADO SPRINGS	HARRISON 2	719-576-8360
COLORADO SPRINGS	LEWIS-PALMER 38	719-488-4700

COLORADO SPRINGS	WIDEFIELD 3	719-391-3000
COMMERCE CITY	ADAMS COUNTY 14	303-289-3950
CONIFER	JEFFERSON COUNTY R-1	303-982-6500
CORTEZ	MONTEZUMA-CORTEZ RE-1	970-565-7282
COTOPAXI	COTOPAXI RE-3	719-942-4131
CRAIG	MOFFAT COUNTY RE:NO1	970-824-3268
CRAWFORD	DELTA COUNTY 50(J)	970-874-4438
CREEDE	CREED CONSOLIDATED 1	719-658-2220
CRESTED BUTTE	GUNNISON WATERSHED RE1J	970-641-7760
CRIPPLE CREEK	CRIPPLE CREEK-VICTOR RE-1	719-689-2685
DE BEQUE	DE BEQUE 49JT	970-283-5597
DEER TRAIL	DEAR TRAIL 26J	303-769-4421
DEL NORTE	DEL NORTE C-7	719-657-4040
DELTA	DELTA COUNTY 50(J)	970-874-4438
DENVER	CHERRY CREEK 5	303-773-1184
DENVER	DENVER COUNTY 1	303-764-3200
DENVER	MAPLETON 1	303-853-1000
DENVER	NORTHGLENN-THORNTON 12	303-451-1561
DENVER	WESTMINSTER 50	303-428-3511
DILLON	SUMMIT RE-1	970-668-3011
DINOSAUR	MOFFAT COUNTY RE:NO1	970-824-3268
DIVIDE	WOODLAND PARK RE 2	719-687-6048
DOLORES	DOLORES RE-4A	970-882-7255
DOVE CREEK	DOLORES COUNTY RE NO.2	970-677-2522
DURANGO	DURANGO 9-R	970-247-5411
EADS	EADS RE-1	719-438-2218
EAGLE	EAGLE COUNTY RE 50	970-328-6321
EASTLAKE	NORTHGLENN-THORNTON 12	303-451-1561
EATON	EATON RE-2	970-454-3402
EDGEWATER	JEFFERSON COUNTY R-1	303-982-6500
EDWARDS	EAGLE COUNTY RE 50	970-328-6321
EGNAR	DOLORES COUNTY RE NO.2	970-677-2522
ELBERT	ELBERT 200	303-648-3030
ELIZABETH	ELIZABETH C-1	303-646-4441
EMPIRE	CLEAR CREEK RE-1	303-567-4467
ENGLEWOOD	CHERRY CREEK 5	303-773-1184
ENGLEWOOD	ENGLEWOOD 1	303-761-7050
ENGLEWOOD	SHERIDAN 2	303-761-8640
ERIE	ST. VRAIN VALLEY RE 1J	303-776-6200
ESTES PARK	PARK (ESTES PARK) R-3	970-586-2361
EVANS	GREELEY 6	970-352-1543
EVERGREEN	CLEAR CREEK RE-1	303-567-4467
EVERGREEN	JEFFERSON COUNTY R-1	303-982-6500
FAIRPLAY	PARK COUNTY RE-2	719-836-3114
FALCON	FALCON 49	719-495-3601
FLAGLER	ARRIBA-FLAGLER C-20	719-765-4684
FLEMING	FRENCHMAN RE-3	970-265-2111
FLORENCE	FLORENCE RE-2	719-784-6312

FORT CARSON	FOUNTAIN 8	719-382-1300
FORT COLLINS	POUDRE R-1	970-482-7420
FORT LUPTON	WELD COUNTY RE-8	303-857-6291
FORT MORGAN	FORT MORGAN RE-3	970-867-5633
FOUNTAIN	FOUNTAIN 8	719-382-1300
FOUNTAIN	WIDEFIELD 3	719-391-3000
FOWLER	FOWLER R-4J	719-263-4625
FRANKTOWN	DOUGLAS COUNTY RE 1	303-688-3195
FRASER	EAST GRAND 2	970-887-2581
FREDERICK	ST. VRAIN VALLEY RE 1J	303-776-6200
FRISCO	SUMMIT RE-1	970-668-3011
FRUITA	MESA COUNTY 51	970-245-2422
FT COLLINS	THOMPSON R-2J	970-669-3940
GALETON	EATON RE-2	970-454-3402
GARDNER	HUERFANO RE-1	719-738-1520
GATEWAY	MESA COUNTY 51	970-245-2422
GEORGETOWN	CLEAR CREEK RE-1	303-567-4467
GILCREST	GILCREST RE-1	970-737-2403
GLENWOOD SPRINGS	ROARING FORK RE-1	970-945-6558
GRANADA	GRANADA RE-1	719-734-5492
GRANBY	EAST GRAND 2	970-887-2581
GRAND JUNCTION	MESA COUNTY 51	970-245-2422
GRAND LAKE	EAST GRAND 2	970-887-2581
GREELEY	GREELEY 6	970-352-1543
GROVER	PAWNEE RE-12	970-895-2222
GUFFEY	PARK COUNTY RE-2	719-836-3114
GUNNISON	GUNNISON WATERSHED RE1J	970-641-7760
GYPSUM	EAGLE COUNTY RE 50	970-328-6321
HAXTUN	HAXTUN RE-2J	970-774-6111
HAYDEN	HAYDEN RE-1	970-276-3864
HENDERSON	BRIGHTON 27J	303-659-4820
HIGHLANDS RANCH	DOUGLAS COUNTY RE 1	303-688-3195
HOEHNE	HOEHNE REORGANIZED 3	719-846-4457
HOLLY	HOLLY RE-3	719-537-6616
HOLYOKE	HOLYOKE RE-1J	970-854-3634
HOOPER	SANGRE DE CRISTO RE 22J	719-78-2321
HOTCHKISS	DELTA COUNTY 50(J)	970-874-4438
HUDSON	KEENESBURG RE-3(J)	303-732-4844
HUGO	GENOA-HUGO C113	719-743-2428
HYGIENE	ST. VRAIN VALLEY RE 1J	303-776-6200
IDAHO SPRINGS	CLEAR CREEK RE-1	303-567-4467
IDALIA	EAST YUMA COUNTY RJ-2	970-332-5764
IGNACIO	IGNACIO 11 JT	970-563-4521
ILIFF	VALLEY RE-1	970-522-0792
INDIAN HILLS	JEFFERSON COUNTY R-1	303-982-6500
JAMESTOWN	BOULDER VALLEY RE-2	303-447-1010
JOES	WEST YUMA COUNTY RJ-1	970-848-5831
JOHNSTOWN	JOHNSTOWN-MILLIKEN RE-5J	970-587-2336

JOLD HILL	BOULDER VALLEY RE-2	303-447-1010
JOLDEN	JEFFERSON COUNTY R-1	303-982-6500
JULESBURG	JULESBURG RE-1	970-474-3365
KARVAL	KARVAL RE-23	719-446-5311
KEENESBURG	KEENESBURG RE-3(J)	303-732-4844
KERSEY	PLATTE VALLEY RE-7	970-352-6177
KIM	KIM REORGANIZED 88	719-643-5295
KIOWA	KIOWA C-2	303-621-2115
KIT CARSON	KIT CARSON R-1	719-962-3219
KREMMLING	WEST GRAND 1-JT	970-724-3217
LA JARA	NORTH CONEJOS RE-1J	719-274-5174
LA JUNTA	EAST OTERO R-1	719-384-6900
LA PORTE	POUDRE R-1	970-482-7420
LA SALLE	GILCREST RE-1	970-737-2403
LA VETA	LA VETA RE-2	719-742-3562
LAFAYETTE	BOULDER VALLEY RE-2	303-447-1010
LAKE CITY	HINSDALE COUNTY RE-1	970-944-2314
LAKE GEORGE	PARK COUNTY RE-2	719-836-3114
LAKEWOOD	JEFFERSON COUNTY R-1	303-982-6500
LAMAR	LAMAR RE-2	719-336-3251
LARKSPUR	DOUGLAS COUNTY RE 1	303-688-3195
LAS ANIMAS	LAS ANIMAS RE-1	719-456-0161
LEADVILLE	LAKE COUNTY R-1	719-486-6800
LIMON	LIMON RE-4J	719-775-2350
LITTLETON	CHERRY CREEK 5	303-773-1184
LITTLETON	DOUGLAS COUNTY RE 1	303-688-3195
LITTLETON	JEFFERSON COUNTY R-1	303-982-6500
LITTLETON	LITTLETON 6	303-347-3300
LIVERMORE	POUDRE R-1	970-482-7420
LOMA	MESA COUNTY 51	970-245-2422
LONGMONT	ST. VRAIN VALLEY RE 1J	303-776-6200
LOUISVILLE	BOULDER VALLEY RE-2	303-447-1010
LOVELAND	THOMPSON R-2J	970-669-3940
LYONS	ST. VRAIN VALLEY RE 1J	303-776-6200
MANASSA	NORTH CONEJOS RE-1J	719-274-5174
MANCOS	MANCOS RE-6	970-533-7748
MANITOU SPRINGS	MANITOU SPRINGS 14	719-685-1235
MANZANOLA	MANZANOLA 3J	719-462-5527
MAYBELL	MOFFAT COUNTY RE:NO1	970-824-3268
MC CLAVE	MC CLAVE RE-2	719-829-4517
MEAD	ST. VRAIN VALLEY RE 1J	303-776-6200
MEEKER	MEEKER RE1	970-878-3701
MERINO	BUFFALO RE-4	970-522-7424
MILLIKEN	JOHNSTOWN-MILLIKEN RE-5J	970-587-2336
MINTURN	EAGLE COUNTY RE 50	970-328-6321
MOFFAT	MOFFAT 2	719-256-4710
MONTE VISTA	MONTE VISTA C-8	719-852-5996
MONTE VISTA	SARGENT RE-33J	719-852-4023

MONTROSE	MONTROSE COUNTY RE-1J	970-249-7726
MONUMENT	LEWIS-PALMER 38	719-488-4700
MORRISON	JEFFERSON COUNTY R-1	303-982-6500
MOSCA	SANGRE DE CRISTO RE-22J	719-378-2321
NATURITA	WEST END RE-2	970-865-2290
NEDERLAND	BOULDER VALLEY RE-2	303-447-1010
NEW CASTLE	GARFIELD RE-2	970-625-1595
NEW RAYMER	PRAIRIE RE-11	970-437-5386
NORTHGLENN	NORTHGLENN-THORNTON 12	303-451-1561
NORWOOD	NORWOOD R-2J	970-327-4712
NUCLA	WEST END RE-2	970-865-2290
OAK CREEK	SOUTH ROUTT RE 3	970-736-2313
OLATHE	MONTROSE COUNTY RE-1J	970-249-7726
ORDWAY	CROWLEY COUNTY RE-1-J	719-267-3117
OTIS	LONE STAR 101	970-848-2778
OTIS	OTIS R-3	970-246-3755
OURAY	OURAY R-1	970-325-4218
OVID	PLATTE VALLEY RE-3	970-463-5414
PAGOSA SPRINGS	ARCHULETA COUNTY 50 JT	970-264-2228
PALISADE	MESA COUNTY 51	970-245-2422
PALMER LAKE	LEWIS-PALMER 38	719-488-4700
PAONIA	DELTA COUNTY 50(J)	970-874-4438
PARACHUTE	GARFIELD 16	970-285-7759
PARADOX	WEST END RE-2	970-865-2290
PARKER	DOUGLAS COUNTY RE 1	303-688-3195
PEETZ	PLATEAU RE-5	970-334-2435
PENROSE	FLORENCE RE-2	719-784-6312
PEYTON	PEYTON 23 JT	719-749-2330
PIERCE	AULT-HIGHLAND RE-9	970-834-1345
PINE	JEFFERSON COUNTY R-1	303-982-6500
PLATTEVILLE	GILCREST RE-1	970-737-2403
PRITCHETT	PRITCHETT RE-3	719-523-4045
PUEBLO	PUEBLO CITY 60	719-549-7100
PUEBLO	PUEBLO COUNTY RURAL 70	719-542-0220
PUEBLO WEST	PUEBLO COUNTY RURAL 70	719-542-0220
RANGELY	RANGELY RE-4	970-675-2207
RED FEATHER LAKES	POUDRE R-1	970-482-7420
RIDGWAY	RIDGWAY R-2	970-626-5468
RIFLE	GARFIELD RE-2	970-625-1595
ROCKY FORD	ROCKY FORD R-2	719-254-7423
RUSH	MIAMI/YODER 60 JT	719-478-2186
RYE	PUEBLO COUNTY RURAL 70	719-542-0220
SAGUACHE	MOUNTAIN VALLEY RE 1	719-655-2578
SALIDA	SALIDA R-32	719-539-4382
SAN LUIS	CENTENNIAL R-1	719-672-3691
SANFORD	SANFORD 6J	719-274-5167
SECURITY	WIDEFIELD 3	719-391-3000
SEDALIA	DOUGLAS COUNTY RE 1	303-688-3195

SEDGWICK	PLATTE VALLEY RE-3	970-463-5414
SEIBERT	HI-PLAINS R-23	970-664-2636
SHERIDAN LAKE	PLAINVIEW RE-2	719-727-4361
SILT	GARFIELD RE-2	970-625-1595
SILVERTHORNE	SUMMIT RE-1	970-668-3011
SILVERTON	SILVERTON 1	970-387-5543
SIMLA	BIG SANDY 100J	719-541-2291
SPRINGFIELD	SPRINGFIELD RE-4	719-523-6654
STEAMBOAT SPRINGS	STEAMBOAT SPRINGS RE-2	970-879-1530
STERLING	VALLEY RE-1	970-522-0792
STRASBURG	STRASBURG 31J	303-622-9211
STRATTON	STRATTON R-4	719-348-5369
SWINK	SWINK 33	719-384-8103
TELLURIDE	TELLURIDE R-1	970-728-6617
THORNTON	MAPLETON 1	303-853-1000
THORNTON	NORTHGLENN-THORNTON 12	303-451-1561
TIMNATH	POUDRE R-1	970-482-7420
TRINIDAD	TRINIDAD 1	719-846-3324
USAF ACADEMY	ACADEMY 20	719-598-2566
VAIL	EAGLE COUNTY RE 50	970-328-6321
VILAS	VILAS RE-5	719-523-6738
VONA	HI-PLAINS R-23	970-664-2636
WALDEN	NORTH PARK R-1	970-723-4391
WALSENBURG	HUERFANO RE-1	719-738-1520
WALSH	WALSH RE-1	719-324-5632
WELDONA	WELDON VALLEY RE-20(J)	970-645-2411
WELLINGTON	POUDRE R-1	970-482-7420
WESTCLIFFE	CONSOLIDATED C-1	719-783-2357
WESTMINSTER	JEFFERSON COUNTY R-1	303-982-6500
WESTMINSTER	NORTHGLENN-THORNTON 12	303-451-1561
WESTMINSTER	WESTMINSTER 50	303-428-3511
WESTON	PRIMERO REORGANIZED 2	719-868-2715
WHEAT RIDGE	JEFFERSON COUNTY R-1	303-982-6500
WHEATRIDGE	JEFFERSON COUNTY R-1	303-982-6500
WIGGINS	WIGGINS RE-50(J)	970-483-7762
WILEY	WILEY RE-13 JT	719-829-4806
WINDSOR	WINDSOR RE-4	970-686-7411
WOODLAND PARK	WOODLAND PARK RE-2	719-687-6048
WOODROW	WOODLAN R-104	970-386-2223
WRAY	EAST YUMA COUNTY RJ-2	970-332-5764
YAMPA	SOUTH ROUTT RE 3	970-736-2313
YODER	EDISON 54 JT	719-478-2125
YUMA	WEST YUMA COUNTY RJ-1	970-848-5831

PRIVATE SCHOOLS

- Colorado has more than 300 private elementary and secondary schools
- 73% of those schools have a religious affiliation
- None of them are military schools
- A number of those schools focus on the special needs of children
- 43% of the schools offer foreign languages in the curriculum
- At least two schools provide support to home schoolers
- Many schools feature specialized curricula such as Montessori, Waldorf, British Primary, and Core Knowledge
- The Denver Metro area has 147 private schools - Boulder has 19 private schools - Colorado Springs has 29 private schools. There are an additional 124 private schools scattered around Colorado from Aspen to Trinidad.

The information available about private schools in Colorado is vast. If you are considering enrolling your child(ren) in a private school it is highly recommended you obtain a copy of *Colorado Private Elementary and Secondary Schools* by Magnolia Street Press, described in Appendix A.

HIGHER EDUCATION

THE COLORADO COMMISSION ON HIGHER EDUCATION

The Colorado Commission on Higher Education, (303) 866-2723, is a nine member lay board, appointed by the Governor and confirmed by the Senate, that acts as a central policy and coordinating board for Colorado public higher education. The Commission meets monthly, on campuses throughout the state, to discuss and act on statewide higher education policy. The Commission works in consultation with governing boards of higher education institutions in the development and implementation of legislative directives and statewide higher education policy. In addition, the Commission receives assistance from an advisory committee that includes legislative, faculty, student, and citizen representation. The responsibilities of the Commission are to:

- Develop long-range plans for an evolving state system of higher education
- Review and approve degree programs
- Establish the distribution formula for higher education funding; recommend statewide funding levels to the legislature
- Approve institutional capital construction requests; recommend capital construction priorities to the legislature
- Develop policies for institutional and facility master plans

- Administer statewide student financial assistance programs through policy development, program valuation, and allocation of funds
- Develop and administer a statewide off-campus (extended studies), community service, and continuing education program
- Determine institutional roles and missions
- Establish statewide enrollment policies and admission standards
- Conduct special studies as appropriate or directed, regarding statewide education policy, finance, or effective coordination.
- Provide the public with various publications concerning all aspects of higher education (see Additional Resources section)

STUDENT FINANCIAL ASSISTANCE PROGRAMS

Colorado student aid is appropriated by the state legislature and allocated by the Colorado Commission on Higher Education to eligible Colorado colleges and universities. Colorado student aid awards are made by institutions to students based upon state guidelines and according to institutional policies and procedures. Any aid received must be used for tuition, fees, room, board, books, and supplies or other expenses related to attendance at Colorado institutions.

General Student Eligibility Requirements:

1. Colorado residency for tuition purposes (A small percentage of Undergraduate Merit and Graduate Fellowship awards may be made to non-residents of Colorado at some institutions)
2. Enrollment in an eligible program at an eligible Colorado postsecondary institution
3. Satisfactory progress toward completion of a course of study
4. No defaulted educational loans or grants

Types of State Aid Available:

Colorado Diversity Grant: Available as part of a statewide effort to increase participation of under-represented groups in the Colorado public higher education system.

Colorado Nursing Scholarships: Designed to provide assistance to individuals seeking nursing education that agree to practice in Colorado. Applications are available from the Colorado Commission on Higher Education annually.

Colorado Part-time Grants: Need-based grants for less than full-time students attending eligible Colorado institutions.

Colorado Student Grants (CSG): Available to qualified undergraduates with documented financial need.

Colorado Student Incentive Grants (CSIG): Available to qualified undergraduates with substantial financial need. (Student grants under this program are comprised of both federal and state funds).

Colorado Work-Study: Part-time employment program designed to assist students with financial need or work experience.

Undergraduate Merit: Available to students who demonstrate superior scholarship or talent as defined by the college or university they attend.

Colorado Graduate Grants: Available to graduate students with financial need.

Colorado Graduate Fellowships: Provide merit based awards to graduate students.

Dependents Tuition Assistance Program: Pays tuition for dependents of Colorado law enforcement officers, fire or national guard personnel killed or disabled in the line of duty, and for dependents of prisoners of war or service personnel listed as missing in action. Dependents of disabled personnel must have demonstrated financial need for the assistance. Applications are available at the Colorado Commission on Higher Education.

Paul Douglas Teacher Scholarships: Federal program designed to encourage outstanding individuals to enter the teaching profession. Federal law stipulates that recipients must be (or have been) in the top 10% of their high school graduating class, or have comparable GED scores.

Contact individual institutions for complete information and details about application procedures and deadlines. Information about other sources of financial aid may be obtained at many local libraries.

DEFINITION OF DEGREES

CERTIFICATES: Requires the completion of a program that would be completed in 30 to 120 credit hours. Includes 1, 2, and 4-year certificate programs, as well as post-bachelor's and postmaster's certificates.

ACADEMIC ASSOCIATE: Normally requires at least 2, but less than 4 years of full-time equivalent college work in an academic field of study.

VOCATIONAL ASSOCIATE: Normally requires at least 2, but less than 4 years of full-time equivalent college work whose expressed intent is to impart work-related knowledge and skills.

BACHELOR: Normally requires at least 4 but not more than 5 years of full-time equivalent college-level work. Includes all bachelor's degrees conferred in a Cooperative or Work-Study Plan or Program. Also includes bachelor's degrees in which the normal 4 years of work is completed in 3 years.

MASTER'S: Requires the successful completion of a program of study of at least the full-time equivalent of 1, but not more than 2 academic years of work beyond the bachelor's degree.

FIRST PROFESSIONAL: Requires completion of a program that meets all three of the following: (1) Completion of the academic requirements to begin practice in the profession; (2) At least 2 years of college work prior to entrance to the program; and (3) A total of at least 6 academic years of college work to complete the degree program, including prior required college work, plus the length of the professional program itself.

COLORADO INSTITUTIONS OF HIGHER EDUCATION

2 Year Colleges and Vocational Schools

Aims Community College	Greeley	970-330-8008
Arapahoe Community College	Littleton	303-794-1550
Colorado Mountain College-Alpine Campus	Steamboat Springs	970-870-4444
Colorado Mountain College-Carbondale Center	Carbondale	970-963-2172
Colorado Mountain College-Roaring Fork	Glenwood Springs	970-945-8691
Colorado Mountain College-Timberline Campus	Leadville	719-486-2015
Colorado N.W. Community College	Rangely	970-675-3220
Community College of Aurora	Aurora	303-360-4700
Community College of Denver	Denver	303-556-2600
Delta-Montrose Voc-Tech	Delta	970-874-7671
Emily Griffith Opportunity Center	Denver	303-575-4700
Front Range Com. College	Westminster	303-466-8811
Front Range Com. College	Fort Collins	970-226-2500
Lamar Community College	Lamar	719-336-2248
Morgan Community College	Fort Morgan	970-867-3081
Northeastern Junior College	Sterling	970-522-6600
Otero Junior College	La Junta	719-384-6831
Pikes Peak Com. College	Colorado Springs	719-576-7711
Pueblo Community College	Pueblo	719-549-3213
Red Rocks Community College	Lakewood	303-914-6100
San Juan Basin Voc-Tech	Cortez	970-565-8457
San Luis Valley Educational Center	Alamosa	719-589-1513
T. H. Pickens Voc-Tech,	Aurora	303-344-4910
Trinidad State Junior College	Trinidad	719-846-5533

4 Year Colleges and Universities

Adams State College	Alamosa	719-589-7936
Colorado School of Mines	Golden	303-273-3000
Colorado State University	Fort Collins	970-491-6317
Fort Lewis College	Durango	970-247-7157
Lesley College	Greely	970-654-1037
Mesa State College	Grand Junction	970-248-1787
Metropolitan State College of Denver	Denver	303-556-2978
University of Colorado	Boulder	303-492-6937
University of Colorado	Colorado Springs	719-262-3266
University of Colorado	Denver	303-556-2844
University of Colorado Health Sciences Center	Denver	303-399-1211

University of Northern Colorado	Greeley	970-351-2817
University of Southern Colorado	Pueblo	719-549-2681
Western State College	Gunnison	970-943-2030

Private Colleges And Universities

Chapman University	Colorado Springs	719-593-0970
Colorado Christian University	Lakewood	303-238-5386
Colorado College	Colorado Springs	719-389-6472
Regis University	Denver	303-458-4135
Denver University	Denver	303-871-2496
University of Phoenix, Denver Campus	Englewood, CO	303-755-9090

Private Vocational Schools

Academy of Beauty Culture	Grand Junction	970-245-5570
Colorado Cranial Institute	Boulder	303-449-0322
Colorado Floral Education Center	Westminster	303-426-6123
Colorado Insurance Education	Denver	303-757-3404
Colorado School of Healing Art	Lakewood	303-986-2320
Columbine Industrial Center	Montrose	970-249-1144
Denver Institute of Technology	Denver	303-650-5050
Denver Paralegal Institute	Colorado Springs	719-444-0190
Denver Paralegal Institute	Denver	303-295-0550
Emery Aviation College	Colorado Springs	719-591-9488
Hair Dynamics Education Center	Littleton	303-798-7772
Hair Dynamics Education Center	Fort Collins	970-223-9943
Healing Arts Institute	Fort Collins	970-223-9741
International Bartending Institute	Denver	303-758-5000
Naomi's Mile High Beauty College	Denver	303-455-3687
Mr. K's Floral Design School	Denver	303-987-2707
Noble School of Cosmetology	Colorado Springs	719-528-8532
Real Estate Training Center	Lakewood	303-421-9078
Real Estate Training Center	Breckenridge	970-453-2160
WDS Truck Driving School	Fountain	719-382-8000

LIBRARIES

Books are vehicles of ideas, instruments of education, vessels of literature and sources of entertainment.[1] The world of books is the most remarkable creation of man. Nothing else he builds ever lasts. Monuments fall, nations perish and civilizations die out. Yet books live on, still as fresh at the day they were written.[2] In the five and a half centuries since the invention of movable type, one thing hasn't changed—the ability of books to move mankind. The book is imagination. It is comfort and companionship. It is solace and inspiration. It

---

[1] Based on remarks in *Book Printing, A Basic Introduction*, by John P. Dessauer, The Continuum Publishing Co., New York, 1989.

[2] From *To Advance Knowledge, A Handbook on American University Press Publishing*, by Gene R. Hawes, American University Press Service, Inc., New York, 1967

is frivolity and formality. It is recipes and revelations. It is a tour down the Danube, a guide to the Louvre, an armchair adventure to the streams of the Rockies.

To learn a craft, professionals must devour huge amounts of information. To excel, they must continue to read. There is virtually nothing, from gardening to home-repairs to constructing an atomic bomb that can not be learned from books. Anyone with average reading ability has the opportunity to learn, to improve and expand her or his base of knowledge, to find the answer to almost any question.

Today's modern libraries are a cross between repositories of books and the latest high-tech computer centers. The "information highway" is here and growing at a phenomenal rate. With the advent of the CD-ROM computer drive and on-line services, there exist no information which can not be located and studied.

One of the intentions for this chapter was to list every public library in Colorado. However, when I discovered there are over 300 such facilities, and because space in this book is limited, I decided to reduce the text presented to information not easily obtained through Directory Assistance or local phone books. Below you will find interesting facts about the newest and best-equipped library in Denver and a list of unique corporate and private libraries which house proprietary, technical and research related material which may be difficult to find elsewhere.

THE NEW DOWNTOWN DENVER LIBRARY

In the Spring of 1995, Denver unveiled its newly renovated and expanded central library (phone: 303-640-6200). The new structure has seven floors above ground and three below for a total of 540,000 square feet. This new library has many special features that include:

Western History and Genealogy Department: Map room with 5,000 maps for browsing and study; computer access to extensive, world-famous photo collection; two-story seminar room; manuscript reading room; separate genealogy collection.

Children's Library and Story Pavilion: Study rooms with word processors; audiovisual study areas; children's story pavilion for special programs; enclosed patio and play area; multi-cultural and foreign language book collections.

Technology: Offers a touch-screen building directory; CD-ROM high-storage jukebox; CARL computerized public access catalog; access to information highways of the world; on-line periodical delivery service; digitized photographic imaging; self-checkout systems; 24-hour dial-up access via modem, to databases; statewide network linking 120 academic and public library catalogs; equipment for people with disabilities.

General: Orientation theater; bookstore and gift shop; centralized reference service; young adult reading room; popular browsing collection; two multipurpose rooms, seating 90 and 100; ten study rooms; seven public meeting rooms, each seating up to 30; full accessibility to people with disabilities; security systems and personnel; four passenger elevators, plus escalators on first through fourth floors.

CORPORATE, SPECIAL AND PRIVATE LIBRARIES

Many large corporations, hospitals, government agencies, and private foundations maintain their own libraries. These special libraries can be an unbelievable source of information not found in public libraries. Although not "public" in nature, most special libraries allow access to material by individuals for specific projects or purposes. This alphabetical list is presented because most special libraries are not listed in any phonebook.

A.T. & T. Gbcs. Library	Denver	303-538-1582
Adolph Coors Company Technical Library	Golden	303-277-3506
Amer. Humane Assoc. Ctr. On Child Abuse	Englewood	303-792-9900
American Legion Auxiliary Library,	Cheyenne Wells	719-727-4006
American Numismatic Association Library	Colorado Springs	719-632-2646
American Water Works Association Info. Services	Denver	303-795-7711
Amoco Production Company Library/Info. Center	Denver	303-830-5336
Arthur Andersen & Company Library	Denver	303-291-9444
Aspen Historical Society	Aspen	970-925-3721
Aspen Institute David Mayer Library	Aspen	970-925-7010
Assoc. Of Operating Room Nurses Library	Denver	303-755-6304
Augustana Lutheran Church Library	Denver	303-388-4678
Ball Aerospace Systems Division Library Service	Boulder	303-939-5755
Beet Sugar Development Foundation	Denver	303-321-1520
Boulder Community Hospital Medical Library	Boulder	303-440-2091
Boulder County Corrections Library	Boulder	303-441-4686
Brega & Winters PC Law Library	Denver	303-866-9400
Career Track Inc. Library/Info Center Resource	Boulder	303-447-2323
Cherry Creek Schools Educators Resource Center	Denver	303-340-5100
Children's Hospital Medical Library	Denver	303-861-6400
Cobe Bct. Inc. Library	Lakewood	303-231-4278
Colorado Dept. Of Education Resource Center	Denver	303-866-6618
Colorado Dept. Of Human Services Library	Denver	303-866-4086
CO Dept. Of Local Affairs State Planning Library	Denver	303-866-2156
Colorado Dept. Of Revenue Office Of Tax Analysis	Denver	303-866-3089
Colorado Dept. Of Transportation Tech. Library	Denver	303-757-9972
CO Developmental Disabilities Planning Council	Denver	303-894-2345
Colorado Div. Of Wildlife Library	Denver	303-297-1192
Colorado Div. Of Wildlife Research Library	Denver	303-484-2836
Colorado Historical Society Stephen H. Hart Library	Denver	303-866-2305
Colorado Legislative Council	Denver	303)866-3521
Colorado Mental Health Institute at Pueblo	Pueblo	719-546-4677
Colorado National Bank - Pueblo Law Library	Pueblo	719-543-1331

COLORADO: A Newcomer's and Resident's Manual

Colorado Springs Fine Arts Center Library	Colorado Springs	719-634-5581
CO Spgs Pioneer Museum Center For Local History	Colorado Springs	719-578-6650
Colorado State Bank Building Law Library	Denver	303-837-0287
Colorado Supreme Court Library	Denver	303-837-3720
Colorado Talking Book Library	Denver	303-727-9277
Community Living Alternatives Inc.	Denver	303-477-4500
Dames & Moore Library	Denver	303-294-9100
Defense Finance & Accounting / Denver Center	Denver	303-676-7566
Denver Art Museum Native Arts Dept. Library	Denver	303-640-1613
Denver Botanic Gardens Helen K. Fowler Library	Denver	303-370-8014
Denver General Hospital Medical Library	Denver	303-436-6360
Denver Medical Library	Denver	303-839-6670
Denver Museum Of Natural History Library	Denver	303-370-6362
Denver Post Newsroom Library	Denver	303-820-1443
Denver Public Schools Ed. Resource Services	Denver	303-764-3692
Denver Wildlife Research Center Library	Denver	303-236-7873
Digital Equipment Corp. Library/Info Center	Colorado Springs	719-548-2113
Econo-Clad Books American Bindery	Littleton	303-798-7063
EG&G Rocky Flats Plant Inc.	Golden	303-966-4809
El Paso Cnty Dept Of Health And Enviro.	Colorado Springs	719-578-3109
El Paso County Law Library	Colorado Springs	719-630-2880
First Presbyterian Church Library	Colorado Springs	719-471-3763
Ft Carson Hq & 4th Infantry Division Grant Library	Ft Carson	719-526-2350
Gates Rubber Company The Information Center	Denver	303-744-4150
Great Sand Dunes National Monument Library	Mosca	719-378-2312
Healthone Aurora Presbyterian Hospital Library	Aurora	303-360-3105
Hewlett Packard Company Fort Collins Site Library	Fort Collins	970-229-3825
Hewlett Packard Company Library	Loveland	970-679-2460
Hewlett Packard S. Colorado Regional Library	Colorado Springs	719-590-2708
Holland And Hart Law Library	Denver	303-295-8091
Dolman Inc. Technical Services & Development Lab	Laporte	303-482-5600
Ntl Fed Of Petroleum & Chem Wkrs Library	Denver	303-333-1543
Efferson Center For Mental Health Library	Lakewood	303-425-0300
Kaman Sciences Corp. Technical Library	Colorado Springs	719-599-1777
Kirkland & Ellis Law Library	Denver	303-291-3045
KRMA-TV Channel 6 Educational Services	Denver	303-892-6666
Lakewood Environmental Library & Central Records	Lakewood	303-987-7678
Lutheran Church of The Master Library	Lakewood	303-988-6400
Lutheran Medical Center Medical Library	Wheat Ridge	303-425-8662
Marathon Oil Co. Production Technology Library	Littleton	303-347-5530
McClelland Center For Child Study	Pueblo	719-543-5271
Memorial Hospital Health Sciences Library	Colorado Springs	719-475-5182
Mental Health Center Of Boulder County Library	Boulder	303-443-8500
Mercy Behavioral Health Center	Durango	970-259-1110
Mesa Verde Research Library Museum	Mesa Verda Park	719-529-4475
Metro Wastewater Reclamation District Library	Denver	303-286-3000
Metrum Information Storage Information Center	Littleton	303-773-4829
Mile High Center Law Library	Denver	303-832-3335
Montrose Memorial Hospital Medical Library	Montrose	970-240-7394
Morrison & Foerster Law Library	Denver	303-592-2259
Museum Of Western Colorado	Grand Junction	970-242-0971
National Archives and Records Adm.	Denver	303-236-0817
National Conference of State Legislatures	Denver	303-830-2200
National Indian Law Library	Boulder	303-447-8760

National Institute of Corrections Info. Center	Longmont	303-682-0213
Ntl. Jewish Center For Immun./Respiratory Medicine	Denver	303-398-1482
National Park Service Library	Denver	303-969-2716
National Renewable Energy Laboratory	Golden	303-275-4215
Parkview Episcopal Medical Center Medical Library	Pueblo	719-584-4582
Penrose St. Francis Healthcare System Library	Colorado Springs	719-630-5288
Platte River Power Authority Library	Fort Collins	970-229-5230
Porter Memorial Hospital Medical Library	Denver	303-778-5656
Poudre Valley Hospital Library	Fort Collins	970-495-7323
Raytheon Engineers & Constructors Inc.	Englewood	303-843-2256
Rocky Mountain News Editorial Library	Denver	303-892-2746
Rose Medical Center Medical Library	Denver	303-320-2160
Schuller International Inc.	Littleton	303-978-5373
Science Apps International Corporate Library	Greenwood Village	303-773-6900
Second Judicial District Law Library	Denver	303-640-2233
Security Life Of Denver Corporate Library	Denver	303-860-2338
Shepard's/Mcgraw-Hill Library	Colorado Springs	719-481-7548
Sherman & Howard L.C.C. Law Library	Denver	303-299-8041
Sixth Judicial District Law Library	Durango	970-259-0258
S. Metro Denver Small Business Development Center	Littleton	303-795-0142
Southeastern Colorado Area Health Education Center	Pueblo	719-544-7833
St. Anthony Hospital Central Medical Ref. Library	Denver	303-629-3790
St. John's Episcopal Cathedral Library	Denver	303-831-7115
St. Joseph Hospital Library	Denver	303-837-7188
St. Mary's Hospital & Medical Center Library	Grand Junction	970-244-2171
Stone & Webster Engineering Tech. Info. Center	Denver	303-741-7323
Storage Tech. Corporation Information Center	Louisville	303-673-5867
Swedish Medical Center Medical Library	Englewood	303-788-6616
Synergen Inc. Library & Information Center	Boulder	303-938-6214
Tri-County Health Department Library	Englewood	303-220-9200
U.S. Bureau Of Land Management Library	Denver	303-236-6649
U.S. Bureau Of Mines Library	Denver	303-236-0474
U.S. Bureau Of Reclamation Library	Denver	303-236-6963
U.S. Bureau Of Census Info. Services Program	Lakewood	303-969-7750
U.S. Court Of Appeals Tenth Circuit Library	Denver	303-844-3591
U.S. Dept. Of Veterans Admin. Med. Center Library	Denver	303-393-2821
U.S. Dept. Of Veterans Affairs Medical Library	Ft. Lyon	719-384-3130
U.S. Dept.Of Interior Geo. Survey Branch Library	Denver	303-236-5774
U.S. EPA Ntl. Enforcemement Investigations Ctr	Denver	303-236-5111
U S. EPA Region VIII Library	Denver	303-293-1444
U.S. National Biological Ecological Science Ctr.	Fort Collins	970-226-9403
U.S. Office Of Surface Mining Library	Denver	303-672-5538
U.S. Olympic Committee Info. Resources Center	Colorado Springs	719-578-4622
U.S. Veterans Affairs Medical Center Library	Grand Junction	970-242-0731
U S West Inc. Research Library	Englewood	303-754-5724
University Of Colorado Technical Reference Center	Boulder	303-492-8774
Ute Mountain Tribal Library	Towaoc	970-565-3751
Wayne Bond Memorial Technical Library	Denver	303-452-6111
Weld County District Court Law Library	Greeley	970-351-7300
Western Interstate Com. For Higher Educa. Library	Boulder	303-541-0285
YMCA Resource Center	Boulder	303-443-0419

ADDITIONAL RESOURCES

Colorado Department of Education, Communications Center, Room 500, 201 East Colfax Avenue, Denver, CO 80203-1799, (303) 866-6937. Call for prices and additional information about these selected publications:

1994-1995 Colorado Education and Library Directory. Lists every school and school administrator in Colorado. Also lists every public library and more. Updated annually.

State Report Card 1994, K - 12 Public Education in Colorado. Updated annually.

Newcomers' Packet, An Overview of Colorado's Public Education System.

Colorado Commission on Higher Education, 1300 Broadway, Second Floor, Denver, CO 80203 (303) 866-2723, offers numerous free reports on all aspects of Colorado's higher education system. Call for details.

Magnolia Street Press, 2600 Magnolia, Denver, CO 80207, (303) 322-2822.
The Guide to Metro Denver Public Schools, 1995-96 Edition
Colorado Private Elementary and Secondary Schools, 1995-96

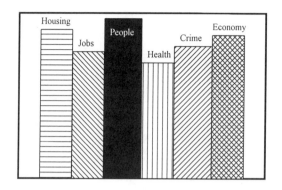

CHAPTER FOUR
THIS MUST BE THE PLACE

STATE-WIDE STATISTICS

General Statistics
Employment
Health Care
Taxes

If you like reading books on world records, technical computer manuals, or actuarial charts, you're going to love this chapter. I have attempted to take a large hodgepodge of data and edit it into a small hodgepodge of data. I have also attempted to integrate narrative material so as not to put the average reader to sleep. This chapter is loosely divided into the four sections shown above. You should keep in mind that many of the charts and figures are based on data which may be 1-3 years old and therefore may not provide an accurate picture. The data used is the most recent available from any source; however, due to the explosive growth Colorado has experienced during the last several years, the information provided should only be used as a basis for general trends or historical reference.

GENERAL STATISTICS
POPULATION GROWTH

Growth! From the smallest rural newspaper to the largest international magazines, the tremendous growth of Colorado is still making headlines. Regardless of which side of the debate you are on—that growth is a blessing or a curse—one thing is undeniable, the boom is not over. Recently released figures from the U.S. Census Bureau show that from 1990 to July 1994 the state's population grew 11 percent. Some counties experienced growth of more than 30 percent. Douglas County was in the lead with a total population increase of 45.8 percent. As a state, Colorado's population grew from 3,294,473 to 3,655,647. That is an additional 361,174 new residents. As of this writing, that figure is probably closer to 500,000!

Many lists of subjects like "The Fastest Growing Counties," "The Largest Counties," and related summaries are available from various sources. For the reasons stated in the beginning of this chapter, no such list should be considered definitive. In addition to the problem of "old" data concerning a rapidly changing subject, there is also the problem of statistical manipulation. This section contains three charts concerning the population growth in Colorado. One runs from 1990 to estimated July 1996 figures. The other two cover the time period of 1995 through 1996; however, one is based on percentage change and the other on numerical change. If one county had a numerical change of 37,000 new residents up from a base of 370,000 it would have a net 10% increase. However, if a small rural county with a base of 1,000 residents gained 110 new residents it would top the list with an 11% increase. You decide which has more growth.

10 LARGEST COUNTIES (1993)

County	Population 1990	Population 1996	Annual Growth Rate 1990-1996
Douglas	60,391	114,817	10.8%
Larimer	186,136	220,106	2.7%
El Paso	397,014	469,013	2.7%
Arapahoe	391,511	452,035	2.3%
Adams	265,038	305, 017	2.3%
Boulder	225,339	258,804	2.2%
Weld	131,821	151,108	2.2%
Jefferson	438,430	494,007	1.9%
Denver	467,610	497,007	1.0%
Pueblo	123,051	130,730	1.0%

(Population figures for 1997 are available but are still in the "challenge" period and thus have not been released as hard data).

10 FASTEST GROWING COUNTIES BASED ON PERCENTAGE CHANGE
1995 - 1996 (ESTIMATED DATA)

County	95 Pop	96 Pop	Change
Archuleta	7,068	7,874	11.4%
Elbert	14,533	16,088	10.7%
Douglas	103,943	114,817	10.5%
Custer	2,699	2,959	9.6%
Park	10,645	11,471	7.8%
Teller	17,387	18,665	7.4%
Lake	7,379	7,860	6.5%
Hinsdale	640	680	6.3%
Mineral	627	663	5.7%
Eagle	28,687	30,140	5.1%

10 FASTEST GROWING COUNTIES BASED ON NUMERICAL CHANGE
1995 - 1996 (ESTIMATED DATA)

County	95 Pop	96 Pop	Increase
Douglas	103,943	114,817	10,874
Arapahoe	443,378	452,035	8,657
Adams	297,869	305,107	7,148
Jefferson	488,017	494,007	5,990
El Paso	463,042	469,013	5,971
Larimer	215,742	220,106	4,364
Denver	492,990	497,007	4,017
Boulder	255,118	258,804	3,686
Weld	147,502	151,108	3,606
Elbert	14,533	16,008	1,555

SUBSTATE POPULATION PROJECTIONS

Colorado is divided into 5 substate regions (see chart in chapter one). The population projections below are an aggregation of all the counties within each region.

REGION	1998	2000	2005
Front Range	3,199,062	3,297,025	3,523,443
Western Slope	424,931	446,052	497,820
Eastern Plains	157,315	164,834	181,431
San Luis Valley	46,327	47,873	51,369
Eastern Mountains	139,354	145,177	158,990
Colorado Total	3,966,989	4,100,961	4,413,055

POPULATION PROJECTIONS

These projections show that the state's population, which has increased by over 100,000 persons/year in the past three years, will continue to increase, but at a slower rate over the next two years

The reasons for the continued growth can be broken down for different parts of the state, and, in particular those for the Front Range, the Western Slope, and then other parts of the state:

Growth in the Front Range in the next several years will be due to the continued increases in certain base industries that have grown in the past three or four years. The largest increases have been in the communications, engineering and business services, chemicals manufacturing, and trucking and warehousing. Other industries that have increased or remained strong in the Front Range have been in electrical machinery and instruments manufacturing, the Federal government, air transportation and construction, which from 1990 to 1993 was significantly related to the new airport. Increases are expected to continue over the next ten years but, in most of these industries, especially construction, at slower rates than have occurred in the last several years.

On the Western Slope, which is actually the fastest growing part of the state, growth is occurring for several reasons. The most obvious is the resort areas in Summit, Eagle (Vail), Pitkin (Aspen), San Miguel (Telluride) and Routt (Steamboat Springs) counties. Here the new construction boom in second-homes and resort facilities has created construction and service jobs for new permanent populations, many of whom are forced to reside in neighboring counties such as Lake, Grand, Garfield, and Montrose. In addition, the attractiveness of the Western Slope cities to small businesses and telecommuters wanting to get away from large metropolitan areas has spawned considerable growth in La Plata (Durango), Montezuma (Cortez), Mesa (Grand Junction), Delta, Montrose, and Chaffee (Salida) counties. Thirdly, the attractiveness of all of these areas and others, Archuleta, for example, to retirees, is also adding population to the region. All of the factors behind these types of growth—the growing number of tourist dollars as the baby-boomers reach middle-age, the desire of many small businesses to move to smaller areas, and the overall number of retirees—are expected to continue or increase throughout the projection period.

Five counties elsewhere in the state have grown or will grow because of the location of new prisons and the effect they have in rural areas of solidifying a local economic base and creating a market for new housing. Fremont County (Canon City) with its large state and Federal (Florence) facilities will continue to provide a very large number of prison-related jobs (as well as house a large number of inmates) for residents of not only Fremont county but also Pueblo, El Paso, and Chaffee counties. In the past five years the economies of Lincoln

(Limon), Crowley (Ordway), and Bent (Lamar) counties have been boosted by the addition of new prisons. Ground has been broken outside the town of Sterling in Logan County for a prison facility that could ultimately house 4,000 prisoners. The 1,000 plus jobs that will result from this will kick off the growth of new residential areas. This will help to provide housing for many workers in other new industries that have had to commute to the county because of the shortage of housing.

The remainder of the state, largely agricultural counties, will grow at slower rates, but this growth is in contrast (in many of these counties) to the declines they have experienced for more than four decades. Growth in the Front Range, elsewhere in the West, and new ties to the Pacific Rim generally will increase the markets for their agricultural goods. In addition, many of these non-metropolitan counties and communities will continue to attract small businesses (some related to agriculture, some not) and new retirees—as they have in the recent past—as part of the overall growth in the multi-state region.

In a broader national context, above average growth is occurring in Colorado because of above average growth in the West and because of new decentralization tendencies away from California, which is the primary destination for an ever-increasing number of immigrants. Since the 1990 Census, the fastest growing states in the country have been Nevada, Idaho, Arizona, Utah, and Colorado with Arizona and Colorado adding the most population—410,000 and 362,000 respectively.

Colorado's potential for gain from these general trends in the West is reinforced by the special attractiveness of the state and the Front Range to businesses and their employees and for other residents. Denver in particular, Colorado Springs, and other metropolitan areas of the Front Range, are ideally situated in the newly emergent international economy. They sit halfway between the trading centers of Chicago, St. Louis, Texas and the Gulf of Mexico and those of the West Coast. They are also favorably juxtaposed between the growing trading centers of Mexico and those of Northwestern Canada. One reason for the growth of the cable television industry in Denver is its central position for satellite relay between Europe and the Pacific Rim.

The Denver International Airport will secure the region's (including Ft. Collins and Greeley) role as a national and international trading center as well as the airport's own role as a transportation hub. The recently completed expansion of the Colorado Springs Airport along with presence of a strong community-based University will also enable that metropolitan area to take advantage of the state's beneficial location and quality of life. Airports in other parts of the state will also be critical in supporting the growth potentials in those areas.

EMPLOYMENT

In February 1995, the Colorado Department of Labor and Employment released its report on Colorado Occupational Employment Outlook 1994-1999. This 35-page report contains data on the growth expected in virtually every occupation. This information is helpful for those contemplating a move to Colorado and to those deciding on educational and career goals. A summary of this report appears below.

Approximately 46% of the jobs created by growth from 1994-1999 is expected to come from two major occupational categories: Professional / Para-Professional / Technical, and Services. Job growth in the Sales, Clerical / Administrative Support, and Blue Collar positions should account for an additional 43% of total new job growth. The remaining 11% will occur in Managerial/Administrative, and Agriculture/Forestry/Fishing.

Professional/Para-Professional/Technical (including Education and Computer Sciences), and the Services Sector are anticipated to continue their dominance as the generator of the largest number of new positions. Although all subsectors, with the exception of Hospitals and Legal Services, are predicted to grow at a rapid pace, almost two-thirds of the new services positions are expected to be created by Business Services, Health Services, and Engineering, Accounting, Research, Management, and Related Services.

The Trade Sector is expected to produce jobs at just over half the rate of the Services sector. The largest increase will be in Restaurants and Bars, Building Materials and Mobile Home Dealers, Apparel and Accessory Stores, and Furniture and Home Furnishings.

Transportation, Communications, and Public Utilities are expected to have the third highest growth rate. Motor Freight Transportation and Warehousing will be the greatest contributor of new positions. Communications is expected to create 522 new jobs per year.

The Finance, Insurance and Real Estate Sector has a predicted growth rate of 1.9% generating 2,080 positions annually. The highest rate is predicted for the Security and Commodity Brokers and Credit Agencies other than banks.

Although **Manufacturing** has been in decline in recent years and roughly one-third of its subsectors are expected to decline over the next five years, this sector, as a whole, is expected to grow at a rate of 2.4% from 1994-1999. The largest increases are projected in Lumber and Wood Products, Machinery, Electrical/Electronic Equipment, and Printing/Publishing. The six declining subsectors include Food Products, Textiles, Chemicals, Transportation Equipment, Instruments/Photographic Equipment, and Miscellaneous Manufacturing Industries.

Overall, the **Mining** industry will be declining at a rate of 1.4% annually with the exception of Bituminous Coal/Lignite Mining and Nonmetallic Minerals which will grow at an annual rate of 0.2% and 0.7% respectively.

The Construction Sector, although expected to incur losses over the next five years, will retain levels considerably higher than the majority of those seen over the past decade. Annual job loss for the entire industry is expected to be 1,160.

Local Government is expected to far exceed State and Federal Government in growth. Anticipated job growth at the local level is 2,680 positions per year. State Government will provide 980 positions annually while another 1,900 new positions are expected from the Federal Government level.

ADDITIONAL RESOURCES

Publications produced (including the one used for this section) by the Labor Market Information Section of the Colorado State Department of Labor and Employment, 1515 Arapahoe St., Denver, CO 80202, (303) 620-4718:

Occupational Employment Survey; Occupational Supply/Demand Report; Occupational Employment Statistics Wage Survey; Job Bank Wage Listing; Colorado Labor Market Information Directory; Occupation Information System (on-line).

COLORADO LARGEST EMPLOYERS

I once interviewed for a high-paying position with an "International Corporation." The interview was conducted in an expensively furnished office and the offers were very generous—too generous. Listening to my intuition, I did some checking and discovered I was dealing with a "paper" corporation with questionable resources and intentions. If you are looking for a position and come across one with United Airlines, Hewlett Packard, UPS or another "household" name, you probably won't have doubts about the offer. Below is a list of many lesser-known regional or statewide companies that employ between 100-16,000 in Colorado. If you like the security of working for a "large and stable" company, this list may help you sort through the classifieds.

ACX Technologies	Candy's Tortilla Factory	First Bank System
Adolph Coors Co	CommNet Cellular Inc.	First Federal Savings
Air Methods Corp.	ConAgra (Monfort)	Fischer Imaging Corp.
ARA Services	Confertech International	Forest Oil Corp.
Ball Corp.	Cyprus Amax Minerals	Gerrity Oil & Gas Corp.
Basin Exploration	Dayton/Hudson Corp.	Good Times Restaurants
Bestop Inc.	Eastman Kodak	Grease Monkey
BI Incorporated	Electromedics Inc.	Hach Co.
Big O Tires Inc.	Exabyte Corp.	Hauser Chem Research

Hugh M. Woods	Mewmont Gold Co.	Storage Technology
Jones Intercable Inc.	Neodata Services	Synergen Inc.
King Soopers	Newmont Mining Corp.	Tele-Communications Inc.
KN Energy Inc.	Norwest Corp.	U.S. West Inc.
Manville Corp.	OEA Inc.	Vicorp Restaurants Inc.
May Co./Foley's	PCL Construction	Western Gas Resources
MCI Communications	Random Access Inc.	
MDC Holdings Inc.	Safeway	
Mercantile Stores	Southland Corp.	

HEALTH CARE

FACTS AT A GLANCE (1990 DATA)

PHYSICIANS: 202 per 100,000 population
HOSPITAL DAILY ROOM CHARGE: $262
DENTISTS: 66 per 100,000 population
INFANT MORTALITY RATE, ALL RACES: 9.3 deaths per 1,000 live births
LEGAL ABORTIONS RATE: 335 per 1,000 live births
DEATHS, ACCIDENTS: 38.4 per 100,000 residents
DEATHS, CANCER: 133.4 per 100,000 residents
DEATHS, HEART DISEASE: 197.7 per 100,000 residents
DEATHS, HOMICIDE: 7.3 per 100,000 residents
DEATHS, LIVER DISEASE AND CIRRHOSIS: 9.5 per 100,000 residents
DEATHS, PNEUMONIA AND FLU: 26.4 per 100,000 residents
DEATHS, SUICIDE: 17.6 per 100,000 residents
AIDS CASES REPORTED, 1989: 315 (RATE): 11.54 per 100,000 residents

HEALTH CARE FACILITIES

To describe every health care facility in Colorado would take 257, 8 1/2 x 11 pages. Suffice it to say, for most of us, having a hospital within an hour of home is good enough. Knowing most ski resorts have some type of emergency facilities and Air Rescue/Ambulance can reach all but the most rugged mountain terrain should ease our fears of injury or serious illness. But what if you or a family member has special medical needs or you are planning a rural move and would like to know what facilities are nearby? There are 20 separate directories available from the Colorado Department of Health and Environment, 4300 Cherry Creek Dr. S., #A200, Denver, CO 80222-1530, (303) 692-2800, which contain complete data. Below is a list of the directories offered. Call the CDHE for the most current pricing and availability.

Alternative Care Facilities	Community Clinics
Ambulatory Surgical Centers	Community Mental Health Clinics

Elderly, Blind, Disabled Facilities
End Stage Renal Dialysis Units
Home Health Agencies
Hospices
Hospitals - Alphabetic
Intermediate Care Facilities
Mammography Facilities
Nursing Homes - Alphabetic

Nursing Homes by City
Nursing Homes by County
Occupational Therapy Facilities
Personal Care Boarding Homes
Physical Therapy Facilities
Portable X-Ray Units
Rural Health Clinics
Swing Beds

TAXES

In addition to Federal income taxes, Colorado residents are subject to Colorado state income taxes, state sales tax and there are some county and city sales taxes and various special taxes.

STATE INCOME TAX

Colorado's personal income tax is 5% of what you claim as your federal taxable income (after all deductions and adjustments). If you work for someone else you will notice state withholding from every paycheck. If you are self-employed, you are responsible for estimated payments and collections just as with federal income tax. This 5% also applies to corporations. Residency determines whether 100% or some lesser proportions is allocated to Colorado. Residents are allowed credit for tax payments to another state.

STATE/COUNTY/CITY SALES TAX

The State of Colorado has a flat 3% sales tax on the purchase price of retail sales of tangible personal property. This tax also applies to used vehicles and certain services such as telephone. Many counties and cities also have sales taxes that vary and can be as high as 4% for counties and 5% in cities. In addition, certain districts have Special Taxes for Public Transportation, Cultural Facilities, Highway Construction and the like. The bottom line is this: in some counties you will pay only 3% sales tax on everything you buy and in others it can be three times that amount. But don't bother going to another county to buy your new $60,000 Range Rover to save the extra $2000 in taxes. Taxes on such purchases are based on your address of record, not where you purchase the vehicle. And if you buy all new furniture in a county without extra taxes and pick it up yourself you are fine. However, if you have it delivered to a county/city with extra taxes, and the retailer has a store there, you pay. The same applies to mail orders when the company has a store in your county/city. Real simple, eh?

HIDDEN TAXES

As mentioned above, you will pay the appropriate amount of sales tax on all vehicle purchases. However, you can also expect to pay additional taxes when you register and title your vehicle. This is better explained in Chapter Five. Every time you have an alcoholic beverage you are paying a hidden tax imposed on the manufacturer. This tax ranges from 8 cents a gallon on beer to 60.27 cents per liter on liquor. If you smoke you pay 20 cents tax per pack and 20% of list price on all other tobacco products. Every time you bet on a horse or tell the dealer to "hit me," you are paying special taxes. And let's not forget about the 22 cents per gallon on gasoline, etc., etc. Call the Department of Revenue with any specific questions.

CHAPTER FIVE
BEHIND THE WHEEL

VEHICLES

Registration/Titles, Tags, Insurance, Emissions, Drivers' Licenses

The information in this chapter was compiled from various sources including, but not limited to, government reports and publications (Federal, State, and Local); materials provided by business and civic organizations; and other books produced by independent Colorado publishers including:

Colorado Revised Statutes 1997, Vehicles and Traffic, Bradford Publishing

For a complete description of the above books and related titles, please see the Publisher's listing in Appendix A.

For a list of legal forms available from Bradford Publishing see Appendix D.

On April 25, 1901, New York became the first state to require automobile license plates; the fee was $1. Today, if you are a resident in the City and County of Denver and purchase a new sport utility vehicle (the vehicle of choice in Colorado) for around $25,000, it will cost you approximately $2,500 for title, taxes, and tags. In addition, you can expect to pay approximately

$600 the following year to renew the tags. This fee is gradually reduced on the 3rd, 5th, and 10th year of ownership.

That is probably why I kept both my Florida driver's license and the Florida tags on my vehicle for almost 5 years after I moved to Denver (which, contrary to what I may state elsewhere in this book, was many, many years ago and I'm sure the Statute of Limitations for my heinous offense has since expired). I was lucky to get away with it as long as I did. This was before the Department of Revenue initiated its violator Hotline. This Hotline was established so people could call and turn in anyone (noisy neighbors, ex-lovers, or anyone from California) who they believed were living in Colorado yet keeping an out-of-state plate or driver's license. The Hotline was flooded with reports and the dreaded "Truant Title and Tag Police" went into action.

It turned out many of the offenders were long-time Colorado residents who registered their $25,000 Chevy Blazers in another neighboring state where the whole shebang only cost about $10 per year. Shame! Shame!

All kidding and serious warnings aside, when I did finally decide (not by choice) to become an officially registered and tagged citizen of Colorado, I found the entire process very confusing and frustrating. I couldn't get my vehicle plates because I did not have an emissions test; I couldn't get an emissions test because my vehicle was titled and tagged in Florida. They wouldn't accept a bill of sale written on a vodka and tonic stained bar napkin and they told me when I went to trade in my Florida Driver's License that someone with *my* name, height, weight and address was already in possession of a Colorado ID card. OK, maybe it wasn't all that bad, but it can be a very frustrating process if you don't know everything "you should have known" before attempting the big switchover.

Hopefully, this chapter will help prevent a great deal of aggravation by providing you with the basic information "you should have known."

NOTE: Everything in this chapter only applies to on-road vehicles. All off-road vehicles (3 or 4 wheel ATV's, Boats, Snowmobiles, et al.,) that are not required to have a tag, are required to have an annual registration sticker. The State Department of Resources, Division of Parks and Recreation, Registration Division, handles this process. Many county offices carry the proper forms or the entire process can be completed through the mail.

> Write or call:
> Division of Parks & Recreation
> Registration Division
> P.O. Box 231
> Littleton, CO 80160
> 303-791-1920

REGISTRATIONS/TITLES

> **Every citizen of Colorado who owns or drives a vehicle is required to have a Colorado Driver's License, Colorado Vehicle Title and Registration, and Colorado Vehicle License Plates.** You establish state residency at the first occurrence of the following: Working at any type of job, owning or operating a business in Colorado, obtaining a Colorado Driver's License or living in the state continuously for 90 days. In other words, unless you are independently wealthy, this means almost immediately upon moving here. There are certain exceptions for special employment situations, military personnel and students. **BEWARE - Effective August 6, 1997 failure to register your vehicle within 30 days of establishing residency may result in substantial fines!** See the section on Drivers' Licenses.

A vehicle registration is that little piece of white paper you only see after you have been asked for it by a police officer. A vehicle title is the more official looking document that proves you own the vehicle (with or without liens). Although these are two separate documents, the information, applications, and fees for both are combined into one process in Colorado.

In all counties except Denver, the County Clerk or Motor Vehicle office handles this process. The end of this section provides a list of County Clerk's phone numbers for each county. Denver has several locations that are also listed. **You must register your vehicle in the county where you reside.**

The requirements for registering and titling a vehicle are covered for three different circumstances: bringing a vehicle in from another state, buying a new or used vehicle from a dealer within Colorado, and buying a used vehicle from a private owner.

TRANSFERRING STATES

To license and register a vehicle from another state, you must have the following:

- Certificate of title for the vehicle
- Current registration
- Vehicle Identification Number (VIN) verification completed by a:
  - Licensed Vehicle Dealer
  - Emissions Testing Station
  - Law Enforcement Agency
- Emissions Test Certificate (where required, see Emissions Section)

BUYING FROM A DEALER

The process here depends on how you pay for your new or used vehicle. If you pay cash, the dealer will issue a temporary tag and hand you the rest of the paperwork. You then have to proceed to the proper office to register the vehicle and obtain your plates. If you have some type of financing, the process is a little different. In this case, the dealer will send the proper information to the lien holder who will take care of the title work. Once the county receives an OK from the lien holder, you will be notified by postcard and will then have to go to the proper office in your county to apply for permanent tags.

Note: Most car dealers are authorized to collect state sales tax, some county and city taxes, and certain fees involved. It's best to make sure you know what taxes and fees are covered in the purchase price so you don't get a rude awakening when you go to apply for tags.

BUYING FROM A PRIVATE OWNER

Let's say you can't exactly afford the new $25,000 Jeep you want so you settle for another used vehicle from a private owner. In this situation, you will need the following to register your vehicle:

- A signed (and possibly notarized, see note below) vehicle title
- A recent (within 120 days) emission test (where required) provided by the seller
- A notarized bill of sale indicating purchase price (see note below)

Titles: Colorado titles issued after January 1, 1990 do not require a notary seal. There is a space on the back where the purchase price is entered. Titles issued before January 1, 1990 require the seller(s) to sign the title in the presence of a notary public. If the vehicle has an out-of-state title you would be well advised to check with your county clerk to verify the requirements. Also, make sure the current title is in the name of the individual selling the car and that nothing has been filled-in or "whited-out" on the back. The powers that be frown upon third party title transfers and whiteout.

Bill of Sale: Although not required, especially for titles issued after January, 1990, it is well worth the effort to obtain a notarized bill of sale showing the vehicle make, model, year, and VIN number along with the purchase price. The amount of sales tax the state, county or city collects is based on your purchase price and they have the option to collect taxes based on the current blue-book value of the vehicle if the purchase price you declare is in doubt and you do not have a notarized bill of sale as proof.

Taxes and fees: There are many taxes and fees involved in transferring a title and getting tags. These include title fee of $5.50, registration fee, license fee based on the weight of the vehicle, ownership taxes based on the age and original value, sales taxes (state and possibly county and city), and depending on the county in which you reside, additional miscellaneous fees. When buying from a private owner, you will have to pay all this when you transfer title and register your vehicle.

PHONE LIST FOR COUNTY CLERKS

ADAMS	303-654-6010	LAKE	719-486-1410
ALAMOSA	719-589-6681	LA PLATA	970-385-0240
ARAPAHOE	303-795-4500	LARIMER	970-498-7878
ARCHULETA	970-264-5633	LAS ANIMAS	719-846-3314
BACA	719-523-4372	LINCOLN	719-743-2444
BENT	719-456-2009	LOGAN	970-522-1544
BOULDER	303-441-3510	MESA	970-244-1667
CHAFFEE	719-539-4004	MINERAL	719-658-2440
CHEYENNE	719-767-5685	MOFFAT	970-824-9104
CLEAR CREEK	303-569-3251	MONTEZUMA	970-565-3728
CONEJOS	719-376-5422	MONTROSE	970-249-3362
COSTILLA	719-672-3301	MORGAN	970-867-5616
CROWLEY	719-267-4643	OTERO	719-383-3020
CUSTER	719-783-2441	OURAY	970-325-4961
DELTA	970-874-2150	PARK	719-836-4222
DENVER	303-576-2882	PHILLIPS	970-854-3131
DOLORES	970-677-2381	PITKIN	970-920-5180
DOUGLAS	303-660-7440	PROWERS	719-336-4337
EAGLE	970-328-8710	PUEBLO	719-583-6507
ELBERT	303-621-2341	RIO BLANCO	970-878-5068
EL PASO	719-520-6240	RIO GRANDE	719-657-3334
FREMONT	719-275-1522	ROUTT	970-870-5557
GARFIELD	970-945-2377	SAGUACHE	719-655-2512
GILPIN	303-582-5321	SAN JUAN	970-387-5671
GRAND	970-725-3347	SAN MIGUEL	970-728-3954
GUNNISON	970-641-1602	SEDGWICK	970-474-3346
HINSDALE	970-944-2228	SUMMIT	970-668-5623
HUERFANO	719-738-2380	TELLER	719-689-2951
JACKSON	970-723-4334	WASHINGTON	970-345-6565
JEFFERSON	303-271-8100	WELD	970-353-3840
KIOWA	719-438-5421	YUMA	970-332-5809
KIT CARSON	719-346-8638		

LICENSE PLATES (TAGS)

The procedure for obtaining license plates is covered in the previous section, Registrations/Titles. This section provides information about the various types of plates available and the requirements for special plates.

There are 47 different types of plates issued in Colorado. Six are for vehicle manufacturers or dealers, six are government-type plates issued to city, county, and state vehicles, with special plates for State Senators, State Representatives, members of Congress, U.S. Senators and members of the

Honorary Consular Corps. Several more are issued to utility companies, farm vehicles, commercial fleets, and tractor/trailer rigs or heavy trucks.

For the rest of us, a wide choice of standard or custom versions is offered. The most common plate is the standard green mountain with white background. A second version called DENIM, is white and blue and shows the Colorado "C". Both versions can be personalized with a 10 - 12 week waiting period. A third type is the "Always Buy Colorado" which is a limited edition of 1,000 plates. All the above come in two classes:

Passenger: Passenger vehicles, station wagons, hearses, ambulances (non-government), passenger vans, buses and motor homes.

Light Trucks: Empty weight less than 16,000 pounds, body designed to transport property with special fees for tow trucks, wreckers, race horse vehicles, veterinary mobile trucks, and special use vehicles.

OTHER VEHICLE CLASSES:

Recreational Truck: Trucks that do not have an empty weight over 6,500 pounds and are not used exclusively for pleasure (non-commercial).

Trailer: Wheeled vehicle without motor power.

Motorcycle: Motor vehicle designed to travel on no more than 3 wheels.

Collector Series: Vehicles at least 25 years old, passenger and trucks, not for commercial use. Plates are issued for a 5-year period.

Street Rod: Issued to passenger and light trucks made in 1948 or earlier.

Horseless Carriage: Manufactured in 1942 or prior. Driving limited to/from auto club functions, to/from repair shops, and occasional leisure drive.

OTHER CUSTOMS PLATES:

Special Organizational: "Naval Reserve"—to individuals in the Naval Reserve. "Honorably Discharged Veteran"—available to any person who has received an honorable discharge from any branch of the U.S. Armed Services. Issued to passenger and light trucks. One set only.

Disabled Veteran: One free set to qualifying applicant (50% or more permanent service connected disability occurring prior to 5/7/75). Issued to passenger, light truck, recreational truck, farm truck or motor home weighing less than 6,500 pounds.

Former Prisoner of War: One free set to qualifying applicant (on active duty with U.S. Armed Forces during a period of armed conflict and was incarcerated by an enemy of the U.S.). Issued to same vehicles as above.

Persons with Disability: Issued to passenger, light truck or mobile homes. Application must be signed by Colorado licensed physician.

Amateur Radio/Commercial Call Letters: Issued to passenger and light trucks with an empty weight of less than 5,000 pounds. One set per amateur call letter, up to 10 sets per commercial call letter.

For additional information concerning special or custom plates, call the State Motor Vehicle Division at 303-205-5607.

VEHICLE INSURANCE

Vehicle insurance is MANDATORY in Colorado. In fact, there are 41 Colorado Revised Statues under Article 7, Motor Vehicle Financial Responsibility Law. When you register your vehicle you must sign a sworn statement indicating you now carry and will continue to carry the proper insurance. The mandatory liability minimum is $25,000 bodily injury, $50,000 per accident, and $15,000 property damage. You are required to have proof of insurance with you at all times when driving and failure to do so can result in a mandatory court appearance and possible fines. The courts in this state tend to go ballistic on people without proper insurance coverage!

The only exception to the above are those who qualify for a certificate of self-insurance. Don't count on it. C.R.S. 42-7-501 reads as follows:

"Any person in whose name more than twenty-five motor vehicles are registered may qualify as a self-insurer. . . when the director [of motor vehicles] is satisfied that such person is possessed and will continue to be possessed of ability to pay all judgments which may be obtained against such person."

EMISSIONS TESTING

You can save yourself a lot of brain damage by skipping this section unless you plan to, or currently live in **or work** in the following counties:

Enhanced Program Area: Adams, Arapahoe, Boulder, Denver, Douglas, El Paso and Jefferson counties.

Basic Program Area: Larimer, Pitkin and Weld counties.

Due to several factors (topography, heavy industry, and an increasing number of automobiles), the front-range of Colorado—especially the greater Denver metro region—suffers from what is known as the "Brown Cloud." When conditions are right, this cloud of pollutants can easily be seen from miles away. In an attempt to reduce the major source of pollutants (automobile emissions), the state's Air Care Colorado Program has recently intensified its effort to reduce emissions by instituting a more stringent testing program along with the older "tailpipe" test which has existed for years.

This effort has not been without its difficulties. The new test and testing facilities have been under attack since their inception from both consumers and some state legislators alike. If you live or work in any of the above listed counties (exceptions noted below), you MUST have a valid emissions test to register your vehicle and a valid emissions sticker on the windshield of your car or truck.

ENHANCED PROGRAM AREA

1981 and older vehicles: A tailpipe test is required each year at an Air Care Colorado Facility or an independent test-only station.

1982 and newer vehicles: An enhanced emission test (on a dynamometer under actual driving conditions) is required at an Air Care Colorado facility every two years.

Change of ownership: An emission test is required when a vehicle is sold or its ownership changes. The seller is responsible for obtaining the test.

Commuters: Vehicles registered outside of the region but which are driven into the six county area 90 or more days a year must also undergo the tests.

Newly manufactured vehicles: Any new, never titled, vehicle is exempt from the emissions test for four years, or until a change of ownership. *(Like, if you sell a brand new car one day after you get it, somehow it magically becomes capable of polluting).*

Cost: $24.25 for 1982 and newer vehicles - 2-year sticker.

$15.00 for 1981 and older vehicles - 1-year sticker.

$45.00 for diesel powered vehicles - 1-year sticker.

Tips to ease the pain:

- Check your emissions sticker for the expiration date and have your vehicle tested promptly.
- Call the Air Care Colorado **Hotline at 303-456-7090** for the best time and most convenient locations (see map).
- Standard hours of operation are M-F, 7:00 a.m. to 7:30 p.m., and Sat., 8:00 a.m. to 3:00 p.m. Closed Sundays and Holidays.
- Avoid the busiest times—the first three days and the last three days of each month, as well as any time during the noon hour.
- Make certain your vehicle has a gas cap.
- Cash and checks are accepted, but **NOT credit cards.**

- **Warm up your engine** thoroughly for at least 15 minutes before testing.
- All-Wheel and four-wheel drive vehicles must use specially marked testing lanes (make sure you don't wait in the wrong lanes).
- If your vehicle fails the test you can have it re-tested free after repairs within 10 days of the initial test.
- In the Enhanced Program Area, test and repairs **are not** done at the same facility.

Now, if that's not confusing enough, there are certain parts of Adams and Arapahoe counties that are completely exempt from any testing. In General, if you live east of Kiowa Creek you are exempt. However, as stated above, if you work west of Kiowa Creek, you need the test. The same degree of confusion applies to the Basic Program Area covered next.

BASIC PROGRAM AREA

In the basic program area (Larimer, Pitkin, and Weld counties), all vehicles, regardless of age (except new, never been titled) are required to have an annual tailpipe test only. There are independent inspection and repair facilities and inspections and repairs **can be** performed at the same facility.

The cost for this test is $15.00 and 1982 and newer vehicles receive a 2 year sticker and 1981 and older a 1 year.

Now, all of Pitkin county participates, a large portion of Larimer county including Loveland, Fort Collins and Poudre Park participates, yet Estes Park, Rustic and Virginia Dale areas are completely exempt. As far as Weld county is concerned, only the city of Greeley is involved, the remainder of the county is exempt from all testing. But remember the Commuters Regulation about working in a covered area. If in doubt, call the Air Care Colorado Hotline at 303-456-7090.

A map showing enhanced testing station locations appears at the end of this chapter.

DRIVER'S LICENSE

Colorado law states you must obtain a Colorado driver's license and vehicle plates immediately upon establishing state residency. The state considers you a resident upon the first occurrence of the following: you work at any type of gainful employment, you own or operate a business in Colorado, you obtain a Colorado drivers' license or you live here continuously for 90 days.

The information presented in this section is intended as a guideline. For complete information please obtain a copy of the *Colorado Drivers' Manual and Supplemental Motorcycle Drivers' Manual.*

Any person 16 years of age or older who operates a motor vehicle or motor driven cycle (including MOPEDS) on the public streets and highways is required to have a valid license. The only exceptions to this are as follows:

Special Employment: Any resident who is employed in another state where the laws of that state require licensing to drive in order to engage in a regular trade or profession, does not need a Colorado driver's license as long as such other license to drive is in force and the employment is not terminated. This exemption applies only if the other state is a member of the Interstate Driver License Compact Agreement.

Other Exemptions: The following need not obtain a Colorado license provided they are 16 years of age or older and possess a valid license from their home state or state of last assignment.

- **Military:** Anyone who is serving as a member of the Armed Forces of the U.S. on active duty including the spouse and children of such member.

- **Foreign Military:** On duty or assigned to temporary duty with the U.S. Armed Forces to include the spouse and children of such member.

- **Students:** Any non-resident who is temporarily residing in Colorado for the principal purpose of furthering his/her education and who is considered a non-resident for tuition purposes. If a student, regardless of the above, also works (even part-time) in Colorado, he/she needs both a Colorado driver's license and plates.

- **Trainees/Instructors:** Any employee of a Colorado licensed company, corporation, organization, school or business who is assigned temporarily in Colorado for the principle purpose of receiving or teaching special training relative to his trade, profession or employment.

- **Non-Resident Aliens:** Foreign tourists, instructors and business persons may drive up to one year with their own personal driver's license. Such foreign driver's license and/or permits issued by foreign countries are recognized when the holder has a valid U.S. Immigration Form 1-94, Arrival/Departure Record, and is driving any private (non-commercial) vehicle including rental vehicles.

Colorado issues five classifications of driver's licenses:

The Class R (basic license) applies to any vehicle with a GVWR of less than 26,001 lbs., as a single unit or in combination, manufactured to transport 15 or fewer passengers including the driver, and not used to transport hazardous materials. The Class R license is valid for chauffeur purposes and for motorized bicycles (MOPEDS).

The Class M (motorcycle) license is valid for any vehicle designed to travel on not more than three wheels in contact with the ground except any such vehicle as may be included within the term farm vehicle or motorized bicycle.

Commercial Driver's License: There are three classes of commercial driver's licenses which are covered in the Colorado Drivers' Manual.

NOTE: If you drive both automobiles and motorcycles, you do not need two licenses. For qualified applicants, a motorcycle endorsement is added to the Class R license.

NEW RESIDENTS WITH A VALID LICENSE

If you are 16 years of age or older and have a valid license in your possession which was issued by another U.S. state, territory or possession, you will normally not be required to take the road performance test nor written examination if the out-of-state license is similar to the Colorado classified driver's license and you surrender the valid out-of-state license.

The driver examiner has a responsibility to require a road performance test, even if you turn in a valid license, if there appears to be a problem with your Physical Aptitude Analysis (obvious disabilities), your Driving Record Analysis, or your Visual Screening (required in all cases).

Should you fail the road performance test, you will be issued an Instruction Permit. When you return to complete the test, both the Instruction Permit and any driver's license must be surrendered.

FEES: $15 for 5-year license, $16 if motorcycle endorsement was part of old licenses. Add $16 for new motorcycle endorsements.

NOTE: If you plan to drive a motorcycle in Colorado and you do not have a motorcycle endorsement on your previous license you will be required to take both the written and motorcycle driving skills test.

Renewal of A Colorado License or Instruction Permit: Once you obtain a Colorado Classified Driver's License or Instruction Permit, you will not normally have to repeat the written or driving test unless:

- You apply for a different class of license or endorsement
- You receive traffic tickets (8 or more points)
- You are driving when a fatality has occurred
- The license or permit is canceled, revoked or denied
- You let the license or permit expire

You Can Lose Your License: All reports of traffic accidents and traffic law violations committed in Colorado are posted to your record. A poor record may be cause for suspension or revocation of your driving privilege.

Suspension may be for any period up to one year. Revocation must be for at least one year.

POINTS ASSESSED

12 Points: Leaving scene of accident, DWI or under the influence of drugs, speed contests, eluding or attempting to elude a police officer

8 Points: Driving while ability is impaired by alcohol, reckless driving

6 Points: Failure to stop for a school bus

4 Points: Careless driving or following too closely, driving on wrong side of road, improper passing, failure to observe traffic sign or signal, failure to yield to emergency vehicle, failure to maintain or show proof of insurance

3 Points: Failure to yield right-of-way, improper turn, driving through safety zone, driving in wrong lane or direction on one-way street, conviction of violations not listed

2 Points: Failure to signal or improper signal, improper backing, failure to dim or turn on lights, operating an unsafe vehicle

Speeding over posted limit

1 Point   1 - 4 m.p.h.
3 Points   5 - 9 m.p.h.
4 Points   10 -19 m.p.h.
6 points   20 - or more m.p.h.

YOUR DRIVING PRIVILEGE MAY BE SUSPENDED/REVOKED/CANCELED IF YOU:

- Are convicted of DUI of alcohol or drugs
- Refuse to be tested for alcohol or drug content
- Leave the scene of an accident without stopping, exchanging information, and rendering aid
- Fail to report an accident to the Colorado Motor Vehicle Division according to the requirements of the financial responsibility law
- Give false information on your drivers' license application
- Fail to settle a judgment against you as a result of an accident while operating a vehicle
- Lend your license to someone else or misuse it in any way
- Alter or deface your license
- Fail to appear for a special reexamination requested by the Motor Vehicle Division
- Use a motor vehicle in committing a felony
- Are convicted of manslaughter as a result of a motor vehicle accident

If you are convicted of driving "while under suspension," your driving privilege will be suspended again effective for ONE YEAR FROM THE DATE YOU WOULD HAVE BEEN REINSTATED.

RE-EXAMINATION OF DRIVERS

You may be required to submit to a reexamination if the Motor Vehicle Division has good cause to believe you are incompetent or otherwise not qualified to be licensed. After you have taken the examination, your license may be returned, suspended, revoked, or you may be issued a restricted license. Refusal to submit to this test is grounds for suspension or revocation of your license.

COLORADO POINT SYSTEM

There are a specified number of points assigned for most traffic law violations. If you accumulate a certain number of points, your license may be suspended for up to one year. Points assessed against your record are not erased when you get a new license.

A driver's license may be classified as a chauffeur license; however, the vehicle must be a public or common carrier. To qualify as chauffeur points, all violations must have been received as a chauffeur of a motor vehicle in use as a public or common carrier of persons or property.

The point accumulations for suspension are as follows:

Minor Driver: More than 5 points in any 12 consecutive months or more than 6 points for period of license.
Provisional Driver: 9 points in any 12 consecutive months or 12 points in any 24 consecutive months or 14 points for the period of the license.
Regular Driver: 12 points in any 12 consecutive months or 18 points in any 24 consecutive months.
Chauffeur Points: 16 points in any 12 consecutive months or 24 points in any 24 consecutive months or 28 points in any 48 consecutive months.

EXPRESSED CONSENT LAW (ALCOHOL & DRUGS)

The Expressed Consent Law provides that if a law enforcement officer suspects that a person is driving under the influence of alcohol or other drug substance and the driver refuses to take the required test, or if the result of such test indicates a blood alcohol concentration (BAC) of .10 or more, the officer will confiscate the driver's license and issue a "Notice of Revocation or Denial" which becomes a seven day driving permit. A request must be made at a drivers' license office, or in writing, within the seven days allotted on the driving permit or the revocation of the license and driving privilege becomes effective automatically. If you do not have a valid driver's license the "Notice of Revocation or Denial" issued by the officer DOES NOT become a seven day driving permit and only allows the person to request a hearing within the seven day period.

IDENTIFICATION CARDS

To obtain a Colorado ID card you must appear in person at any drivers' license office. You must present at least two (2) documents of identification to support your true name and correct birthday, such as a state certified birth certificate, marriage certificate, or other legal documents. Documented proof of a Social Security number is required. If you are under 60 years of age you will be required to pay the ID card fee.

THE DRIVER EXAMINATION

There are five separate tests to take in order to receive a driver's license: Driving Record Analysis, Physical Aptitude Analysis, Vision Screening, Basic Written Test, and Driving Test.

OFFICE LOCATIONS

MAIN OFFICE

1881 Pierce Street, Lakewood, CO 80214 (303) 205-5600

EXPRESS OFFICES (NO TESTING)

Colorado Springs (719) 598-2929: Chapel Hills Mall, 1520 Brairgate Blvd
Denver (303) 839-1829: 8:30 - 4:30, M-F, 1560 Broadway
Denver (303) 292-9310: 8:30 - 4:30, M-F, 2736 Welton St.
Littleton (303) 973-2926: Southwest Plaza Mall, 8501 W. Bowles Ave.
Westminster (303) 426-9683: Westminster Mall, 5433 W. 8th Ave.
Aurora (303) 337-5872: Buckingham Square Mall, 1307 Joliet.
Arvada (303) 425-4638: 7450 W. 52nd Ave., Unit O, (offers written test).
Aurora S.E.(303) 693-4652: 13736 E. Quincy Ave., (offers written test).

BRANCH OFFICES (HOURS/DAYS VARY, CALL FOR DETAILS AND LOCATION)

(Location given if phone number unavailable)

Akron	(970) 345-2484	Alamosa	(719) 589-4274
Aurora	(303) 344-8400	Avon	(970) 949-3156
Bailey	(303) 838-4280	Boulder	(303) 442-3006
Brighton	(303) 659-5055	Buena Vista	Senior Center
Burlington	(719) 346-8638	Calhan	Fire Station
Canon City	(719) 275-5617	Castle Rock	(303) 688-4625
Cheyenne Wells	(719) 767-5685	Colorado Springs	(719) 594-8701
Conejos	(719) 376-5919	Cortez	(970) 565-9779
Craig	(970) 824-5447	Creede	(719) 658-2440
Denver	(303) 937-9507	Del Norte	(719) 657-2708
Delta	(970) 874-9795	Dove Creek	(970) 677-2283
Durango	(970) 247-4591	Eads	(719) 438-5421
Estes Park	(303) 586-5331	Evergreen	(303) 674-4152

Fowler	City Hall	Frisco	(970) 668-5015
Ft. Collins	(970) 223-3648	Ft. Morgan	(970) 867-2647
Georgetown	(303) 569-2005	Glenwood Springs	(970) 945-8229
Granby	(970) 887-3875	Grand Junction	(970) 248-7010
Greeley	(303) 352-5845	Gunnison	(970) 641-1052
Holyoke	(970) 854-3131	Hotchkiss	Town Hall
Hugo	(719) 743-2796	Julesburg	(970) 474-3346
Kiowa	(303) 621-3125	Kremmling	Public Library
La Junta	(719) 384-2801	Lake City	(970) 944-2223
Lakewood	(303) 986-2742	Lamar	(719) 336-2670
Las Animas	County Courthouse	Leadville	(719) 486-0888
Littleton	(303) 795-5954	Longmont	(303) 776-4073
Loveland	(303) 667-6497	Meeker	(970) 878-5548
Montrose	(970) 249-5426	Norwood	(970) 327-4226
Nucla	City Hall	Ordway	311 Main Street
Ouray	(970) 325-4323	Pagosa Springs	(970) 264-6088
Pueblo	(970) 543-5164	Rangely	(970) 675-2881
Rifle	(970) 625-2044	Saguache	(719) 655-2512
Salida	(719) 539-2802	San Luis	(719) 672-3372
Security-Widefield	(719) 392-6101	Silverton	(970) 387-5671
Springfield	(719) 523-4372	Steamboat Springs	(970) 879-0715
Sterling	(970) 522-5982	Strasburg	County Building
Thornton	(303) 287-8033	Trinidad	(719) 846-4348
Walden	(970) 723-4334	Walsenburg	(719) 738-2807
Westcliffe	(719) 783-2282	Woodland Park	(719) 687-2447
Wray	(970) 332-5855		

Air Care Colorado Centers

Longmont Center
4040 Walker Way
Longmont
near Airport Rd.
& Nelson Rd.

Air Care Colorado
Because we care for cleaner air

Boulder Center
5655 Airport Blvd.
Boulder
near Foothills Pkwy.
& Valmont Rd.

Broomfield Center
11609 Teller St.
Broomfield
120th & Pierce

Northglenn Center
1950 E. 112th Ave.
Northglenn
112th & Irma

Arvada Center
5185 N. Marshall St.
Arvada
Near I-70 & Wadsworth

Commerce City Center
5000 E. 62nd Ave.
Commerce City
Near Mile High Kennel Club

Denver
International
Airport

Golden Center
15335 W. 44th Ave.
Golden
44th & McIntyre

Aurora Center
12042 E. 30th Ave.
30th & Peoria

Denver Center
2300 S. Lipan St.
Near W. Evans Ave.

Denver Southeast Center
10190 E. Warren Ave.
Havana & Parker Rd.

Sheridan Center
2802 W. Mansfield Ave.
Sheridan
Near Federal & Hampden

County Line Center
8494 S. Colorado Blvd.
County Line Rd. & Colorado Blvd.

Ken Caryl Center
10727 Centennial Rd.
Near Kipling & Chatfield

Parker Center
10199 Park Glenn Way
Parker
Near Parker Rd. & Lincoln

Castle Rock Center
541 Topeka Way
Castle Rock

For more information call:
456-7090

12 miles
AdMap-Denver, 1995

CHAPTER SIX
SEND LAWYERS, GUNS, AND MONEY

LAWS, RULES AND REGULATIONS

The information in this chapter was compiled from various sources including, but not limited to, government reports and publications (Federal, State, and Local); materials provided by business and civic organizations; and books produced by independent Colorado publishers including:

Friendly Divorce Guidebook for Colorado
Landlord & Tenant Guide to Colorado Evictions, both by Bradford Publishing

For a complete description of the above books and related titles, please see the Publisher's listing in Appendix A.

For a list of legal forms available from Bradford Publishing see Appendix D.

You just got married a month ago to your 15-year-old cousin who now wants a divorce and half of your winning Lotto ticket. So you go out to buy some liquor at the nearest drive-through using a check you know you can't cover and while having a few belts in the parking lot you get busted for DUI. On top of that, your landlord served you an eviction notice and the transaction on your new "For Sale by Owner" house is null and void because of bad paperwork. Maybe you should have read this chapter first. As the saying goes, "Ignorance of the law is no excuse."

DUI/DWAI

This section won't be a lecture on drinking and driving. However, a word of warning is warranted. In addition to the legal implications, DWI in Colorado can be quite hazardous to your health. A great number of people tend to drink and drive while on a weekend getaway to the mountains. DON'T! Imagine driving down unfamiliar, unlit, very narrow and slick mountain roads. Now imagine it after a couple of drinks.

In Colorado, a driver with a Blood Alcohol Content (BAC) between 0.05% and 0.09% is, by law, driving with ability impaired (DWAI). If a driver's BAC is 0.10% or higher, they are, by law, driving under the influence (DUI). The penalties for DWAI/DUI are tough. First offense DWAI can result in 8 points on your license, a $500 fine, up to 180 days in jail and 48 hours community service. You can be arrested for DWAI/DUI if you are in your car sitting in a parking lot, in an alley or parked on the street. Unlike some states, Colorado DOES acknowledge DUI offenses on private property.

LIQUOR LAWS

Colorado has some unique liquor and beer codes. In California, I can walk into a 7-11 and buy liquor and munchies too. In Colorado, the only alcoholic beverage you can buy outside a liquor store or bar is 3.2% beer. Conversely, liquor stores can't sell food, snacks or anything else not directly related to the consumption of alcoholic beverages. The legal drinking age is 21; however, someone at least 18 years old can handle, dispense or sell drinks if acting as an employee for a liquor licensee.

Liquor and drug stores may sell alcoholic beverages from 8:00 a.m. until midnight but may not sell on Sunday or Christmas. All bars, restaurants and taverns may sell drinks from 8:00 a.m. until 2:00 a.m. 365 days a year.

BAD CHECKS

Colorado is not the place to write a bad check—intentionally or unintentionally. This is covered under statues 18-5-205 of the Colorado Criminal Code. In essence, the law states that if any person, knowing he has insufficient funds, issues a check for the payment of services, wages, rent, property, etc., that person commits fraud by check. Depending on the amount of the check, the charge can range from a class 3 misdemeanor to a class 6 felony. Even if you bounce a $5.00 check, you are subject to a fine of $100 or 3 times the amount of the check, whichever is greater.

EVICTIONS

Colorado has very clear laws and procedures in regard to evictions, although technically, there is no such thing in the state. None of the courts or legal forms uses the term "eviction." All such actions are referred to as "Unlawful Detainer," and are covered under the Forcible Entry and Detainer (FED) Statute (13-40-101 et seq. C.R.S.).

Whether you are a landlord or a tenant, it pays to know the laws concerning this matter if you are faced with a possible eviction. There are state statutes in place to protect the rights of both parties. Landlords need to know how to give proper notice, complete, file and serve the necessary forms and avoid violating any tenant rights. Tenants should know the legal defenses to an eviction, how to file an Answer or Counterclaim, and the laws regarding Security Deposits.

A written lease is of utmost importance to both parties. In almost all situations where there is a conflict between the common law and lease provisions, the lease will control. This is particularly important in regard to notice, security deposits and rental liability issues.

The factual and legal issues involved in an eviction are far too complicated to cover in this section. Before you lease property as a landlord, or, as a tenant you find yourself on the receiving end of a possible eviction (for any reason), I highly recommend the *Guide to Colorado Evictions* by Bradford Publishing. I have seen cases won in court by a wrongful party simply because they knew the laws and the innocent party did not.

MARRIAGE

Requirements for a legal marriage vary widely from state to state. Below are the basic requirements to become married in Colorado.

Marriage License Requirements: Licenses can be issued in any county seat and are valid throughout the state. There is no waiting period after the license is issued; however, the license must be used within 30 days of issuance. The fee for the license is $20 cash; checks are not accepted.

Age Requirements: The legal age without parental consent is 18 years of age. Ages 16-17 require a notarized consent form from either both parents, a parent having sole custody or a guardian having legal custody of the minor. If these do not apply then judicial approval is required. Applicants 15 and under must obtain a court-granted judicial approval in the county where residency has been established.

Identification: Acceptable forms of identification and proof of age are: driver's license, Passport, Baptism Certificate, Military ID or a state issued ID card.

Blood Test: No blood test is required in Colorado.

Application Form: Both male and female applicants must appear in person to complete and sign the license application. If one party can not appear due to illness, travel or incarceration, he or she must obtain an absentee application in a county seat. This form must be completed, notarized and returned before a license will be issued. Applicants do not need to be residents of Colorado.

Ceremonies: A judge or public official who is authorized to perform a marriage ceremony may do so. Also, a person in accordance with any mode of solemnization, recognized by a religious denomination, Indian tribe or nation, may perform the marriage. Clergy from out of state need not be registered in the state to perform the ceremony.

Prohibited Marriages: A person may not re-marry unless a divorce is absolutely final. Proof of divorce is required if it has been granted within 30 days prior to application for marriage license. Marriage between ancestor, descendent, brother, sister, uncle, aunt, niece or nephews is prohibited, whether the relationship is by half or whole blood. Marriages between first cousins and further relations are permitted. Contact your county clerk for additional information.

DIVORCE

Although everyone would like to think their marriage was made in heaven and will last forever, statistics beg to differ. Over half of all marriages end in divorce in Colorado. Depending on issues such as financial assets and children, there are four ways you can handle the process. You can do it all yourselves; do it yourselves with limited assistance from a legal center or attorney; do it yourselves with mediation; or have an attorney do it for you. Regardless of method, I recommend *The Friendly Divorce Guidebook for Colorado* also by Bradford Publishing. In Colorado, whether and how you use a lawyer in your divorce is up to you, but having the proper information is invaluable.

Before running to the courthouse to file for a divorce, you may want to consider the various other options available in Colorado. Marriage counseling, marital mediation, physical or trial separation, legal separation, annulment, and finally the legal dissolution of marriage (divorce) are all available and legal.

For a legal separation or divorce the process begins by filing a petition with the clerk of the **district** court. You must have been domiciled in Colorado for at least 90 days before filing your first papers. A waiting period of 90 days, required by law, begins once you have filed the petition. The 90 day waiting period is mandatory as a "cooling off" time so both parties can give the action serious consideration before making it final.

Couples usually use the 90 days to work out their final divorce plan which, when written, is called the separation agreement. A separation agreement must cover all the following: property division, payment of debts, maintenance (alimony), custody and support of children, taxes and medical and life insurance. A separation agreement must be presented to the court at the time you ask for a final decree. A final decree can be obtained by affidavit without appearing before the court if no minor children are involved, or, if there are children, both parties must be represented by counsel. Those who do not qualify for divorce by affidavit, and those seeking a decree of legal separation, must appear at a final hearing in court.

After your divorce or legal separation has been granted, the court retains continuing jurisdiction over your children (custody, support, higher education costs).

One final note: Colorado recognizes common law marriages. You have a common law marriage if you have lived together while "holding yourselves out" as being married, meaning that you acted as though you were married. Typical proof of this is you introduced each other as wife and husband, used the same last name, or filed married/joint tax returns AND neither of you was still married to someone else, either by a marriage license and a ceremony or by common law. A common law marriage and a marriage with a license and a ceremony are legally equal and subject to the same requirement for divorce.

REAL ESTATE

Almost all aspects of real estate transactions are regulated by the Division of Real Estate, (303) 894-2166. The Division administers the real estate recovery fund, which can be used by persons to recover sums lost because of the actions of a licensee. Persons who obtain a final judgment against a broker or salesperson can regain their actual loss suffered in a transaction up to $15,000 per claimant and up to $50,000 in the aggregate against any one licensee. The Division also regulates all time-share projects sold in Colorado and regulates developers of subdivisions consisting of 10 or more residential sites, tracts or lots.

Real estate agents and brokers in Colorado are required to "declare their allegiance" in any transaction. They must state up front whether they are working for a seller or a buyer. This law was put in to place to protect consumers from being misled by agents claiming to be on their side while they were actually looking out for the best interest of someone else.

Finally, if you are looking to buy rural property (acreage), there are many considerations which may not be apparent: water rights, well permits, test for septic permits, mineral rights (especially in Colorado), mining patents, legal access, road maintenance, zoning restrictions, utilities, and drastic changes in seasons to list a few. My wife and I looked at a beautiful 6-acre plot for $36,000. However, it would have cost at least $10,000 to install electricity $10,000 for well/septic, and $25,000 to grade the dirt road. Now the price was over $80,000 before we laid the first brick. If you are serious (or just not sure) about moving out of the city, get copies of *Discover the Good Life In Rural America (The City Slicker's Guide To Buying Country Real Estate Without Losing Your Shirt)*, and *Country Bound! (Trade Your Business Suit Blues for Blue Jean Dreams)*, both by Communication Creativity. See Appendix A for details.

LOTTO

Colorado has lottery (scratch cards), lotto & Keno. The cash prizes for Keno are preset with a maximum of $50,000 for matching 10 out of 20 numbers. Lotto has a progressive pot that starts at $1.5 million. When you purchase a Lotto ticket you must choose a payment option of either a 25-year annuity or the Cash Value (40% before taxes).

You can check with any Lottery retailer for the previous day's drawing results. Winning numbers for games are also available by calling the Lottery Luck Line at (303) 759-LUCK (5825) in Denver, (719) 542-LUCK in Pueblo and toll free at 1-800-283-LUCK outside of the Denver Metro area. These numbers may also appear in local newspapers and are available at your Lottery retailer. You may begin claiming winning tickets the morning following the drawing.

If you win, immediately sign the back of your ticket if you haven't already done it. To claim prizes up to $599, simply present your ticket at any Keno/Lotto retailer within 180 days of the winning drawing. To claim prizes over $600, you must visit one of the Lottery offices in Pueblo, Denver, Ft. Collins or Grand Junction. Or mail the signed ticket and a completed claim form available at all Lottery retailers to the Colorado Lottery, P.O. Box 7, Pueblo, CO 81002-0007 for payment by mail. Lotto jackpot winners (6 of 6) will be paid only at Denver or Pueblo Lottery offices.

Every time you play, Colorado wins. Between July 1, 1996 and June 30, 1997 more than $94 million was distributed for local and state park and recreation projects, outdoors and wilderness projects, and for state public buildings and facilities.

You must be 18 or older to purchase tickets. Tickets may be given as gifts to anyone of any age, and they may win. All prize claims are subject to validation. Federal and State laws require a minimum 32% tax withholding on individual winnings over $5,000.

CHAPTER SEVEN
CHANGES IN LATITUDES,
CHANGES IN ATTITUDES

THE TEN FASTEST GROWING
COUNTIES IN COLORADO

The information in this chapter was compiled from various sources including, but not limited to, government reports and publications (Federal, State, and Local); materials provided by business and civic organizations and The Colorado Economic and Demographic Information System (CEDIS) maintained by the Colorado Division of Local Government.

Explosive growth! I have used that term numerous times in this book. I can't think of a better way to describe it. Much like a bomb, the growth of Colorado has been sudden, unexpected, uncontainable and, in some respects, devastating to the state's resources (natural, economic and social).

I was drawn to Colorado more than a decade ago. The natural beauty, wide-open spaces, un-crowded cities (for the most part), and friendly, laid-back attitudes of Colorado's residents were all factors in my move from Florida.

Downtown) was a place you did not want to be after dark, traffic in and out of Denver was only congested on rare occasions, mountain land could be had for a song, and there were distinct, natural divisions between one city and the next—all a memory now.

The state's population has increased by over 100,000 people a year for the last 3 years. Between 1990 and 1994 the population grew 11%. While most of the increase was centered in the six-county Denver metro area, many of the rural and mountain communities have also seen tremendous growth. There have been numerous news reports lately concerning the unwanted effects this growth has had in many areas. Several of the state's one-time "wildlife" areas no longer have much wildlife due to a constant onslaught of hikers, campers, hunters and the like. The long-time residents of some smaller, rural areas are up in arms because newcomers are destroying the assets and beauty of their home-turf. Many small areas have been populated by affluent new arrivals that, once situated, demand improvements in roads, utilities and conveniences so their new home will be more like the one they couldn't wait to leave.

Because they began to see the writing on the wall, a group of state leaders held a conference recently in an attempt to stop a disaster waiting to happen. On January 25-26, 1995, over one thousand Coloradans from different communities and backgrounds—elected officials, community, agricultural and business leaders, educators and students—met at the Colorado Leadership Summit on Smart Growth in Denver to tackle the tough issues raised by the state's explosive growth. Summit participants listened to a number of presentations and participated in small breakout groups to identify and discuss problems, opportunities, ideas, barriers and solutions related to growth and development issues. At the end of the conference, participants had developed 14 guiding principles or goals concerning Smart Growth and Development.

I would ask everyone who reads this book, newcomer and life-long citizen alike, to review the principles below and work together to keep Colorado the wonderful, beautiful, exciting, and prosperous state it has always been.

GUIDING PRINCIPLES FROM THE COLORADO LEADERSHIP SUMMIT ON SMART GROWTH AND DEVELOPMENT

1. **Our vision and the process we take to get there should fully develop the human potential of all our citizens.** We must strive to make our communities places where all kids and adults can fully develop their human capacities— their minds and bodies. We should work together to ensure that strong families and communities, as well as great educational opportunities, cultural resources, good jobs, adequate food, clothing, and health care are available for all of our citizens. Colorado communities must sustain and enhance the lives of families and individuals today and for the future.

2. **We need to enhance the quality of our place.** We must identify and emphasize both the physical and the human elements of our communities that are important to us. We must make our communities more livable by keeping crime off our streets, making all our neighborhoods attractive, protecting our natural resources and celebrating the magnificence of our setting. We also must cultivate an ethic of community, preserving towns and neighborhoods where we know and care for each other, where we respect cultural and ethnic diversity and the value of the environment, and where a child can grow up with a healthy body and healthy values.

3. **At the local and regional level, we should better coordinate growth planning with the provision of services such as schools, water, infrastructure and transportation.** A more cooperative effort between governments, communities and the private sector to make sure services accompany growth will guarantee the provision of services for new development, avoid duplication and inefficient use of services, allow for the fairer allocation of the cost of development, account for non-fiscal costs of development, help encourage urban in-fill and discourage sprawl, and allow us to preserve cherished areas we may not want to develop. Better coordination locally and regionally will also make it easier to plan for the long-term, increase citizen participation and enhance our sense of community.

4. **We need to expand the opportunities—such as better jobs, education, housing and health care—that result from growth, and help Coloradans take advantage of those opportunities.** Economic development can and should bring many benefits to Colorado. Clearly, affordable housing, improved education, better health and expanded job choices ought to be among the measurable results of growth in Colorado. Just as clearly, growth should generate increased cultural and recreational opportunities for Colorado citizens. To the extent possible, smart growth must strengthen the identity of Colorado's diverse neighborhoods, communities and regions. We must empower local governments to attract and help create "good" growth, and we must help Colorado residents—including low and moderate income residents-receive the benefits resulting from growth.

5. **We need to provide the structures so that we can effectively make the decisions that need to be made within each community, region and the state.** We must make decisions as locally as it is possible for them to be effective. Therefore, we need to identify more ways to support regional and local priorities while simultaneously assuring a positive response to the crucial statewide issues of air quality, transportation, telecommunications, and water quality. We need to foster collaborative and supportive relationships at every level of decision making, by making governmental structures more flexible, reducing institutional barriers to cooperation and input, creating more opportunities for citizens to be involved, cultivating partnerships between

97

government and the private and non-profit sectors, empowering grass-roots activism, and taking into account overlapping areas of commercial and ecological interest.

6. **We must continuously reform our tax, revenue and regulatory framework.** Without creating an unpredictable regulatory environment, we must constantly rethink our tax and regulatory structure. Fees, licenses, permits, regulations such as zoning, taxes and tax revenue, should encourage and empower—not impede—state, regional and local efforts to provide services, as well as manage resources and plan for infrastructure, telecommunications and land use. We also must encourage non-regulatory approaches such as collaborative decision-making, facilitation and negotiation to foster cooperation and dialogue among public, private sector and community groups regarding growth initiatives.

7. **We need to protect, enhance and promote the value of our public lands, our open spaces, our natural resources, our wildlife, our parks, our recreational opportunities and our historical facilities.** We must take personal and community responsibility for ensuring that growth supports and facilitates the protection and enhancement of Colorado's public assets. They enrich our lives. We need to cultivate improved relationships between state and federal land management and regulatory agencies, regional and local governments, community groups and the private sector in order to protoect assets that are valuable to our environment, our history and our communities.

8. **We need to foster a sustainable agricultural economy.** Agricultural lands are not merely open space. We must acknowledge the importance of Colorado's agriculture lands and communities to the state's economy, as well as the benefits that go beyond the primary purpose of farms and ranches, such as aesthetics, cultural contributions and wildlife habitat. Development of a sustainable agricultural economy should be given emphasis in state, regional and local growth strategies.

9. **We need to protect Colorado from pollution.** The health of our citizens and our environment is vital to our high quality of life and our economic strength. Individual citizens, community groups, government and the private sector must collaborate to reduce and prevent pollution and protect and conserve our natural resources, without disregarding local circumstances or disrespecting private property rights.

10. **We need to continue to develop economically.** We need a business climate that fosters quality jobs in stable or growing industries like telecommunications, promotes growth in areas that want it, and allows us to withstand boom and bust cycles. Smart growth is good business: long-range planning can help strike a balance between Colorado's "haves" and "have-

nots," achieve economic diversity throughout the state and ensure a stable economy for many years into the future.

11. **We must always be conscious of the need for sustainability.** We must meet the economic, social and environmental demands of the present without compromising the ability of future generations to meet their needs. We must also work to mitigate the problems that have resulted from past actions.

12. **We need to foster a sustainable system of water management, in terms of treatment, storage and the regulation and determination of usage.** Water is the most important resource in Colorado, as it applies to growth and the environment. We also need to develop a conservation ethic as a state, within communities and as individuals.

13. **Smart growth must be an inclusive and cooperative process.** Direct citizen input at all levels of decision-making is crucial to viable growth management. Education and information about all the costs and benefits of growth as well as the needs and values of different communities around the state, must be available. We also must remember that the private and non-profit sectors can be very effective partners with government, and planning decisions should be made with as much input, support and collaboration as possible. This is a cooperative venture, so we should share data and experiences, learn from each other's mistakes and share in each other's successes.

14. **We all must be conscious of our rights and responsibilities as individuals.** Planning decisions always must honor and respect private property rights and the need for compensation of all individuals, including business people, farmers and ranchers. At the same time, we all must take responsibility for the impacts our private actions and decisions have on other individuals, communities or shared resources. **For more information about the Summit contact the Colorado Department of Local Affairs at 1-800-899-GROW or (303) 866-2817.**

For those considering a move, this chapter contains basic information about the ten fastest growing counties in the state. These counties were picked from two separate statistical lists (numerical and percentage changes). The counties appear alphabetically, not in order of growth (**Adams, Arapahoe, Boulder, Denver, Douglas**, Elbert, El Paso, **Jefferson**, Larimer, and Weld), with the six counties of the Greater Metro Region being shown in bold. You should keep in mind some data presented may be several years old (although it is the most recent available), and since the population of some counties has increased 20-45 percent since the release of the data, it should be used as a basic guide only (public school statistics for example). It is interesting to note that when this book was released in 1995 that 9 of the 10 fastest growing counties have remained the same. More recent (unreleased) figures may be available from the individual counties or agencies in question.

ADAMS COUNTY

LARGEST CITIES/TOWNS/COMMUNITIES

Aurora, Bennett, Brighton, Broomfield, Commerce City, Federal Heights, Northglenn, Thornton and Westminster

POPULATION ESTIMATES BY AGE GROUPS, 1998-2005

AGE GROUP	1998	2000	2005
0 to 4 years old	25070	25016	25131
5 to 18	71484	73543	76853
19 to 34	72348	73773	81828
35 to 64	122581	130754	146208
65 to 89	27189	28949	33181
90 and over	560	597	780
Total	319232	332632	363982

LOCAL COMMUNITY DESCRIPTION

Adams County stretches from the foothills of the Rockies to the eastern Colorado plains, making up the northern tier of the six-county Denver metropolitan area. Western urbanized Adams County includes all or portions of the cities of Arvada, Aurora, Brighton, Broomfield, Commerce City, Federal Heights, Northglenn, Thornton and Westminster. Situated in a fast-growing area, Adams County is a diverse, cosmopolitan county supported by a broad base of business and industry. A wide price range of housing is available for the county's diverse work force.

ADDRESS: 450 South 4th Avenue, Brighton, CO 80601, 303-659-2120
DATE OF INCORPORATION: 1901, COUNTY SEAT: City of Brighton

LOCAL EMERGENCY SERVICES

Aurora, Bennett, Brighton, Broomfield, Commerce City, Federal Heights, Northglenn, Thornton and Westminster are served by fire departments.

LAW ENFORCEMENT: 380 staff, 120 vehicles, Phone: (303) 654-1850

EMERGENCY MEDICAL SERVICE: Private ambulances, fire districts, municipalities

LOCAL AMENITIES

HUMAN SERVICES: Adams County Social Services (303) 287-8831 ext. 595, 7190 Colorado Blvd., Commerce City, CO 80022 **RECREATIONAL:** Barr Lake State Park, Adams County Regional Park and Fairgrounds, 3 Golf Courses, 6 Health Clubs, 7 Movie Theaters, Water World.

CLIMATE

January Temperature (in degrees Fahrenheit)	30.0
July Temperature (in degrees Fahrenheit)	73.0
Annual Precipitation (in inches)	15.0
Annual Snowfall (in inches)	54.0
Elevation (in feet)	5300
Area (in square miles)	1197.8

TAXES

1993 PROPERTY TAXES: Mill Levy	27.332
1993 SALES TAXES: Adams County	.50%
Other (RTD, Stadium, Cultural Facilities, etc.)	.60%
State	3.00%

LOCAL ECONOMIC DEVELOPMENT CONTACTS

Major firms in area: **GOVERNMENT**: Adams County, Cities of Brighton, Commerce City, Westminster, Northglenn, and Thornton, **MANUFACTURING**: Sundstrand Aviation, Whirlpool Kitchens, Fischer Imaging, **WHOLESALE TRADE**: APS, Associated Grocers, Silver Engineering Works **RETAIL TRADE**: Barber Poultry, ITT Continental Baking, JC Penney, K-Mart, King Soopers, Livtak Meat, NAPA, Peavey Conagra, Target **SERVICES**: Holiday Inn, Humana Valley View Hospital, Frederic Printing **HI-TECH**: Security Pacific Info. Sys., Melco Industries. Adams County has a diverse economy but major segments are services, manufacturing (electronics), and government.

1995 PUBLIC SCHOOL INFORMATION

District Name	# of Students	# of Schools	# of Teachers	Students /Teacher
Adams County 14	6162	13	293	21.0
Adams-Arapahoe 28J	28,492	44	1,502	19.0
Bennett 29J	1,055	3	61	17.4
Brighton 27J	4,562	9	233	19.6
Byers 32J	420	2	29	14.5
Deer Trail 26J	195	2	19	10.3
Mapleton 1	5,154	11	244	21.1
Northglenn-Thornton	25,604	39	1291	19.8
Strasburg 31J	501	3	28	18.2
Westminster 50	11,360	25	639	17.8
Wiggins RE-50(J)	570	2	37	15.4
State of Colorado	673,438	1,483	36,398	18.5

Nearest four-year college: University of Northern Colorado (Greeley)
Nearest community college: Community College of Aurora
Nearest vocational center: T.H. Pickens Voc-Tech (Aurora)

LOCAL TRANSPORTATION

NEAREST SCHEDULED AIR SERVICE: Denver International Airport
LOCAL BUSES, TRUCKS, AND TRAINS: Greyhound, Alpine Charter,
RTD, Grayline of Denver, Variety of truck lines providing local, interstate,
and intrastate service. Freight: Colorado Southern, Denver and Rio Grande,
Chicago Rock Island Pacific, Union Pacific, Burlington Northern. Passenger:
Amtrak.

LOCAL UTILTIES

LOCAL WATER INFORMATION: Lost Creek Groundwater Mgmt.,
Northgate and Shaw Heights Water, Central Colo. Water Conservancy,
Central Colo. Groundwater Mgmt., N. Kiowa Bijou Groundwater Mgmt.,
Hazeltine Heights Water District.

LOCAL SEWER INFORMATION: Beebe Draw, Bennett Sanitation, Hi-
land Acres, Himalaya, Metro Denver Sewage Disposal, Industrial Park,
Berkeley, Box Elder, Central Adams County, Crestview, Eastlake, North
Pecos

LOCAL LANDFILL INFORMATION: BFI of Colorado, Waste
Management of Colorado

LOCAL ELECTRICITY INFORMATION: United Power

LOCAL GAS INFORMATION: Public Service Company of Colorado

ARAPAHOE COUNTY

LARGEST CITIES/TOWNS/COMMUNITIES

Aurora, Englewood, Greenwood Village, Littleton

POPULATION ESTIMATES BY AGE GROUPS, 1998-2005

AGE GROUP	1998	2000	2005
0 to 4 years old	31902	30902	29295
5 to 18	98107	97928	94858
19 to 34	95841	94629	102474
35 to 64	196570	203969	209261
65 to 89	38415	40542	46833
90 and over	743	783	1039
Total	461578	468753	483760

103

LOCAL COMMUNITY DESCRIPTION

Arapahoe County is a rapidly growing area with several cities including Aurora, Englewood, Greenwood Village, and Littleton. It was one of the original 17 counties in the Colorado Territory and today has the highest number of up-scale communities in the greater metro area. Arapahoe County has its own business airport and encompasses a great portion of the Denver Technological Center.

ADDRESS: 5334 South Prince Street, Littleton, CO 80166, 303-795-4630
DATE OF INCORPORATION: 1901, COUNTY SEAT: City of Littleton

LOCAL EMERGENCY SERVICES

City and local fire districts: For details contact County.
LAW ENFORCEMENT: 450 staff, 190 vehicles, Phone: Sheriff: Patrick J. Sullivan, Jr. (303) 795-4711. Hospitals: 8 in area (see Healthcare below).

LOCAL AMENITIES

HUMAN SERVICES: Comitis, Arapahoe House, Social Services Department, Veterans Services, Child Care Food Program, Weatherization, Senior Transportation, Homemakers, Arapahoe Volunteers, Inter-Faith Task Force **ENTERTAINMENT:** Fiddlers Green Theater, Littleton Theater, **HEALTHCARE:** Aurora Presbyterian, Aurora Regional Medical Center, Colorado Mental Health, Craig Hospital, Littleton Hospital/Porter, Porter Memorial Hospital, Spalding Hospital, Swedish Medical Center **LODGING:** Ramada, Heritage, Holiday Inn, Days Inn, Brock Residence Inn, **CHURCHES:** Episcopal, Baptist, Catholic, Lutheran, Methodist, Christian, Presbyterian, Congregational **ORGANIZATIONS:** Jaycees, Lions Club, Kiwanis, Rotary, Knights of Columbus, Sertoma, Optimists, Elks, Federated Women's Club, Junior League.

CLIMATE

January Temperature (in degrees Fahrenheit)	34.0
July Temperature (in degrees Fahrenheit)	79.0
Annual Precipitation (in inches)	15.0
Annual Snowfall (in inches)	52.0
Elevation (in feet)	5400
Area (in square miles)	805.5

TAXES

1993 PROPERTY TAXES: Mill Levy	16.973
1993 SALES TAXES: Arapahoe County	0.00%
Other (RTD, Stadium, Cultural Facilities, etc.)	.60%
State	3.00%

LOCAL ECONOMIC DEVELOPMENT CONTACTS

Major firms in area: **UTILITIES**: Mountain Bell, Public Service **SERVICES**: Stearns-Rogers, Inc., IBM, United Airlines, Honeywell, Inc., Amoco Product Co. **FINANCE, INSURANCE, REAL ESTATE**: Allstate Insurance. The leading source of income is Office/light-industrial near Centennial Airport.

1995 PUBLIC SCHOOL INFORMATION

District Name	# of Students	# of Schools	# of Teachers	Students /Teacher
Adams-Arapahoe 28J	28,492	44	1,502	19.0
Bennett 29J	1,055	3	61	17.4
Byers 32J	420	2	29	14.5
Cherry Creek 5	37,128	44	2,018	18.4
Deer Trail 26J	195	2	19	10.3
Englewood 1	4,588	11	227	20.2
Littleton 6	16,044	24	856	18.8
Strasburg 31J	501	3	28	18.5
State of Colorado	673,438	1,483	36,398	18.5

Nearest four-year college: Metropolitan State College of Denver, University of Colorado (Auraria Campus - Denver)
Nearest community college: Community College of Aurora
Nearest vocational center: T.H. Pickens Voc-Tech (Aurora)

LOCAL TRANSPORTATION

NEAREST SCHEDULED AIR SERVICE: Denver International Airport
LOCAL BUSES, TRUCKS, AND TRAINS: Continental Trailways, Greyhound, RTD. All major truck lines serve Arapahoe County and the surrounding metropolitan area. Freight: Union Pacific, Denver and Rio Grande Western, Burlington-Northern. Passenger: Amtrak (in Denver).

LOCAL UTILITIES

LOCAL WATER INFORMATION: Local City Water Departments

LOCAL SEWER INFORMATION: Local City Sewer Departments

LOCAL LANDFILL INFORMATION: Charles Bailey (303) 373-0155.

LOCAL ELECTRICITY INFORMATION: Public Service Company of Colorado, Yvonne Hill (303) 571-3036

LOCAL GAS INFORMATION: Public Service Company of Colorado, Yvonne Hill (303) 571-3036

BOULDER COUNTY

LARGEST CITIES/TOWNS/COMMUNITIES

Boulder, Broomfield, Lafayette, Longmont, Louisville

POPULATION ESTIMATES BY AGE GROUPS, 1998-2005

AGE GROUP	1998	2000	2005
0 to 4 years old	16682	16996	17168
5 to 18	51923	53781	56879
19 to 34	69507	71005	76471
35 to 64	113134	120954	136825
65 to 89	20149	21321	25138
90 and over	704	739	828
Total	272099	284796	313309

LOCAL COMMUNITY DESCRIPTION

Boulder County houses the University of Colorado's main campus in Boulder, with an enrollment of 26,000 undergraduate, graduate, and professional students. In addition, the county is the center for research and high technology manufacturing. Nestled against the foothills of the Front Range, Boulder County is also a prime recreation area for activities including backpacking, hiking, cycling, water sports, and skiing. The territory within Boulder County first became part of the United States in 1803 with the Louisiana Purchase. Today Boulder County remains diversified, with both rural and urban settings. The County encompasses 753 square miles and is situated on the eastern slope of the Rocky Mountains. Elevations within the boundaries of the County vary from the 5,000-foot level of the plains to the 14,000-foot peaks of the Continental Divide.

ADDRESS: P. O. Box 471, Boulder, CO 80306, 303-441-3500
DATE OF INCORPORATION: 1861, COUNTY SEAT: City of Boulder

LOCAL EMERGENCY SERVICES

All jurisdictions are served by fire departments - please contact them for details.

LAW ENFORCEMENT: 200 staff, 72 vehicles. Phone: (303) 441-3636

EMERGENCY MEDICAL SERVICE: 5 hospitals in area.

LOCAL AMENITIES

AVAILABLE NEARBY: The Denver Metro Area has a variety of recreation areas/facilities, attractions and major hotels and motels available **CHURCHES:** All denominations of churches **HEALTHCARE:** Mental

Health Center, Public Health, Developmental Disabilities Center **HUMAN SERVICES:** Housing Authority, Social Services **LODGING:** A great number of major hotels and motels exist in Boulder **ORGANIZATIONS:** Veterans, CAP **ENTERTAINMENT:** 8 Golf Courses, 23 Movie Theaters.

CLIMATE

January Temperature (in degrees Fahrenheit)	31.0
July Temperature (in degrees Fahrenheit)	73.0
Annual Precipitation (in inches)	16.0
Annual Snowfall (in inches)	93.0
Elevation (in feet)	6100
Area (in square miles)	751.4

TAXES

1993 PROPERTY TAXES: Mill Levy	22.245
1993 SALES TAXES: Boulder County	.359%
Other (RTD, Stadium, Cultural Facilities, etc.)	.60%
State	3.00%

LOCAL ECONOMIC DEVELOPMENT CONTACTS

Major firms in area: **HI-TECH**: IBM, Rockwell, Storage Technology Corp., Ball Aerospace, Neodata, NBI, NCAR, Valley Lab, Syntex **MANUFACTURING**: Monsanto/Head, Dieterich Standard, Flatiron Co. **GOVERNMENT**: University of Colorado, St. Vrain Valley School District, Boulder County, US Department of Commerce, City of Boulder, City of Longmont, FAA **FOOD PROCESSING**: Celestial Seasonings, Boulder Beer, Longmont Foods **SERVICES**: Boulder Community Hospital **UTILITIES**: Public Service, Mountain Bell. The leading sources of income are manufacturing, services, tourism.

1995 PUBLIC SCHOOL INFORMATION

District Name	# of Students	# of Schools	# of Teachers	Students /Teacher
Boulder Valley RE 2	25,648	51	1,373	18.7
Park R-3	1,349	3	77	17.5
St. Vrain Valley RE	17,459	32	885	19.7
Thompson R-2J	13,787	26	717	19.2
State of Colorado	673,438	1,483	36,398	18.5

Nearest four-year college: University of Colorado (Boulder)
Nearest community college: Front Range Community College (Westminster)
Nearest vocational center: Boulder Valley Voc-Tech (Boulder)

LOCAL TRANSPORTATION

NEAREST SCHEDULED AIR SERVICE: Fort Collins-Loveland Municipal Airport, Fred Anderson Jr., 4824 Earhart Road, Loveland, CO 80538,)970) 669-7182

LOCAL BUSES, TRUCKS, AND TRAINS: Continental Trailways, RTD, BDT, Consolidated Freightways, Globe Truck Line, Yellow Freight, American Freight. Freight: Burlington Northern, Union Pacific. Passenger: Amtrak in Denver, CO (30 miles)

LOCAL UTILITIES

LOCAL WATER INFORMATION: This community did not provide this information.

LOCAL SEWER INFORMATION: This community did not provide this information.

LOCAL LANDFILL INFORMATION: This community did not provide this information.

LOCAL ELECTRICITY INFORMATION: Please contact municipalities.

LOCAL GAS INFORMATION: Please contact municipalities.

CITY AND COUNTY OF DENVER

LARGEST CITIES/TOWNS/COMMUNITIES

This county consists of the City of Denver.

POPULATION ESTIMATES BY AGE GROUPS, 1998-2005

AGE GROUP	1998	2000	2005
0 to 4 years old	44182	44306	42148
5 to 18	100592	10634	119284
19 to 34	95236	88232	95289
35 to 64	200163	209289	207968
65 to 89	62886	61939	59720
90 and over	2665	2713	2880
Total	505724	512821	527888

LOCAL COMMUNITY DESCRIPTION

The heart of Colorado is the six-county Greater Metropolitan Area around the City and County of Denver (the only City and County in the State). Denver is a mix of the downtown business district, neighborhood businesses, residential areas, industrial parks and the new Denver International Airport. Being the capital city of Colorado with a very rich historical background, Denver is home to many amenities and recreational and cultural facilities including the Denver Center for the Performing Arts with nine theaters which seat nearly 100,000 people, the Denver Art Museum, the Denver Museum of Natural History, the Denver Zoo, and the Denver Botanical Gardens. Its newly revitalized LoDo (lower downtown) area includes many restaurants, brew-pubs, Coors Field, and Elitch Gardens.

ADDRESS: 110 16th Street, Suite 400, Denver, CO 80202, 303-640-5555
DATE OF INCORPORATION: 1902, COUNTY SEAT: Denver

LOCAL EMERGENCY SERVICES

FIRE PROTECTION: This community did not provide this information.
POLICE PROTECTION: Denver Police Department
EMERGENCY MEDICAL SERVICE: 15 hospitals in the area.

LOCAL AMENITIES

Denver is the largest city in Colorado and offers a full-range of amenities.

CLIMATE

January Temperature (in degrees Fahrenheit)	29.9
July Temperature (in degrees Fahrenheit)	73.0
Annual Precipitation (in inches)	15.5
Annual Snowfall (in inches)	59.9
Elevation (in feet)	5280
Area (in square miles)	154.8

TAXES

1993 PROPERTY TAXES: Mill Levy	33.088
1993 SALES TAXES: Denver	3.50%
Other (RTD, Stadium, Cultural Facilities, etc.)	.60%
State	3.00%

LOCAL ECONOMIC DEVELOPMENT CONTACTS

The downtown business district alone has 7,000 employers.

1995 PUBLIC SCHOOL INFORMATION

District Name	# of Students	# of Schools	# of Teachers	Students /Teachers
Denver County 1	66,331	116	3,198	20.7
State of Colorado	673,438	1,483	36,398	18.5

Nearest four-year college: Metropolitan State College of Denver, University of Colorado - Denver (Auraria Campus - Denver)
Nearest community college: Community College of Denver (Auraria Campus - Denver)
Nearest vocational center: Several schools (Denver)

LOCAL TRANSPORTATION

NEAREST SCHEDULED AIR SERVICE: Denver International Airport
LOCAL BUSES, TRUCKS, AND TRAINS: All major carriers serve the greater Denver Metropolitan Area.

LOCAL UTILITIES

Public Service Company of Colorado, U.S. West

DOUGLAS COUNTY

LARGEST CITIES/TOWNS/COMMUNITIES

Castle Rock, Parker, Highlands Ranch

POPULATION ESTIMATES BY AGE GROUPS, 1998-2005

AGE GROUP	1998	2000	2005
0 to 4 years old	10741	11048	11690
5 to 18	27108	28954	32926
19 to 34	28934	29280	32737
35 to 64	51240	26049	65800
65 to 89	5688	6368	8523
90 and over	79	97	164
Total	123789	131797	151840

LOCAL COMMUNITY DESCRIPTION

Located between the Denver and Colorado Springs metropolitan areas on Colorado's Front Range, Douglas County is experiencing significant development. In fact, from 1990 to 1994, Douglas County had a total population increase of 45.8 percent. Offering open terrain ranging from rolling grasslands on the east, to pine forests and rock canyons, the county has a wide potential for growth. There are 21 planned communities in the County offering a choice of lifestyle from remote rural to adult condominium and suburban neighborhoods. Elevation of the county ranges from 6300 to 9800 feet. One third of the county is in federal, state and local public lands.

ADDRESS: 101 Third Street, Castle Rock, CO 80104, (303) 660-7400

COUNTY SEAT: Town of Castle Rock

LOCAL EMERGENCY SERVICES

All have service—for details please call Douglas County Fire Chiefs Association, (303) 770-3720.

LAW ENFORCEMENT: 80 staff, 40 vehicles, Phone: (303) 660-7505

EMERGENCY MEDICAL SERVICE: This community did not provide this information.

LOCAL AMENITIES

CHURCHES: 30 churches **ENTERTAINMENT**: Douglas County Arts and Humanities Group, County Choir and Orchestra **FESTIVALS**: Renaissance Festival at Larkspur, Douglas County Fair at Castle Rock, Parker Days at Parker **GOLF TOURNAMENTS**: Senior Champions of Golf Tournament at Plum Creek, Tournament of Players Club, International PGA Tournament at Castle Pines, 7 PGA rated golf courses **HUMAN SERVICES**: County Extension Service, Senior Citizen Programs **ORGANIZATIONS**: Parker and Castle Rock Chambers of Commerce, Jaycees, Lions, Rotary, Civation, 4-H, Eagles **PARKS**: Pike National Forest, Castlewood Canyon State Park, Chatfield State Park, Roxborough State Park, Daniels Park.

CLIMATE

January Temperature (in degrees Fahrenheit)	28.0
July Temperature (in degrees Fahrenheit)	73.0
Annual Precipitation (in inches)	14.0
Annual Snowfall (in inches)	57.0
Elevation (in feet)	5900
Area (in square miles)	842.8

TAXES

1993 PROPERTY TAXES: Mill Levy	18.774
1993 SALES TAXES: Douglas County	.17%
Other (RTD, Stadium, Cultural Facilities, etc.)	.60%
State	3.00%

LOCAL ECONOMIC DEVELOPMENT CONTACTS

Major firms in area: **GOVERNMENT**: Douglas County School District, Douglas County **MANUFACTURING**: Marquest Manufacturing, Racquet World-Inverness, Industrial Textiles, Moly Corp., Denver Brick, E.I. DuPont, Inventive Packaging, Saltzgitter Machinery, Inc., Ensign Bickford, Toyota **HI-TECH**: Information Handling Systems, Honeywell, Hewlett-Packard, Tektronix **FINANCE, INSURANCE, REAL ESTATE**: Hartford Insurance,

SERVICES: Mercy Medical Center, Tournament of Players UTILITIES: Intermountain Rural Electric Association, Mountain Bell. The leading sources of income are technology and communications services, construction.

1995 PUBLIC SCHOOL INFORMATION

District Name	# of Students	# of Schools	# of Teachers	Student /Teacher
Douglas County RE 1	24,495	37	1,330	18.4
State of Colorado	673,438	1,483	36,398	18.5

Nearest four-year college: Metropolitan State College of Denver, University of Colorado (Auraria Campus - Denver)
Nearest community college: Arapahoe Community College (Littleton)
Nearest vocational center: Several schools (Denver)

LOCAL TRANSPORTATION

NEAREST SCHEDULED AIR SERVICE: Denver International Airport
LOCAL BUSES, TRUCKS, AND TRAINS: Continental Trailways - 5 buses/day, RTD to Parker. All truck lines that service Denver and Colorado Springs. Santa Fe RR Piggyback Center in county. Freight: Santa Fe, Rio Grande, Burlington Northern. Passenger: Amtrak available in Denver CO (25 miles).

LOCAL UTILITIES

LOCAL WATER INFORMATION: There are twenty different water and sanitation districts serving Douglas County.

LOCAL SEWER INFORMATION: There are twenty different water and sanitation districts serving Douglas County.

LOCAL LANDFILL INFORMATION: County managed waste transfer stations to regional landfills, County Highway Dept. (303) 660-7480.

LOCAL ELECTRICITY INFORMATION: Public Service Company of Colorado, Intermountain Rural Electric Association, Mountain View Electric Association.

LOCAL GAS INFORMATION: Public Service Company of Colorado, Intermountain Rural Electric Association, Mountain View Electric Association.

ELBERT COUNTY

LARGEST CITIES/TOWNS/COMMUNITIES

Elizabeth, Kiowa and Elbert

POPULATION ESTIMATES BY AGE GROUPS, 1996-2005

AGE GROUP	1996	2000	2005
0 to 4 years old	1477	1882	2490
5 to 18	4085	4625	6134
19 to 34	5003	5844	6993
35 to 64	7800	9184	12615
65 to 89	1170	1345	1778
90 and over	31	36	44
Total	19566	22915	30053

LOCAL COMMUNITY DESCRIPTION

The community did not provide this information.

LOCAL EMERGENCY SERVICES

The community did not provide this information.

LOCAL AMENITIES

The community did not provide this information.

CLIMATE

January Temperature (in degrees Fahrenheit)	28.0
July Temperature (in degrees Fahrenheit)	84.0
Annual Precipitation (in inches)	15.0
Annual Snowfall (in inches)	52.7
Elevation (in feet)	6300
Area (in square miles)	1851.0

TAXES

1993 PROPERTY TAXES: Mill Levy	32.305
1993 SALES TAXES: Elbert County	0.00%
Other (RTD, Stadium, Cultural Facilities, etc.)	0.00%
State	3.00%

LOCAL ECONOMIC DEVELOPMENT CONTACTS

The community did not provide this information.

1995 PUBLIC SCHOOL INFORMATION

District Name	# of Students	# of Schools	# of Teachers	Students /Teachers
Agate 300	111	2	14	8.2
Big Sandy 100J	355	3	25	14.5
Calhan RJ-1	500	3	33	15.3
Douglas County RE-1	24,495	37	1,330	18.4
Elbert 200	279	2	23	12.1
Elizabeth C-1	2,339	5	135	17.3
Kiowa C-2	333	2	24	13.9
Limon RE-4J	619	2	31	20.0
Miami/Yoder	287	2	17	16.9
Peyton 23 JT	543	3	36	15.3
State of Colorado	593,030	1,367	33,093	17.9

Nearest four-year college: University of Colorado (Colorado Springs)
Nearest community college: Pikes Peak Community College (Colorado
    Springs)
Nearest vocational center: Several schools (Colorado Springs)

LOCAL TRANSPORTATION

NEAREST SCHEDULED AIR SERVICE: Colorado Springs Municipal Airport, Gary Green, 719-596-0188
LOCAL BUSES, TRUCKS, AND TRAINS: Greyhound, Continental Trailways, A & A, ABF, ANR, American Freight, Consolidated Freightways, Edson, Ellis, McLean, and Yellow Freight. Freight: Santa Fe, Rio Grande

LOCAL UTILITIES

LOCAL WATER INFORMATION: The community did not provide this information.

LOCAL SEWER INFORMATION: The community did not provide this information.

LOCAL LANDFILL INFORMATION: The community did not provide this information.

LOCAL ELECTRICITY INFORMATION: The community did not provide this information.

LOCAL GAS INFORMATION: The community did not provide this information.

EL PASO COUNTY

LARGEST CITIES/TOWNS/COMMUNITIES

Colorado Springs, Manitou Springs, Fountain, Palmer Lake

POPULATION ESTIMATES BY AGE GROUPS, 1998-2005

AGE GROUP	1998	2000	2005
0 to 4 years old	45537	44491	44018
5 to 18	105390	111703	123710
19 to 34	126070	129534	141643
35 to 64	170661	178498	193375
65 to 89	39936	42072	47029
90 and over	903	944	1175
Total	488497	507242	550950

LOCAL COMMUNITY DESCRIPTION

Primarily rolling plains, El Paso County is located south of the Palmer Divide, which separates it from Douglas County. The Federal Government owns most of the southwestern part of the county for use by the U.S. Army located at Fort Carson. The largest city in the county is Colorado Springs, which also has the second largest population in the state.

ADDRESS: 27 East Vermijo, Colorado Springs, CO 80903, 719-520-6444
COUNTY SEAT: City of Colorado Springs

LOCAL EMERGENCY SERVICES

Air Force Academy, Peterson Air Force Base, Calhan, Colorado Springs, Fort Carson, Manitou Springs, Fountain, Palmer Lake.

LAW ENFORCEMENT: 246 staff, 94 vehicles + 6 fire units, phone: (719) 520-7207

EMERGENCY MEDICAL SERVICE: This community did not provide this information.

LOCAL AMENITIES

HUMAN SERVICES: More than forty-five organizations provide human services in this community HEALTHCARE: Ambicab, Brockhurst Ranch Adolescent Chemical Dependency Treatment Center, Cedar Springs Psychiatric Hospital, Hospice, Inc., Mental Health, Planned Parenthood, Rape Crisis Service, Visiting Nurses Association ORGANIZATIONS: More than fifty associations, organizations and clubs are active in the area; some are headquartered here PROFESSIONAL SERVICES: Institute for Business and Industrial Technology **ENTERAINMENT:** Imperial Hotel and Melodrama, Iron Springs Chateau Dinner Theater.

CLIMATE

January Temperature (in degrees Fahrenheit)	27.0
July Temperature (in degrees Fahrenheit)	78.0
Annual Precipitation (in inches)	16.0
Annual Snowfall (in inches)	59.0
Elevation (in feet)	6500
Area (in square miles)	2129.7

TAXES

1993 PROPERTY TAXES: Mill Levy	12.000
1993 SALES TAXES: El Paso County	1.00%
Other (RTD, Stadium, Cultural Facilities, etc.)	0.00%
State	3.00%

LOCAL ECONOMIC DEVELOPMENT CONTACTS

Major firms in area: **GOVERNMENT:** Ft. Carson, Peterson/NORAD/Space Command, Air Force Academy, City Governments, School District 11, County Governments, Harrison School District, US Postal Service, Academy School District, Widefield School District **HI-TECH:** Hewlett-Packard Co., Digital Equipment Corp., TRW Inc., Current Inc., Ampex Corp., Inmos Corp., Honeywell Inc., Ford Aerospace, Kaman Corp., Texas Instruments Inc. **SERVICES:** Penrose Hospitals, Broadmoor Hotel Inc., Memorial Hospital, St. Francis Hospital **RETAIL TRADE:** King Soopers, Safeway, Sears, Schoollage Lock Co. **FINANCE, INSURANCE, REAL ESTATE:** Farmers Insurance Group **UTILITIES:** Mountain Bell, Colorado Interstate Gas. The leading sources of income are high tech and military.

1995 PUBLIC SCHOOL INFORMATION

District Name	# of Students	# of Schools	# of Teachers	Students /Teachers
Academy 20	14,715	20	805	18.3
Big Sandy 100J	355	3	25	14.5
Calhan RJ-1	500	3	33	15.3
Cheyenne Mountain 1	3,458	8	174	19.9
Colorado Springs 11	33,175	59	1,696	19.6
Edison 54 JT	47	2	6	7.8
Ellicott 22	658	2	40	16.3
Falcon 49	3,998	8	233	17.2
Florence RE-2	1,972	3	121	16.4
Fountain 8	4,712	10	272	17.3

Hanover 28	157	2	15	10.5
Harrison 2	10,590	19	658	16.1
Lewis-Palmer 38	3,787	7	177	21.4
Manitou Springs 14	1,399	4	75	18.6
Miami/Yoder 60 JT	287	2	17	16.9
Peyton 23 JT	543	3	36	15.3
Widefield 3	8,370	15	447	18.7
State of Colorado	673,438	1,483	36,398	18.5

Nearest four-year college: University of Colorado (Colorado Springs)
Nearest community college: Pikes Peak Community College (Colorado Springs)
Nearest vocational center: Several schools (Colorado Springs)

LOCAL TRANSPORTATION

NEAREST SCHEDULED AIR SERVICE: Colorado Springs Municipal Airport, Gary Green, 719-596-0188
LOCAL BUSES, TRUCKS, AND TRAINS: Greyhound, Continental Trailways, AandA, ABF, ANR, American Freight, Consolidated Freightways, Edson, Ellis, McLean, Yellow Freight. Freight: Santa Fe, Rio Grande

LOCAL UTILITIES

LOCAL WATER INFORMATION: City of Colorado Springs (719) 636-5300, City of Fountain (719) 382-7591, City of Manitou Springs (719) 685-5597, Town of Calhan (719) 347-2586

LOCAL SEWER INFORMATION: City of Colorado Springs (719) 636-5300, Fountain Sanitation (719) 382-5719, Calhan Sewage District (719) 347-2338, Monument Sewage District, Palmer Lake Sewage District (719) 481-2732

LOCAL LANDFILL INFORMATION: See individual municipalities.

LOCAL ELECTRICITY INFORMATION: City of Colorado Springs (719) 636-5300, City of Fountain (719) 392-9088, Mountain View Electric Association (719) 332-9881

LOCAL GAS INFORMATION: City of Colorado Springs (719) 636-5300, City of Fountain (719) 392-9088, Mountain View Electric Association (719) 332-9881

JEFFERSON COUNTY

LARGEST CITIES/TOWNS/COMMUNITIES

Mountain View, Wheat Ridge, Lakewood, Arvada, Bow Mar, Broomfield, Edgewater, Golden, Lakeside, Morrison

POPULATION ESTIMATES BY AGE GROUPS, 1998-2005

AGE GROUP	1998	2000	2005
0 to 4 years old	32182	31361	30275
5 to 18	102058	102058	99245
19 to 34	104963	106403	117393
35 to 64	221261	229481	239583
65 to 89	45371	48061	55823
90 and over	1184	1259	1500
Total	507020	518622	543820

LOCAL COMMUNITY DESCRIPTION

Jefferson County is situated in the north central portion of the state where the eastern plains rise to meet the Rocky Mountains. The County forms the western and southwestern extension of Colorado's principle urban center, the six county Denver metropolitan area. Prairies, valleys, mountains and forests offer a varied physical appearance to the county whose chief landmark is the rock formation near Morrison that forms Red Rocks Amphitheater. Jefferson County's growth has led to increases in small business and professional services, the expansion of industrial operations, the creation of shopping centers and the enlargement of the regional operations of many federal government agencies. Economic expansion has created the opportunity for diverse lifestyles among the County's residents and has resulted in one of the nation's finest public education systems and a nationally acclaimed program for the preservation of open space. Golden, the county seat, was the state's first capital.

ADDRESS: 100 Jefferson County Pkwy., Golden, CO 80419, 303-271-8525
DATE OF INCORPORATION: 1861, COUNTY SEAT: City of Golden

LOCAL EMERGENCY SERVICES

Mountain View, Wheat Ridge, Lakewood, Arvada, Bow Mar, Broomfield, Edgewater, Golden, Lakeside, Morrison are served by fire departments.
LAW ENFORCEMENT: Staff: 529, Vehicles: 140, Phone: (303) 271-5697

LOCAL AMENITIES

HUMAN SERVICES: Jefferson County Social Services - Bill Hales (303) 232-3632, JEFFCO Employment and Training Services, Jefferson Animal

Shelter, Cooperative Extension Service, Prospect Recreation District **PUBLIC FACILITIES**: Public Library - 9 branches, bookmobile; CHURCHES: all denominations available **RECREATIONAL AREAS**: Pike National Forest, Arapahoe National Forest, Roosevelt National Forest, Red Rocks Park, Golden Gate State Park, Means Meadow, White Ranch Park, Mt. Falcon Historic Park, (16,000 acres of open space park and recreational areas) **TOURIST ATTRACTIONS**: Hiwan Homestead Museum, Nature and Conference Center - Lookout Mountain, Buffalo Bill's Grave, Coors Brewery, Heritage Square - amusement rides, craft and specialty shops, Jefferson County Fairgrounds - July 4th Festival of the West Celebration, Morrison - antique and craft shops **ACTIVITIES**: Swimming, Fishing, Boating, Camping, Windsailing, Hiking, Equestrian Trails **LODGING**: Denver West - Marriott Hotel, Motel 6, Comfort Inn, Holiday Inn, many others.

CLIMATE

January Temperature (in degrees Fahrenheit)	29.0
July Temperature (in degrees Fahrenheit)	75.0
Annual Precipitation (in inches)	16.0
Annual Snowfall (in inches)	50.0
Elevation (in feet)	5500
Area (in square miles)	778.2

TAXES

1993 PROPERTY TAXES: Mill Levy	25.584
1993 SALES TAXES: Jefferson County	.50%
Other (RTD, Stadium, Cultural Facilities, etc.)	.60%
State	3.00%

LOCAL ECONOMIC DEVELOPMENT CONTACTS

Major firms in area: **MANUFACTURING**: Martin Marietta, Rockwell International, Cobe Laboratories, Sunstrand, Ball Metal Container, International Business Machines **ENERGY**: Rocky Mountain Energy, Amax Inc., Mobile Premix **FOOD PROCESSING**: Jolly Rancher, Adolph Coors Company **SERVICES**: General Cable, Mountain Bell, ATT, Public Service Company of Colorado **FINANCE, INSURANCE, REAL ESTATE**: Rocky Mountain Banknote **OTHER**: Statitrol **GOVERNMENT**: Federal Government, Jefferson County, R-1 School District., Federal Center **RETAIL TRADE**: King Soopers **TRANSPORTATION**: United Airlines. Local banks have $3,200,000,000 in assets.

1995 PUBLIC SCHOOL INFORMATION

District Name	# of Students	# of Schools	# of Teachers	Students /Teacher
Jefferson County R-1	86,670	150	4,134	21.0
State of Colorado	673,438	1,483	36,398	18.5

Nearest four-year college: Colorado School of Mines (Golden)
Nearest community college: Arapahoe Community College (Littleton)
Nearest vocational center: Columbine Beauty School, Mile Hi College
   (Lakewood)

LOCAL TRANSPORTATION

NEAREST SCHEDULED AIR SERVICE: Denver International Airport
LOCAL BUSES, TRUCKS, AND TRAINS: Greyhound, Continental Trailways, RTD. A full array of truck lines serve the Denver Metro area and Jefferson County. Freight: Denver and Rio Grande Railway, Great Western Railway. Passenger: Amtrak

LOCAL UTILITIES

LOCAL SEWER, WATER & LANDFILL INFORMATION: This community did not provide this information.

LOCAL ELECTRICITY INFORMATION: Public Service Company of Colorado, Intermountain Rural Electric Association

LOCAL GAS INFORMATION: Public Service Company of Colorado

LARIMER COUNTY

LARGEST CITIES/TOWNS/COMMUNITIES

Berthoud, Estes Park, Fort Collins, Loveland, Timnath, Wellington

POPULATION ESTIMATES BY AGE GROUPS, 1998-2005

AGE GROUP	1998	2000	2005
0 to 4 years old	14994	15714	17196
5 to 18	46228	47137	49439
19 to 34	62058	65017	72523
35 to 64	86024	91073	103257
65 to 89	20104	20607	22459
90 and over	711	745	847
Total	230120	240292	265721

LOCAL COMMUNITY DESCRIPTION

Larimer County is located on the eastern edge of the Rocky Mountains in northern Colorado. Major urban areas in the county are arranged along scenic foothills, with a backdrop of spectacular mountain peaks. The county extends to the Continental Divide and includes several mountain communities and Rocky Mountain National Park. Lifestyle opportunities in Larimer County are as varied as the terrain and include sophisticated urban areas with established cultural facilities, productive agricultural lands, small-town environments and a wealth of outdoor recreation areas enjoyed by urban and rural residents alike. The area benefits from its proximity to the Denver metropolitan area, but has retained its own identity and unique quality of life. Colorado State University is located in Larimer County, which together with Colorado University in adjacent Boulder County has established the area as a center of advanced research and learning. The unique environment has attracted a variety of businesses, both large and small, which have generally prospered, so growth of existing business is a more important source of new jobs than those created by new industry.

ADDRESS: P. O. Box 1190, Fort Collins, CO 80522, 970-498-7000
DATE OF INCORPORATION: 1861, COUNTY SEAT: City of Fort Collins

LOCAL EMERGENCY SERVICES

Berthoud, Estes Park, Fort Collins, Loveland, Timnath, and Wellington are served by fire departments.

LAW ENFORCEMENT: 183 staff, 78 vehicles, phone: (970) 221-7107

LOCAL AMENITIES

CHURCHES: 110 churches in the community HEALTHCARE: Foothills Gateway Rehabilitation Center, Hospice, Inc., Human Development, Mental Health, Public Health ORGANIZATIONS: Boy Scouts, Girl Scouts, Multiple Sclerosis Society of Colorado, Neighbor to Neighbor, United Service Organization, Right to Life, Birthright, HUMAN SERVICES: More than thirty organizations provide human services in the area ADDITIONAL INFORMATION: contact Larimer County Parks and Recreation at 970-669-4077; LODGING: several major hotels in major municipalities

CLIMATE

January Temperature (in degrees Fahrenheit)	23.0
July Temperature (in degrees Fahrenheit)	71.0
Annual Precipitation (in inches)	14.0
Annual Snowfall (in inches)	58.0
Elevation (in feet)	5400
Area (in square miles)	2634.0

TAXES

1993 PROPERTY TAXES: Mill Levy	21.723
1993 SALES TAXES: Larimer County	0.00%
Other (RTD, Stadium, Cultural Facilities, etc.)	0.00%
State	3.00%

LOCAL ECONOMIC DEVELOPMENT CONTACTS

Major firms in area: **MANUFACTURING**: Woodward Governor, Teledyne Water Pik, Hewlett Packard, Eastman Kodak, Anheuser Busch **GOVERNMENT**: Colorado State University, Poudre Valley Schools, Larimer County, City of Fort Collins **SERVICES**: Poudre Valley Hospital **UTILITIES**: Mountain Bell, **PLEASE NOTE**: All of the above employers have more than 500 employees. The leading source of income is high tech manufacturing.

1995 PUBLIC SCHOOL INFORMATION

District Name	# of Students	# of Schools	# of Teachers	Students /Teacher
Johnstown-Milliken	1,280	4	84	15.2
Park R-3	1,349	3	77	17.5
Poudre R-1	21,922	43	1,101	19.9
St. Vrain Valley RE	17,459	32	717	19.7
Thompson R-2J	13,787	26	717	19.2
State of Colorado	673,438	1,483	36,398	18.5

Nearest four-year college: Colorado State University (Fort Collins)
Nearest community college: Aims Community College (Greeley)
Nearest vocational center: Larimer County Voc-Tech (Fort Collins)

LOCAL TRANSPORTATION

NEAREST SCHEDULED AIR SERVICE: Fort Collins-Loveland Municipal Airport, Fred Anderton Jr., 4824 Earhart Road, Loveland, CO 80538, (970) 962-2852

LOCAL BUSES, TRUCKS, AND TRAINS: Continental Trailways, TWX, American Freight Systems, Consolidated Freightways, CHandW Transportation Co., Ryder. Freight: Union Pacific, Colorado and Southern

LOCAL UTILITIES

LOCAL WATER INFORMATION: Arkins Water Association, Inc., Bald Mountain Water Association, East Larimer County Water (ELCO), Fort Collins-Loveland Water, Laporte Water, Sunset Water, Little Thompson Water

LOCAL SEWER INFORMATION: Boxelder Sanitation, Cherry Hills Sanitation, Estes Park Sanitation, Laporte Sanitation, Mountain View Sanitation, South Fort Collins Sanitation

LOCAL LANDFILL INFORMATION Frank Lancaster (303) 221-7712

LOCAL ELECTRICITY INFORMATION Poudre Valley Rural Electric Authority, 226-1234, Public Service Company of Colorado

LOCAL GAS INFORMATION Poudre Valley Rural Electric Authority, 226-1234, Public Service Company of Colorado

WELD COUNTY

LARGEST CITIES/TOWNS/COMMUNITIES

Greeley, Evans, Platteville, Fort Lupton

POPULATION ESTIMATES BY AGE GROUPS, 1998-2005

AGE GROUP	1998	2000	2005
0 to 4 years old	11762	11686	12138
5 to 18	34145	34869	36307
19 to 34	41372	43692	48747
35 to 64	55022	57923	65392
65 to 89	14604	14961	16229
90 and over	553	578	634
Total	157457	163709	179447

LOCAL COMMUNITY DESCRIPTION

Weld County represents a highly diversified economy with excellent growth potential. Weld County offers an outstanding quality of life. Within a 60-mile radius are located 4 major universities with their attendant cultural and athletic events. The Denver metro-area forms the county's southern boundary and 6 major ski areas are located within a 2 hour drive and the county will soon be home to the largest performing arts center in Northern Colorado.

ADDRESS: P. O. Box 758, Greeley, CO 80632, (970) 356-4000
DATE OF INCORPORATION: 1861, COUNTY SEAT: City of Greeley

LOCAL EMERGENCY SERVICES

See individual municipalities

LAW ENFORCEMENT: 180 staff, 38 vehicles, phone: (970) 356-4000 x4631, contact Ed Jordan.

LOCAL AMENITIES

ORGANIZATIONS: American Cancer Society, Cystic Fibrosis Foundation, Leukemia Society of America, Multiple Sclerosis Society, National Kidney Foundation, National Association of Sickle Cell Disease **HEALTHCARE**: Crisis Pregnancy of Weld County, North Colorado Medical Center, Weld County Health Department, Island Grove Regional Treatment Center, Northern Colorado Center on Deafness, Rape Crisis Team, Schaefer Rehabilitation Center, Weld Mental Health Center, Patient Advocacy Team, Northeast Home Health Care Service **HUMAN SERVICES**: Battered Women's Helpline, Catholic Community Services, Chemical Families Support Services, Child Abuse Resource and Education, Parent Child Learning Center, Partners, Inc., SAVE, Salvation Army, The Sycamore Tree, United Way of Weld County, Women's Place, Weld County Community Center Foundation, Weld County Social Services, Weld County Human Services, Weld County Health Department, Weld Information and Referral Service, Colorado Christian Services, Colorado Civil Rights Commission, Volunteer Resource Bureau; **CHURCHES**: All major denominations **LODGING**: Holiday Inn, Raintree Hotel and Conference Center, Heritage Hotel **PERFORMING ARTS CENTER** (soon to be completed); **PHILHARMONIC ORCHESTRA** (oldest philharmonic orchestra west of the Mississippi River).

CLIMATE

January Temperature (in degrees Fahrenheit)	29.0
July Temperature (in degrees Fahrenheit)	75.0
Annual Precipitation (in inches)	13.0
Annual Snowfall (in inches)	37.0
Elevation (in feet)	4900
Area (in square miles)	4021.8

TAXES

1993 PROPERTY TAXES: Mill Levy	22.038
1993 SALES TAXES: Weld County	0.00%
Other (RTD, Stadium, Cultural Facilities, etc.)	0.00%
State	3.00%

LOCAL ECONOMIC DEVELOPMENT CONTACTS

Major firms in area: **MANUFACTURING**: Eastman Kodak, Monfort of Colorado, Hewlett Packard, ConAgra, Electronic Fab **GOVERNMENT**: School District #6, University of Northern Colorado, Aims College, Weld County, City of Greeley, Federal Government, State of Colorado, School District #8, School District #4 **SERVICES**: North Colorado Medical Center, Mountain Bell, Golden Recycling (Coors) **FINANCE, INSURANCE, REAL ESTATE**: State Farm Insurance **RETAIL TRADE**: Safeway, Toddys, K-

Mart **CONSTRUCTION**: Hensel Phelps (contractor) **TRANSPORTATION**: Steinbecker Brothers (motor freight transport.) **OTHER**: Northwest Publishing, Greeley Publishing. The leading sources of income are agriculture, oil and gas, meat products, film, computers. Local banks have $497,330,000 in assets.

1995 PUBLIC SCHOOL INFORMATION

District Name	# of Students	# of Schools	# of Teachers	Students /Teacher
Ault-Highland RE-9	860	3	54	15.9
Briggsdale RE-10	120	2	13	9.2
Brighton 27J	4,562	9	233	19.6
Eaton RE-2	1,355	4	79	17.2
Fort Lupton RE-8	2,655	5	156	17.1
Greeley 6	13,662	25	736	18.6
Johnstown-Milliken	1,280	4	84	15.2
Keenesberg	1,434	4	84	17.1
Platte Valley RE-7	1,019	2	62	16.4
Prairie RE-11	133	2	16	8.5
St. Vrain Valley RE	17,459	32	885	19.7
Thompson R-2J	13,787	26	717	19.2
Weld RE-1	1,970	6	123	16.0
Weldon Valley RE-20	144	3	16	9.1
Wiggins RE-50 (J)	570	2	37	15.4
Windsor RE-4	2,116	5	128	16.5
State of Colorado	673,438	1,483	36,398	18.5

Nearest four-year college: University of Northern Colorado (Greeley)
Nearest community college: Aims Community College (Greeley)
Nearest vocational center: Larimer County Voc-Tech (Fort Collins)

LOCAL TRANSPORTATION

NEAREST SCHEDULED AIR SERVICE: Fort Collins-Loveland Municipal Airport, Fred Anderton Jr., 4824 Earhart Road, Loveland, CO 80538, (970) 962-2852
LOCAL BUSES, TRUCKS, AND TRAINS: Greyhound, Estes Park Bus Company, Greeley Bus, Weld County Mini-Van System, Continental Trailway, Airport Shuttle. MOST MAJOR TRUCKLINES. Freight: Great Western, Union Pacific, Burlington Northern. Passenger: AMTRAK.

LOCAL UTILITIES

LOCAL WATER / SEWER INFORMATION: Contact city or town

LOCAL ELECTRICITY INFORMATION: Home Light and Power, Public Service Company of Colorado, Union Rural Electric Authority

LOCAL GAS INFORMATION: Greeley Gas

CHAPTER EIGHT
MONEY FOR NOTHING

SMALL AND HOME-BASED BUSINESS START-UP

The information in this chapter was compiled from various sources including, but not limited to, government reports and publications (Federal, State, and Local); material provided by business and civic organizations; and books produced by independent Colorado publishers including:

Big Ideas for Small Service Businesses and *Country Bound! Trade Your Business Suit Blues for Blue Jean Dreams*, both by Communication Creativity

For a complete description of the above books and related titles, please see the Publisher's listing in Appendix A.

For a list of legal forms available from Bradford Publishing please see Appendix D.

So you want to be your own boss? Do you want to be self-employed or own your own business? There are 21.5 million small businesses in the United States that employ 54% of the private workforce. Of the 1.9 million new jobs created in 1993, small businesses produced an estimated 71% of those jobs.

In the United States, small businesses account for 52% of all sales. In Colorado, during 1993 and 1994, there were 31,000 new businesses created. However, a full 17%—or 2,644—of the 15,425 for-profit businesses started in 1993 are no longer in business.

I have been self-employed since I turned in my parachute, beret, and uniform and became a civilian again in 1979. I can tell you from experience, the "American Dream" of owning your own business is not always what it's cracked-up to be. It takes a special type of person to make it successfully. There is the hard work, the uncertain financial return, the responsibility, and the ever-increasing burden of rules, regulations and laws.

This chapter is designed to help you determine if starting your own small or home-based business is really what you want to do and to give you as much information and resources as space permits. While all federal laws concerning this subject are uniform throughout the country, most states have unique laws, rules and regulations of which you need to be aware. The simple self-quiz below should help you decide whether to skip this chapter or not.

SO YOU WANT TO BE AN ENTREPRENEUR?

There is no way to eliminate all the risks associated with starting a small business. However, you can improve your chances of success with good planning and preparation. A good starting place is to evaluate your strengths and weaknesses as the owner and manager of a small business. Carefully consider each of the following questions.

Are you a self-starter? It will be up to you, not someone else telling you, to develop projects, organize your time, follow through on details.

How well do you get along with different personalities? Business owners need to develop working relationships with a variety of people including customers, vendors, staff, bankers and professionals such as lawyers, accountants or consultants. Can you deal with a demanding client, an unreliable vendor or cranky staff person in the best interests of your business?

How good are you at making decisions? Small business owners are required to make decisions constantly, often quickly, under pressure and independently.

Do you have the physical and emotional stamina to run a business? Business ownership can be challenging, fun and exciting. But it's also a lot of work. Can you face 12-hour work days six or seven days a week? How well do you plan and organize? Research indicates many business failures could have been avoided through better planning. Good organization—of financial inventory, schedules, and production—can help avoid many potential pitfalls.

Is your drive strong enough to maintain your motivation? Running a business can wear you down. Some business owners feel burned out by having to carry all the responsibility on their shoulders. Strong motivation to make the business succeed will help you survive slowdowns as well as periods of burnout.

How will the business affect my family? The first few years of business start up can be hard on family life. The strain of an un-supportive spouse may be hard to balance against the demands of starting a business. There also may be financial difficulties until the business becomes profitable, which could take months or even years. You may have to adjust to a lower standard of living or put family assets at risk.

Is it worth it? For many, yes! While there are numerous reasons not to start your own business, there are many advantages that, for the right person, far outweigh the risks. For starters, you get to be your own boss. Your hard work and long hours directly benefit you, rather than increasing profits for someone else. Your earnings and growth potential are far less limited. A new venture—your new venture— is exciting and running a business will provide endless variety and challenge and won't settle into a dull routine.

Assuming you have seriously considered each of these questions and have decided to go for it, the next step is to plan your new venture using the checklist below.

CHECK-LIST FOR NEW BUSINESS START-UP

You should be fully aware of the implications of owning your own business. The best advice for anyone starting or operating a business is to EDUCATE YOURSELF. This chapter is only a first step. It outlines only the basic information you will need to start your business. To obtain complete information, there are dozens of books available, many specific to Colorado business operation. Highly recommended is the Colorado Business Start-up Kit available free of charge from the Colorado Business Assistance Center.

- Decide upon the legal structure of your business and register your business and tradename with the appropriate state and/or federal agencies. **If you plan to open a business checking account you must have a tradename registration.** Refer to the Legal Structure and Registration section of this chapter.

- If your business will have employees, you must open federal, state and local wage withholding and payroll tax accounts. See the Employers Responsibilities section of this chapter.

- If your business will be selling, renting or leasing tangible personal property, obtain state and local sales tax licenses. If you rent accommodations for less than 30 days, a sales tax license is also required. Refer to the Colorado Sales Tax Licenses section.

• Be aware of the personal and business tax implications of starting your own business. Refer to the Income and Property Taxes section.

• Define the products or services you will provide. **Is there actually a need for what you will provide in today's marketplace. Is the demand great enough to be profitable! What is your competitive advantage? Develop your marketing strategy first!**

• Are there any special licenses required for the business you are starting? The Colorado Business Assistance Center has information on federal, state, and local business licensing.

• Find the best location for your business. The Colorado Department of Transportation has information on traffic patterns on state highways. Some local governments have information on city and county roads. They may also have information on local population demographics. Observe pedestrian movement during business hours to estimate walk-in potential.

• Check with the local city and county government regarding any special business regulations, sales taxes, personal property taxes and zoning restrictions.

• Seek management advice and counseling. Assemble your team of professional advisors, e.g., an accountant, an attorney, an insurance broker, a real estate agent, etc. Business organizations, business consultants, your local Small Business Development Center, the Small Business Administration, trade associations, and your local Chamber of Commerce are good resources. Refer to the Additional Resources section.

• **Develop a sound business plan with specific goals and objectives. A business plan should show where you are, where you want to go and how you will get there.** There are numerous books and software packages designed to assist you in every step of formulating a business plan—well worth the investment!

• Develop a financial plan. Include profit and loss projections, cash flow analysis and capital requirements.

• Obtain adequate insurance coverage. Protect your business activities for enough in advance to cover your growth. See the Business Insurance section.

• **Protect your ideas, products, symbols and logos through the proper registration and maintenance.** The Colorado Business

Assistance Center has information on Trademarks, Patents, and Copyrights.

NEW, ESTABLISHED, OR FRANCHISE

There are typically three avenues available to start a new business: starting a new venture from scratch, buying an existing business, or buying a franchise.

STARTING A NEW VENTURE: A new start up is typically pursued when you have a unique idea that requires special equipment, specialized talents or a new way of doing things. A new venture may also be pursued when there is a customer base you can serve, or you are aware of an unfilled market. Factors you need to consider when forming a new venture include legal structure, location, facilities, equipment, employees, taxes, marketing and advertising, a records system, and capital. **Be warned: recent estimates suggest investors lose $500 million annually in franchise and work-at-home schemes.** There are several free brochures available from the Federal Trade Commission including, "Job Ads, Job Scams and '900' Numbers," "Work At Home Schemes," and "Telemarketing Fraud."

BUYING AN ESTABLISHED BUSINESS: Buying an existing business can have its advantages. By purchasing a business that is already established, you may eliminate some of the problems associated with starting a new business. However, when you acquire an existing business, you may also acquire the business's debts. Purchasing an existing business can be fairly complex. The following is a brief summary of some of the concerns of which you should be aware to avoid commercial fraud.

Avoiding Commercial Fraud

- Do you know why the seller is selling the business? If the business has not been profitable, find out why. Do you have a plan to make it profitable?

- Does your purchase agreement include the sale of the business name? The property? The equipment and inventory? The debts? Be sure the exact terms of the sale are explained clearly before you buy. It is highly recommended you have your own attorney review all parts of the agreement.

- Ask the seller about outstanding claims on inventory, equipment and fixtures. Whose responsibility is it to settle these claims? Are there liens against the property you are buying? Check with the seller and the county clerk and recorder's office in the county where the business and the seller are located. Also check with the Colorado Secretary of State, Uniform Commercial Code Section for records of any security interests that may have been filed as liens against the property or assets of the business.

- Will the owner of the building transfer the lease to you? What are the terms and restrictions of the lease?

- Review the business's past and current financial statements. Are they in good order? Also, examine any existing contracts that affect the business's operations.

- Can you transfer the existing phone number(s)? The phone service may require information from both you and the seller. See the U.S. West heading under the Additional Resources Section.

If there are employees in the business, you will be responsible for withholding tax, unemployment insurance, workers' compensation and social security (FICA). You must open new employee payroll accounts unless you buy out the stock of an existing corporation and do not set up a new corporation. In every case the unemployment history established under the former owners will transfer to your account. When you purchase the business, the former owner should file form UILT-2 to report the change in ownership. For more information on payroll tax requirements see the Employer Responsibilities section.

Tax Liabilities: If you purchase a retail business you may be liable for sales tax debts of the business. As a precaution, you should get a tax status letter from the Department of Revenue before buying. The current owner using form DR0096 must request the tax status letter. Tax status letters may be requested on all state collected tax accounts including sales tax, wage withholding and corporate income tax accounts. There is a $10 charge for each tax status record requested. If you purchase a corporation, you may have the option of keeping the same sales tax account with the Department of Revenue. If you purchase a sole proprietorship or a partnership, you are required to open a new sales tax account.

When you purchase tangible property as part of a business, such as furniture, fixtures or equipment (new or used) for which you have not paid sales tax, you must pay a state use tax. For further information about state tax liabilities when purchasing a business contact the Colorado Department of Revenue.

Many cities and counties also collect a use tax. All county use taxes and most city use taxes are collected by the state. Large 'home rule' cities may collect use taxes directly. There may be additional liabilities for personal property taxes imposed by the county. Contact the local city clerk, the county assessor and/or the county treasurer's offices for more information regarding local use and personal property taxes.

BUYING A FRANCHISE: Franchising offers a unique opportunity for individuals interested in operating a business. It allows you to both own and operate a business while drawing from the resources of the parent company.

This arrangement may reduce some of the risks of going into business for yourself depending upon the quality and stability of the franchiser. It should be noted that while a franchise is a method for going into business it is NOT a form of legal structure. The franchiser—the business with the plan and structure—and the franchisee—you—must determine the appropriate form of legal structure. See the next section on Legal Structure and Registration for more information.

Once you have decided you are able to meet the requirements for purchasing a franchise, you may want to shop around for the best investment. There are various publications and franchise directories available from bookstores and public libraries. Many times the classified sections of your local newspaper or magazines have listings of franchise offers.

Exercise Caution: Before you agree to invest in a company that promises you large financial returns, you should exercise some caution. **Colorado lacks specific laws to protect you should you need recourse.** There are, however, general provisions governing "good business practices." These protections against deceptive and unfair trade practices are stated in the _Colorado Consumer Protection Act_ and the _Uniform Consumer Credit Code._ The Federal Trade Commission's Franchise Rule requires franchisers to provide prospective buyers with a detailed disclosure statement regarding the company's history, background and operations. This document should also describe the costs and responsibilities of both the franchiser and the franchisee and must be made available to you at least ten days before any agreements are signed, or at the first face to face meeting, whichever comes first.

The Franchise Opportunities Handbook, published by the US Department of Commerce is available for $21.00 from the Government Printing Office Bookstore by calling (303) 844-3964.

Disclosure Requirements and Prohibitions Concerning Franchising and Business Opportunity Ventures (The Franchise Rule), is available free from the Federal Trade Commission by calling (303) 844-2271.

LEGAL STRUCTURE AND REGISTRATION

Choosing The Right Legal Structure: When starting your own business you must carefully choose the appropriate legal structure for your business. You should examine the characteristics of each structure as well the needs of and desires you have for your business.

A Sole Proprietor is a single individual who owns and operates the business. There is no legal separation between the individual and the business. She or he benefits from 100% of the profits and is personally responsible for 100% of all the debts and liabilities of the business.

A General Partnership is very similar to a sole proprietorship except there are two or more individuals who own the business. A general partnership offers the means for pooling all resources and sharing control of a business. There is relatively little formality required to establish and run the business, and control remains with the partners. However, all partners remain 100% responsible for all the debts and liabilities of the business, regardless of any partnership agreement outlining work responsibilities and shares of profit.

A Limited Partnership is a partnership in which some of the partners have given up their right to manage the business. In return, their liability is limited. They are "limited" partners, as opposed to "general" partners.

A Corporation is a legal entity separate from the owners of the business. There are significant formalities that must be observed to properly operate a corporation. The corporation provides a wall of liability protection between the business and the owners. It has the ability to raise capital by issuing stock.

While the limited liability enjoyed by shareholders may appear attractive, most lenders will probably require a personal guarantee as collateral anyway. The corporation must pay its own taxes, and the owners who work in the business are normally classified as employees. A corporation must comply with the Colorado Corporation Code. Among the requirements of the Code are the following:

- "Articles of Incorporation" must be filed with the Secretary of State
- The corporation must adopt bylaws
- A corporation must adhere to certain corporate formalities including procedures for shareholder meetings, the election of the board of directors, maintenance of corporate records and proper filings with the Secretary of State

Complete corporate kits are available from Bradford Publishing, see Appendix D for details.

A Subchapter S Corporation is not actually a separate form of legal structure, but rather a special tax status granted by the IRS to tax business's income more like that of a partnership or a sole proprietorship. While an S corporation is not subject to double taxation as is a regular corporation, it may lose the ability to deduct the full cost of medical insurance as a business and business losses are treated differently. A competent tax advisor should be consulted before applying for S Corporation tax status. It is important to note the corporation must file the "Articles of Incorporation" with the Secretary of State before it can apply to the IRS for Subchapter S status.

For more specific information about qualifying and applying for filing as a Subchapter S Corporation, contact the IRS.

Non-Profit Corporations are not covered in this chapter. If you are interested in forming an NPO, all information can be obtained through the office of the Secretary of State. It should be noted that an individual might form a Not-for-Profit Corporation in Colorado for approximately $50.

A Limited Liability Company (LLC) allows you to combine the benefits of liability protection such as a corporation provides with the more simplified tax structure that a partnership can employ. **However, Limited Liability Companies are a new form of business structure that is not recognized throughout the United States. Many questions regarding tax, legal and liability issues have not yet been completely clarified.**

A Limited Liability Partnership (LLP) was approved for use in Colorado in mid-1995. It is basically the same as an LLC except it is for use by partnerships.

As you decide upon your legal structure, you should carefully evaluate both your present and future needs for operating your business. To avoid duplication of legal expenses, licensing and paperwork, analyze your various options and choose the business structure that will meet your long term needs rather than choosing a business structure solely for its short-term convenience.

WHERE TO REGISTER YOUR NEW BUSINESS

Department of Revenue: If you are a sole proprietor or general partnership and will be doing business under a name other than your own legal name(s), you must register a trade name with the Department of Revenue. Registration of the trade name does not grant exclusive rights to the use of the trade name. Sole proprietors and general partnerships gain exclusive rights to the use of a trade name only through the use of the name over a period of time. If you want to find out if a name is already being used, call the Department of Revenue.

There are two forms that you may use to register a trade name. If your business will not have any sale of tangible products or any employees, you may use form DR0592, "Trade Name Registration." If you will have employees or sales of taxable goods, you should use the "Colorado Business Registration" form. This form will register your trade name as well as open your sales tax license, state wage withholding and unemployment insurance accounts. The appropriate form can be obtained from the Department of Revenue or through the Small Business Hotline. Completed forms may be filed via mail or in person. Please note that if forms are mailed you will receive confirmation in approximately 4-6 weeks. In person, accounts will be established immediately.

Secretary of State: If your business will be a Limited Partnership, Limited Liability Company or Corporation, you must file with the Secretary of State.

You should not register trade names for these businesses with the Department of Revenue. If you do business under an additional name, you must file a "Certificate of Assumed or Trade Name" with the Secretary of State. If you are outside the Denver metro area, you can obtain the original filing paperwork and trade name forms for the Secretary of State through the Small Business Hotline.

Internal Revenue Service: All forms of legal structure, except sole proprietors with no employees, must obtain a Federal Employer Identification Number (FEIN). The FEIN is your federal tax ID number. You can obtain your FEIN by filing the SS-4 form with the IRS, Ogden, UT 84201. If it is necessary to obtain your FEIN immediately, complete the form and call (801) 620-7645. This form can be obtained from the IRS or through the Small Business Hotline. If you fax your form you will receive your FEIN in approximately 10-14 days. A sole proprietor with no employees may use their social security number as their Federal Tax ID number.

COLORADO SALES TAX LICENSES

If you sell, rent or lease tangible personal property in Colorado, you must obtain a sales tax license. The type of license you need and the amount of tax you are required to collect depends upon to whom you are selling and where and how you are doing business. A license is also required to rent accommodations to others for periods of less than 30 days.

Retailer License: A retailer license is required if you are selling, renting or leasing your product to the end user of the product. If you will be generating wholesale and retail sales you need only a retailer license. A retailer license costs $16 for a two-year period plus a one-time $50 deposit. The deposit will be automatically refunded to you once you have collected and remitted a total of $50 in state sales tax to the Department of Revenue. 501(c)(3) charitable organizations are not required to pay the $50 deposit when they obtain their license.

Wholesaler License: A wholesaler license is required if you are selling your product to another business that will resell your product or use it as an ingredient in another product to be resold. A wholesaler license costs $16 for a two-year period. If your business is primarily wholesale, you may have up to $1,000.00 in retail sales per year and will not be required to obtain a retailer license. If you will have more than $1,000 in retail sales per year, you should get a retailer license and record your wholesale sales under your retail license.

Single Event: If you plan to attend a single event as a vendor at a location other than your regular business location, you must obtain a single event license. A single event license costs $8.00 unless you already have a wholesaler or retailer license; then there is no charge.

Multiple Event License: If you attend more than one event during a two-year period, you should obtain a multiple event license. A multiple event license costs $16, unless you already have a wholesaler or retailer license, and then there is no charge.

Local License: Most city sales taxes are collected for the city by the state. However, there are 43 home rule cities in Colorado that have their own city sales tax license for retail sales conducted within their jurisdiction (see Collecting Sales Taxes below).

Fees: All state sales tax licenses are $16 and are issued for the same two-year period. Each two-year period is divided into four six-month 'quarters'. The actual cost of your initial license will be pro-rated depending upon the quarter in which you start your business.

COLLECTING SALES TAXES

If you will be selling a product to the end user, you must collect sales tax. The amount of sales tax you collect depends upon the taxing districts where your business is located, the type of business you are in and how the transaction is completed. To determine the amount of tax you must collect, check with the Department of Revenue.

You may also be required to collect county, city, Regional Transportation District, and other special taxes. You should obtain a retail sales tax license to collect all state taxes and you may need several city sales tax licenses from the home rule cities where you do business. Department of Revenue Publication DRPl002, Colorado Sales/Use Tax Rates, lists all state, county and city sales tax rates as well as addresses and phone numbers for home rule cites with separate licensing and collection procedures. Also note special situations below:

Mail Order and Delivery: When you have a mail order business or you sell a product contingent upon delivery to another location within the state, you must collect the taxes you have in common with the delivery location. Check with the Department of Revenue for details.

Mobile Businesses: If your business involves sales at your client's address or is mobile, you must collect the appropriate tax for each sales location. This applies to such businesses as mobile locksmiths, mobile dog grooming, interior decorators and the like. If this situation applies to you, you will not have a principle place of business and must collect the appropriate tax for each point of sale.

Craft Shows: If you will be selling at events you must have a state multiple events license. If the event is held in a city that collects its own city sales tax, you may be required to obtain an additional city sales tax license.

Flea Markets: Flea markets that operate more than three times per year are considered to be a retail location. If you sell at a flea market, you may not use an event license. All vendors should obtain retail licenses.

Multiple Permanent Business Locations: If your business has multiple permanent branch locations, each branch must have its own license and collect the appropriate tax. Exception: vending machine operators are only required to have one state license and report the appropriate tax collection under a single license. Although, each machine is required to display a sales tax decal and may still be subject to local licensing requirements.

Small Home Businesses: If you operate a small business from your home and your total annual sales are less than $1,000 per year, you do not have to obtain a state sales tax license. However, you must collect all applicable sales taxes and file a "Combined Annual Retail Sales Tax Return," DRO1OOA, at the end of each year. In addition, you will not be able to purchase inventory or supplies at wholesale without a license. If you are located in a home rule city, contact your city officials regarding your local sales tax requirements.

EMPLOYER RESPONSIBILITIES

As your business grows you may ask, "Should I hire full or part-time employees or should I hire subcontractors to perform specific jobs on an as-needed basis?" If you hire contract labor, your paper work is much easier. But just calling someone contract labor doesn't make her/him so and if you incorrectly classify those working for you, you may end up paying substantial penalties and back taxes to the IRS and the State of Colorado.

Most individuals who work for you will be considered either common law employees or independent contractors. Unfortunately, there are many state and federal laws that are used to define an employment relationship and to determine whether an individual who performs services for you is an "employee" or an "independent contractor." The following are general definitions for common law employees and independent contractors.

Common Law Employees: Common law employees are individuals who perform services subject to the control of an employer, regarding what, where, when and how something must be done. It does not matter if the employer gives the employee substantial discretion and freedom to act, so long as the employer has the legal right to control both the method and results of service. Employers are responsible for withholding all state and federal taxes and all common law employees must be covered by workers' compensation insurance.

Independent Contractors: Persons in a trade, business or profession such as law, accounting or construction who offer their services to the general public are usually considered independent contractors. The most important characteristics of independent contractors are freedom from control and financial risk. An independent contractor is responsible for his or her own self-employment taxes and any necessary insurance.

The IRS uses a list of 20 factors to determine whether a worker is a common law employee or an independent contractor. The Colorado Unemployment Insurance - Liability Unit and the Division of Workers' Compensation use similar guidelines.

Statutory Employees: Commissioned delivery drivers, insurance agents, full-time commissioned sales agents and individuals who do piece work with materials supplied by the employer are considered to be statutory employees by the IRS. The employer is not required to withhold federal income tax from payments. However, if the contract states an individual must perform the services personally, that the individual will perform the service on a continuing basis and that the equipment will be supplied by the employer, then the payments are subject to FICA. Payments to commissioned delivery drivers and sales agents are subject to unemployment insurance tax. Because statutory employees are similar in some respects to both common-law employees and independent contractors, you should contact the Colorado Division of Workers' Compensation directly regarding your workers' compensation liability.

Children And Spouses: If your business is a sole proprietorship, your children who work for your business are not considered to be employees by the IRS and are not subject to FICA and Medicare taxes until age 18. If a child is paid for domestic work in the parent's home, wages are not subject to social security and Medicare taxes until the child reaches age 21. Federal unemployment does not cover services performed by children under the age of 21 who work for their parents. It is not necessary for the children to be claimed as dependents. All wages paid to children may still be subject to income tax withholdings. Wages paid by a sole proprietor to a spouse are subject to income tax withholding and social security taxes (FICA), but not to federal unemployment insurance taxes. All wages paid to a child or a spouse are subject to withholding taxes, FICA and state and federal unemployment insurance taxes if the parent/spouse's business is a partnership or a corporation, unless each partner is parent of a child. Workers' Compensation insurance must be provided for family member/employees.

Corporate Officers: Generally, working corporate officers are considered employees by the IRS and may not be paid through a distribution of dividends only. They must be paid a "reasonable wage or salary." All wages are subject to federal and state wage withholding, FICA, and unemployment insurance taxes. Corporate officers who own more than a 10% share of the business may elect to reject workers' compensation coverage. These rules apply to the corporate officers in both C and S corporations.

Leased Employees: An alternative to hiring your own employees is to contract for workers from a temporary employment agency or an employee-leasing agency. You pay the agency a fee to provide the number and type of employees you need and specify the conditions they must work under, but the individual workers remain employees of the agency. The agency is responsible for all payroll taxes, unemployment insurance, and workers' compensation. However, if a leasing company defaults in payment of unemployment insurance, the client company is then responsible for payment of unemployment insurance. A temporary agency is used when workers are needed for a "short" period of time. Leasing agencies provide employees under contract on a permanent basis.

Household Employees: If you hire someone to work in your own home, you may have responsibilities as a household employer. If the employee earns over $50 during a quarter, you are responsible for social security and Medicare taxes. If the employee earns over $1,000 during a quarter, you will also be responsible for unemployment insurance. The law does not require that you withhold federal or state income taxes for your employee; however, you may do so voluntarily if requested by your employee and she or he completes Form W-4. Workers' compensation insurance must be obtained for household employees who work 40 or more hours per week or 5 or more days per week. For additional information regarding your responsibilities as a household employer, call the IRS to request Publication 926, "Employment Taxes for Household Employers." NOTE: The rules regarding household employees are under consideration for revision by congress and subject to change.

PAYROLL TAX FILING REQUIREMENTS AND FORMS

Wage Withholding And Social Security/Medicare Taxes: If you have employees, you will be responsible for withholding income taxes and social security/Medicare taxes from your employees' wages. As the employer, you must pay an equal share of social security/Medicare taxes. Also, you must withhold Colorado withholding tax from all employees working in Colorado, including non-residents.

Unemployment Insurance: Unemployment insurance is a fund established by law to provide benefits to employees who lose their jobs through no fault of their own. As an employer, you will be required to pay both state and federal unemployment insurance taxes.

Employee W-2s: At the end of the year, you are responsible to report wage and tax withholding information with W-2 forms. Copies of the W-2 must be sent to your employee no later than January 31. Copy A of form W-2 must be sent to the Social Security Administration (SSA) by February 28 with form W-3. For your Colorado employees, you must file DR 1093, Transmittal of State W-2s.

Independent Contractor 1099s: If you have determined your workers are independent contractors, you are not required to withhold or pay any taxes on their behalf. However, you must keep track of how much you pay them and file form 1099 for each person to whom you paid over $600 during the year. The independent contractor must be sent her/his form 1099 by January 31. Copy A of form 1099 must be sent to the IRS by February 28 with form 1096.

Payroll Records And Audits: It is important to keep complete and accurate employee/payroll records and to retain the records for at least five years. The IRS, the Immigration and Naturalization Service, the Colorado Department of Revenue and the Colorado Department of Labor & Employment all have the authority to audit your records. Remember that your liabilities begin as soon as you hire an employee.

Workers' Compensation: Workers' Compensation is mandatory insurance that provides coverage for medical expenses and lost wages due to a job-related injury or occupational disease. The employer must pay the cost of coverage for employees. All employees must be covered beginning with the very first employee. Corporate officers who actively work in a Corporation and members who work in a Limited Liability Company must be covered unless they own at least ten percent of the business and they formally elect in writing to reject coverage. The election to reject coverage is filed with the insurance carrier. If there are no other employees, the election to reject coverage should be filed using form WC43 with the Division of Workers' Compensation. According to state law, sole proprietors and partners in a partnership have the option of electing coverage for themselves although a prime contractor may require it. However, this election may significantly affect health insurance coverage. Carefully discuss this election with your insurance agent before making your decision.

BUSINESS INSURANCE

Before starting your business, you should be aware of the potential liabilities that may be incurred. You should look into what types of insurance may be required or may be in your best interest.

General Business Liability: General Business Liability is the broadest form of coverage which can protect you against losses when injury, damage or even death result to another person or her/his property because of business negligence. Your obligations may even extend beyond the general liability for which you assume you are responsible. Read the terms of the insurance contract carefully.

Product Liability Insurance: If you manufacture a product, product liability insurance can also cover the goods you produce. Insurance coverage typically relates to the product itself, but may also protect you, as the manufacturer should someone experience personal injury or property damage from the use of your product.

Completed Operations Insurance: If you are a contractor, you can become insured for events that may occur after you leave the job site. Problems that may be covered include personal injuries or damage to someone's property due to something on which you worked going wrong. This is called Completed Operations Liability Insurance.

Health Insurance: Employers are not required by federal or state law to provide health coverage to their employees. However, if you do provide health benefits, certain laws will determine the nature of the plan and how it is administered. Effective January 1995, Colorado health insurers in the small group (employers with 2-50 employees) market must at least provide a basic or standard health benefit plan to an entire small group, regardless of the health status of its employees. Other consumer protections that apply to small group policies include guaranteed renewals, underwriting restrictions, and stringent premium rating rules. Starting in January 1996, all of the above will apply to even one-person businesses.

Property Insurance: This coverage is especially important if you own the property or building where your business is located. As the mortgagee, you can be protected against losses and a loss of income in the event your business experiences damage as a result of natural disaster, fire, burglary or vandalism that may destroy all or part of your property.

Business Interruption Insurance: (Also referred to as "Specific Time Element Coverage") can pay losses of income as a result of personal property damage that might occur to your business from either environmental factors, natural disasters or destruction by others until you are able to begin operating again.

Errors and Omission/Professional Liability Insurance: E & O insurance is often recommended for employees, owners and directors of the business. Errors and omissions and professional liability coverage offer protection for employees and owners of the business against lawsuits that many arise as a result of their actions or failure to act for duties performed during the course of business.

Bonding: Bonding is not an insurance contract; however, there are several types of surety bonds you can purchase which cover a wide range of losses. Fidelity bonds are designed to protect a business or employer from losses due to the dishonesty of employees, partners or officers in the business. Performance bonds guarantee a business' performance because of an obligation or contractual agreement. Colorado Law requires certain occupations (such as construction work or motor vehicle dealers) post a bond before they can be licensed or before they are awarded a state contract. Bonding is usually not a mandatory requirement; however, many companies do require that you post a bond before beginning work.

INCOME AND PROPERTY TAX

Corporations: If your business is a corporation located in or "doing business" in Colorado, it is subject to state and federal corporate income taxes. If you will be filing as an S corporation, your business's income will be taxed as a partnership and will be exempt from corporate income taxes, although a corporate income tax return must still be filed. Working corporate officers are still treated as employees, even in an S corporation, and must be paid a reasonable wage that is subject to all payroll taxes.

Every corporation, including S corporations, "doing business" in Colorado or deriving income from Colorado sources, must file a corporate income tax return with Colorado.

If you expect your federal tax liability to be $500 or more and/or your state tax liability to be $5,000 or more, you are required to file and pay estimated taxes during the year. A Corporation that owes more than $500 in federal income tax or $5,000 in state income tax may be subject to penalties and interest.

Partnerships: If your business is a partnership, you must file state and federal partnership income tax returns. The partnership as a whole is not required to pay income tax. Each partner in the partnership is responsible for her or his own self-employment taxes as an individual. If you and your spouse run your business together and share in the profits, your business may be considered a partnership. You should record your respective shares of partnership income or loss separately for self-employment taxes. Doing this will usually not increase your total tax, but will give each spouse credit for social security earnings on which retirement benefits are based. IRS Publication, *Tax on Partnerships*, is a useful guide regarding partnership filing requirements and the allocation of income to the partners.

Self-Employment Taxes: If you are a sole proprietor or a partner in a partnership, you must file your own estimated self-employment taxes. When you work for others as an employee, your employer withholds your taxes from your paycheck. As an employee, your employer pays half of your social security taxes and you pay half. When you are self-employed, you must pay the entire amount. Estimated taxes are normally paid quarterly on actual income. If you do not have taxable income, you do not have to pay estimated taxes. If you expect to owe the IRS more than $500 in federal taxes, you must make federal estimated tax payments. IRS Publication 533, *Self-Employment Tax,* is a useful guide in determining your estimated federal tax liability. If you expect to owe Colorado more than $1,000 in state taxes, you must pay state estimated tax payments. Estimated payments are made using federal form 1040-ES and Colorado form 104-ES.

Property Taxes: Property taxes are assessed on any real and/or personal property (land, buildings, furniture, equipment, etc.) which directly or indirectly produce income within your business. The County Assessor will mail a declaration schedule for property taxes after January 1st. Taxes must be paid by April 15th unless an extension has been obtained. The County Treasurer is responsible for mailing and collecting the actual property tax bill. Agricultural and natural resources are treated somewhat differently

Enterprise Zones: An Enterprise Zone is defined as an economically depressed area of Colorado in which special tax incentives are offered to businesses that expand or locate in the zone. There are currently 16 Colorado enterprise zones. An individual zone may include all of several counties in rural areas or small portions of a single county in urban areas. You should call the Department of Revenue for more information regarding tax incentives.

ADDITIONAL RESOURCES

The Office of Regulatory Reform (ORR) was established to serve as an ombudsman for the small business community in Colorado. The office is charged with identifying and working to eliminate unnecessary, duplicative, and burdensome regulation. The office maintains a database of comprehensive (federal, state and local) regulatory requirements. In conjunction with the Office of Business Development and the Department of Revenue, ORR operates the Small Business Hotline and the Colorado Business Assistance Center which together assist over 6,000 new, expanding and existing Colorado businesses each month.

DBE Certification: An additional service provided by ORR is Disadvantaged Business Enterprise (DBE) certification. The certification process determines the eligibility of minority and women owned businesses to participate as DBEs on projects for the Colorado Department of Transportation, the Regional Transportation Distinct and the Denver Water Board.

The Office of Business Development (OBD) works with companies starting, expanding or relocating in Colorado. The Colorado First training program provides job training assistance as an incentive for companies to expand within Colorado or relocate to the state. OBD manages a Revolving Loan Fund that serves existing businesses in rural areas.

The Small Business Office coordinates start-up and existing small business programs and activities that include the Colorado Leading Edge Training

Program that teaches new and existing businesses how to develop a comprehensive business plan during a 10-12 week intensive education program.

The Minority Business Office provides assistance to ethnic minority-owned businesses in areas of procurement, marketing, training and technical assistance programs. The office works as an advocate for minority businesses and is a point of contact for current bid information and maintains a database of ethnic minority-owned businesses.

Small Business Development Centers (SBDC) offer free one-on-one counseling services in the areas of business financing information, research and marketing, business plan preparation and other small business subjects, as well as specialized seminars on many small business topics. There are twenty-one community-based SBDC branches co-sponsored by OBD. Services are provided for new and existing businesses. In addition to general services listed above, local SBDCs also specialize in international trade, government procurement, and home-based business and technology resources. The SBDCs are a cooperative venture of the US Small Business Administration, the State of Colorado Community Colleges and Chamber of Commerce.

Local Small Business Development Centers:

Alamosa	719-589-7372	Aurora	303-341-4849
Boulder	303-442-1475	Cañon City	719-275-5335
Colorado Springs	719-592-1894	Craig	970-824-7078
Delta	970-874-8772	Denver	303-620-8076
Durango	970-247-7009	Fort Collins	970-498-9295
Fort Morgan	970-867-3351	Glenwood Springs	970-928-0120
Grand Junction	970-243-5242	Greeley	970-352-3661
Lakewood	303-987-0710	Lamar	719-336-8141
Littleton	303-277-1840	Pueblo	719-549-3224
Stratton	719-348-5596	Trinidad	719-846-5644
Westminster	303-460-1032		

For more information regarding the programs administered by the Offices previously described call (303) 892-3840.

Colorado Community Colleges and Occupational Educational System: Colorado offers a wide variety of education and training programs for youth and adults through the Colorado Community College and Occupational Education System. The system provides training in more than 400 specific occupations ranging from basic entry level skills to highly technical positions and develops industry specific training programs for employers for entry level employees or upgrading of current employees.

Access Colorado Library and Information Network (ACLIN) is a project of the Colorado library community in partnership with Colorado Supernet—a Colorado access point to the information superhighway. ACLIN provides access to the information resources of the libraries in the state to support education, business, health, social services, and personal growth activities of the residents of Colorado. It creates a statewide library computer network that links the automated systems and on-line catalogs of participating libraries in a single network which includes academic, public, private and specialized (medical, legal, etc.) library participants. The service also provides free access to over 130 library catalogs, which list over 11 million books, as well as over 35 other information databases. ACLIN connects users via a single phone call, local or toll-free, using a computer and a modem from home, office, school or library. For additional information about ACLIN, contact your local public library.

To access ACLIN, use the local access number for your area or if outside a local calling area, use the 800 number. NOTE: if you attempt to use the 800 number from an area with a local number, your call will be blocked. At the first two prompts (user name and annex) type "ac" then follow the on-line instructions.

ACLIN Phone Numbers: Toll Free within Colorado   1-800-748-0888

Alamosa	719-589-0505	Boulder	303-440-9969
Colorado Springs	719-575-0200	Denver	303-294-7260
Durango	970-385-4949	Fort Collins	970-498-9199
Glenwood Springs	970-928-0055	Grand Junction	970-243-4441
Greeley	970-353-2225	Gunnison	970-641-4446
Pueblo	719-543-8811	Salida	719-530-0365
Sterling	970-521-0718	Summit County	970-968-2267
Telluride	970-728-4448		

The Small Business Administration (SBA) is a federal agency which offers a wide variety of services for new and expanding businesses, including an all-day business seminar on advertising/marketing, financial sources, record keeping, insurance needs, legal considerations and computers. Reservations may be required and there is usually a nominal charge. The SBA also offers free counseling to small businesses through SCORE (Service Corps of Retired Executives) and ACE (Active Corps of Executives). For more information on these and other programs please contact The Small Business Administration at (303) 844-3985 or SCORE toll-free 1-800-634-0245.

Colorado Department of Labor & Employment (DOLE) operates a statewide network of Job Service Centers (JCSs) providing a number of employer services including Screening and Referral, Mass Recruitment, Affirmative Action Hiring, Layoff Assistance, and the Interstate Job Bank.

Local Job Service Centers:

Alamosa	719-589-5118	Aurora	303-3061946
Bear Valley	303-922-2450	Boulder	303-441-3985
Brighton	303-659-4250	Broomfield	303-439-8161
Burlington	719-346-5331	Canon City	719-275-7408
Colorado Springs	719-473-6220	Cortez	970-565-3759

Craig	970-824-3246	Delta	970-874-5781
Denver	303-830-3000	Durango	970-247-0308
Edwards	970-926-4440	Fort Collins	970-223-2470
Fort Morgan	970-867-9401	Frisco	970-668-5360
Glenwood Springs	970-945-8638	Golden	303-271-4850
Grand Junction	970-248-7350	Greeley	970-353-3800
Gunnison	970-641-0031	Lakewood	303-922-8422
Lamar	719-336-2256	Littleton	303-798-7787
Longmont	303-449-6643	Loveland	970-667-4261
Monte Vista	719-852-5171	Montrose	970-249-7783
Pueblo	719-546-5627	Rocky Ford	719-254-3397
Salida	719-539-6523	Steamboat Springs	970-879-3075
Sterling	970-522-9342	Trinidad	719-846-9221
Walsenburg	719-738-2372		

The Governor's Job Training Office (GJTO) provides opportunities for both employees and employers by offering programs through the Job Training Partnership Act. The goal is to prepare unemployed individuals, both youth and adult, for entry into the labor force and to assist with job training for those individuals who require this assistance to prepare them for productive employment. To achieve this goal, local service areas develop training programs that meet the needs of local employers as well as eligible clients. Employers may receive financial reimbursement for hiring and helping train eligible participants.

Local GJTO service areas:

Adams County	303-289-6500	Arapahoe County	303-752-5820
Boulder County	303-441-3985	Denver County	303-893-3382
Jefferson County	303-271-4600	Larimer County	970-223-2470

All others: (303) 866-4900

Local Economic Development Offices provide variety of different services to the businesses in their area, including permitting assistance; relocation, demographics, and site location information; and counseling and support services. A few offices administer small loan programs. Some are agencies of local city or county governments. Some are independent, non-profit organizations that receive funding from local governments and/or Chambers of Commerce. Check with your local Chamber of Commerce office to locate the **LEDC** nearest you.

Chambers of Commerce: Chambers of Commerce provide a number of opportunities for business owners. Primarily, your local chamber of commerce is where you can meet and "network" with other business owners from your community. Some chambers provide additional services including counseling, training programs and guest speakers on useful business topics.

Minority Chambers of Commerce:

Asian	303-595-9737	Hispanic	303-534-7783
Black	303-341-1296	Indian	303-446-2422
Black-Colorado Springs.	719-260-9535	Latino-Pueblo	719-542-1704
Gay & Lesbian	303-595-8042	Women's	719-442-2007

Geographic Chambers of Commerce:

Akron	970-345-6842	Alamosa County	719-589-3681
Antonito	719-376-5443	Aspen	970-925-1940
Aurora	303-755-5000	Avon/Beaver Creek	970-949-5189
Basalt	970-927-4031	Berthoud	970-532-4762
Boulder	303-442-1044	Breckenridge	970-453-2913
Brighton	303-659-0223	Broomfield	303-466-1775
Brush Area	970-842-2666	Buena Vista	719-395-6612
Burlington	719-346-8070	Canon City	719-275-2331
Carbondale	970-963-1890	Castle Rock	303-688-4597
Central City	303-582-5077	Colorado Spring	719-635-1551
Conifer	303-838-0178	Copper Mountain	800-530-3099
Cortez	970-565-3414	Craig	970-824-5689
Crawford Area	97-921-4725	Creede-Mineral	800-327-2102
Crested Butte	800-545-4505	Cripple Creek	800-526-8777
Del Norte	719-657-2845	Delta	970-874-8616
Denver, Greater	303-534-8500	Denver, N. Metro	303-450-0335
Denver, S. Metro	303-795-0142	Divide	719-687-2246
Dolores	970-882-4018	Dove Creek	970-677-2272
Durango	970-247-0312	Eagle Valley	970-328-5220
Elizabeth	303-646-4287	Estes Park	970-586-4431
Evans Area	970-330-4204	Evergreen Area	303-674-3412
Florence	719-784-3544	Florissant-Lk George	719-748-8000
Fort Collins	970-482-3746	Fort Lupton	303-857-4474
Fort Morgan	800-354-8660	Fountain	719-390-4066
Fowler	719-263-4609	Franktown	303-688-9226
Fruita	970-858-3894	Georgetown	303-569-2888
Gilpin County	303-582-5077	Glenwood Springs	970-945-6589
Golden	303-279-3113	Granby	800-325-1661
Grand Junction	970-242-3214	Grand Lake	800-531-1019
Greeley/Weld	970-352-3566	Gunnison	970-641-1501
Haxtun	970-774-6600	Hayden	970-276-3737
Holyoke	970-854-3517	Hotchkiss	970-872-3226
Huerfano County	719-738-1065	Idaho Springs	303-567-0607
Jefferson- West	303-233-5555	Johnstown-Milliken	970-587-4671
Julesburg	970-474-3504	Keenesburg	303-732-4246
Kremmling	970-724-3472	La Junta	719-384-7411
La Veta	719-742-3676	Lafayette	303-666-9555
Lake City	800-569-1874	Lakewood	303-233-5555
Lamar	719-336-4379	Las Animas	719-456-0453
Leadville	800-933-3901	Limon	719-775-2373
Logan County	800-544-8609	Longmont	303-776-5295
Louisville	303-666-5747	Loveland	970-667-6311
Lyons	303-823-5215	Manitou Springs	800-642-2567
Meeker	970-878-5510	Monte Vista	719-852-2731
Montrose County	800-249-5515	Monument	719-481-3282
Nederland	800-221-0044	Newcastle	970-984-2311

North Park	970-723-4600	Norwood	970-327-4707
Olathe	970-323-5601	Ordway	719-267-4012
Ouray County	303-325-4746	Pagosa Springs	800-252-2024
Palisade	970-464-7458	Paonia	970-527-3886
Parker	303-841-4268	Platteville	970-785-2265
Pueblo	719-542-1624	Rangely	970-675-5290
Rico	970-967-2861	Rifle	970-625-2085
Rocky Ford	719-254-7483	Salida	719-539-2068
Silverton	800-752-4494	Snowmass	800-598-2004
South Fork	719-873-5512	Springfield	719-523-4061
Steamboat Springs	970-879-0882	Summit County	800-530-1515
Telluride	800-525-3455	Trinidad	719-846-9285
Vail	970-949-5189	Vallecito Lake	970-884-9782
West Yuma	970-848-2704	Westcliffe	719-783-9163
Windsor	970-686-7189	Winter Park	970-726-4118
Woodland Park	719-687-9885	Yuma	970-848-2704

Colorado Small Business Incubators: Small business incubators are designed to assist business start-ups during the most critical formative years (embryo stage). These incubators provide workshops to teach business skills and to improve knowledge of business operations and management. Other benefits of utilizing an incubator include formal and informal networks of business assistance, consulting services, multi-tenant office space, shared office services and improved access to financial resources. Call the following incubator sites for more information:

Denver Enterprise Center	(303) 296-9400
Jefferson County Business and Innovation Center	(303) 238-0913
Western Colorado Business Development Corporation	(970) 243-5242
Fremont County EDC and Business Development Center	(719) 275-8601
Colorado Bio-Venture Center	(303) 237-3998

US West Home Office Consulting Center: Virtually all local phone service in Colorado is handled by US West. Recently they created the Home Office Consulting Center that offers free advice and service from consultants who are specially trained to provide creative, cost-efficient ideas for work-at-home professionals and entrepreneurs. I can tell you that from experience they really know their stuff. With so many new services available it really pays— although you won't have to—to have one of these professionals work out the best system for your home-office. Call 1-800-872-4658.

AT&T Home Business Resources: Same as above except for long-distance services. Call 1-800-473-7687 and ask for an information package and a free subscription to AT&T Powersource, a quarterly magazine loaded with useful and up-to-date information.

Rocky Mountain Home-Based Business Association: This non-profit association offers networking opportunities, educational seminars, a quarterly newsletter, and special events designed specially for those with home-based businesses. Call (303) 367-1918 for more information.

Additional Resources

Active Corps of Executives (ACE)	303-844-3985
Aurora Small Business Development Center	303-361-0847
Census Bureau	303-969-7750
Colorado Business Assistance Center	303-592-5920
Colorado Compensation Insurance Authority	303-782-4000
Colorado Department of Business Development	303-892-3840
Colorado Department of Revenue	303-866-3091
Colorado Department of Revenue - Income & Sales Tax	303-844-2271
Colorado Department of Transportation	303-757-9488
Federal Employer I.D. Numbers	801-625-7645
Federal Wage & Hour Division	303-844-4405
Front Range Community College Small Business Development	303-466-8811
Government Printing Office Bookstore	303-844-3964
Immigration and Naturalization Service	303-371-3041
Internal Revenue Service	303-825-7041
International Trade	303-844-6623
Jefferson Co. Employment & Training Services	303-271-4600
Minority Business Assistance Office	303-892-3840
Occupational Safety and Health Administration	303-844-5285
Recorded Tax Information	800-829-4477
Red Rocks Community College Small Business Development	303-987-0710
Secretary of State	303-894-2251
Small Business Hotline	303-592-5920
Tax Form & Publication Assistance	800-829-3676
U. S. Department of Commerce	303-844-3964
U. S. Department of Labor	303-844-1256
U. S. Postal Service-Requirements and Permits	303-297-6120
U. S. Small Business Administration Services	303-844-3985
University of Colorado Business Advancement Center	303-444-5723

CHAPTER NINE
GET OUT OF DENVER

STATE-WIDE RECREATION, ENTERTAINMENT AND CULTURE

Communing With Nature, Winter Activities, Water Sports, Bicycling, Sky-High Adventure, Weekend Getaways, Tours, Professional Sports, Downtown Denver, Leisure, Fun & Unusual Things To Do, The Arts & Culture

Looking for something to do in Colorado? Try: Arts, Amusement Parks, Archaeological Tours, Ballet, Ballooning, Bed & Breakfast, Bicycle Touring, Boating, Brew-Pubs, Camera Safari, Camping, Concerts, Cross-country Skiing, Dog Sledding, Downhill Skiing, Festivals And Events, Flying, Four-Wheel-Drive Trips, Gambling, Glider Rides, Gold Panning, Golf, Hang Gliding, Hiking/Backpacking, Historic Tours, Horseback Riding, Hot Springs, Ice Climbing, Ice Skating, Kayaking, Llama Trekking, Mine Tours, Mountain Biking, Mountaineering, Museums, Narrow-gauge Train Rides, Nature Walks, Opera, Paragliding, Plays, Planetariums, Professional Baseball, Basketball, Football, or Hockey, River Rafting, Rock Climbing, Running, Sailing, Scenic Drives, Scuba Diving, Skydiving, Sleigh Rides, Snowshoe Walks, Snowboarding, Snowmobiling, Swimming, Tennis, Trail Walks, Water Skiing, Weekend Getaways, Windsurfing, Winery Tours, Zoos.

As you can see, there are unlimited options when it comes to things to do in Colorado. You might also guess it would be impossible to adequately cover all these options in this book. The intent of this chapter is to provide an overview of the possibilities and direct you to sources of more complete information. In fact, there are dozens of books available on Colorado's cultural and recreational activities. If you are interested in a particular activity, I recommend the books listed throughout this chapter.

When you think of New York City, you imagine skyscrapers, crowded streets and rude taxi drivers. When you think of Florida, you imagine vast stretches of beach, palm trees and water sports. When you think of Colorado, you imagine thousands of square miles of wilderness and all the activities that go with them. Colorado has 2 national parks, 6 national monuments, 12 national forests, 43 state parks, 2 national recreation areas, 24 ski areas/resorts, and dozens of large lakes and reservoirs. These areas offer a multitude of things to do during all four seasons.

COMMUNING WITH NATURE

Camera Safaris/Nature & Trail Walks; Camping; Hiking/Backpacking; Horseback Riding; Llama Trekking; Mountaineering; Rock Climbing

Recommended Reading: Colorado Publishers produce excellent books on these subjects, please see these listings in Appendix A: Fulcrum Publishing, Johnson Books, Outdoor Books & Maps, Pruett Publishing, Roberts Rinehart Publishing, University Press of Colorado, Westcliffe Publishing

Please observe the following rules while visiting or camping in any National Park, National Monument, or National Forest (check with each location for additional rules and regulations):

1. Leash laws for pets vary from location to location: check any posted signs pertaining to containment.
2. Do not feed or touch wild animals (do not keep food in tents).
3. Hunting is allowed in designated areas by permit only.
4. Picking wildflowers and plants is allowed by permit only.
5. Harassment of wildlife is prohibited.
6. Fishing requires a valid Colorado state fishing license.
7. Camping is restricted to designated areas in National Parks, however most National Forests are considered open area.
8. A permit is required for all overnight stays in National Parks, but not in National Forests.
9. Fires may be built only in picnic areas and campsites with grates in National Parks, however most National Forests are considered open area. Be sure to check the Fire Danger signs where posted.
10. Vehicles must remain on designated roadways or in parking areas.

11. Trail bikes, snowmobiles, and all other vehicles are restricted to designated trails.
12. Remove all your own trash from picnic areas and campsites.

Mesa Verde National Park: MVNP is located in southwestern Colorado. Established in 1906, the park contains ancient cliff dwellings dating back to 1200 A.D. The most notable of the cliff dwellings are Cliff Palace in Cliff Canyon, which contains more than 200 rooms and 23 kivas (ceremonial chambers); Spruce Tree House in Spruce Tree Canyon, with 114 rooms and 8 kivas; and Balcony House in Soda Canyon, a small cliff dwelling of at least 30 rooms. The Park covers 81.4 square miles and includes two museums and a 494-unit campground. For additional information call 970-529-4465.

Rocky Mountain National Park: RMNP is located 62 miles (as the crow flies) Northwest of Denver. Covering 414 square miles, the park includes 113 named peaks above 10,000 feet including Longs Peak at 14,255 feet. The Park has 57 miles of paved road (including Trail Ridge Road), 14 miles of gravel road, and 355 miles of hiking trails. RMNP has 5 campgrounds with a total of 500 sites. For additional information call 970-586-1206.

NATIONAL MONUMENTS (NM)

National Parks & Monuments – Main Number		303-969-2500
Black Canyon of the Gunnison NM	Montrose	970-641-2337
Colorado NM	Fruita	970-858-3617
Dinosaur NM	Dinosaur	970-374-3000
Florissant Fossil Beds NM	Florissant	719-748-3253
Great Sand Dunes NM	Mosca	719-378-2312
Hovenweep NM	Mesa Verde NP	970-749-0510

NATIONAL FORESTS (NF)

Rocky Mountain Region National Forest Service		303-275-5350
Arapahoe National Forest	Ft. Collins	970-498-2770
Grand Mesa National Forest	Delta	970-874-6600
Gunnison National Forest	Delta	970-874-7691
Pawnee National Grassland	Greeley	970-353-5004
Pike National Forest	Pueblo	719-545-8737
Rio Grande National Forest	Monte Vista	719-852-5941
Roosevelt National Forest	Ft. Collins	970-498-2770
Routt National Forest	Steamboat Springs	970-879-1870
San Isabel National Forest	Pueblo	719-545-8737
San Juan National Forest	Durango	970-247-4874
Uncompahgre National Forest	Delta	970-874-6600
White River National Forest	Glenwood Springs	970-945-2521

NATIONAL RECREATION AREAS

Arapahoe National Recreation Area	Ft. Collins	970-498-2770
Curecanti National Recreation Area	Gunnison	970-874-6600

WILDERNESS AREAS

WILDERNESS	+- ACRES	MANAGEMENT
Black Canyon / Gunnison	11,180	Black Canyon of the Gunnison NM
Buffalo Peaks	43,410	Pike, San Isabel NF
Byers Peak	8,095	Arapaho NF
Cache La Poudre	9,308	Roosevelt NF
Collegiate Peaks	118,900	Gunnison, San Isabel, White River NF
Comanche	66,901	Roosevelt NF
Eagles Nest	133,915	Arapaho, White River NF
Flat Tops	235,230	Routt White River NF
Fossil Ridge	33,060	Gunnison NF
Great Sand Dunes	33,450	Great Sand Dunes NM
Greenhorn Mtn	22,040	San Isabel NF
Holy Cross	123,410	San Isabel, White River NF
Hunter-Fryingpan	82,780	White River NF
Indian Peaks	70,894	Arapahoe, Roosevelt NF, Rocky Mtn. NP
La Ganta	129,626	Gunnison, Rio Grande NF
Lizard Head	41,496	San Juan, Uncompahgre NF
Lost Creek	120,151	Pike NF
Maroon Bells-Snowmass	183,871	Gunnison, White River NF
Mesa Verde	8,100	Mesa Verde NP
Mt. Evans	74,401	Arapaho, Pike NF
Mt. Massive	28,047	San Isabel NF
Mt. Sneffels	16,527	Uncompahgre NF
Mt. Zirkel	160,648	Routt NF
Neota	9,924	Roosevelt, Routt NF
Never Summer	21,090	Arapaho, Routt NF
Platte River	743	Roosevelt NF
Powderhorn	60,100	Bureau of Land Management
Ptarmigan Peak	13,175	Arapaho NF
Raggeds	65,430	Gunnison, White River NF
Rawah	73,886	Roosevelt, Routt NF
Sangre de Cristo	226,455	Rio Grande, San Isabel NF
Service Creek	47,140	Routt NF
South San Juan	158,790	Rio Grande, San Juan NF
Uncompahgre	102,790	Uncompahgre NF
Vasquez Peak	12,300	Arapaho NF
Weminuche	492,418	Rio Grande, San Juan NF
West Elk	176,412	Gunnison NF

COLORADO STATE PARKS

FEES: A valid parks pass is required on every vehicle entering a state park. A daily pass is $4; an annual pass—good for the entire calendar year at all state parks—is $40. Camping permits are $6-$12 per night, depending on the facilities available. Day-use areas are generally open for 5 a.m. to 10 p.m. and campgrounds (when open) are open 24 hours a day.

For additional information call 303-866-3437. For camping reservations call 303-470-1144 or 1-800-678-CAMP. Before using any state parks you should request a copy of the State Park Regulations. All state parks are listed below:

Park Name	Location	Phone Number
Arkansas	Salida	719-539-7289
Barbour Ponds	Loveland	970-678-9402
Barr Lake	Brighton	303-659-6005
Bonny Lake	Idalia	970-354-7306
Boyd Lake	Loveland	970-669-1739
Castlewood Canyon	Franktown	303-688-5242
Chatfield	Littleton	303-791-7275
Cherry Creek	Aurora	303-690-1166
Colorado State Forest	Walden	970-723-8366
Crawford	Crawford	970-921-5721
Eldorado Canyon	Eldorado Springs	303-494-3943
Eleven Mile	Lake George	719-748-3401
Golden Gate Canyon	Golden	303-582-3707
Harvey Gap (no pets)	Rifle	970-625-1607
Highline	Loma	970-858-7208
Island Acres	Palisade	970-434-3388
Jackson Lake	Orchard	970-645-2551
Lake Pueblo	Pueblo	719-561-9320
Lathrop	Walsenburg	719-738-2376
Lory	Belivue	970-493-1623
Mancos	Mancos	970-883-2208
Mueller	Divide	719-687-2366
Navajo	Arboles	970-883-2208
North Sterling	Sterling	970-522-3657
Paonia	Crawford	970-921-5721
Pearl Lake	Clark	970-879-3922
Ridgway	Montrose	970-626-5822
Rifle Falls	Rifle	970-625-1607
Rifle Gap	Rifle	970-625-1607
Roxborough (no pets)	Littleton	303-973-3959
San Luis	Mosca	719-378-2020
Spinney Mountain	Lake George	719-748-3401
Stagecoach	Oak Creek	970-736-2436
Steamboat Lake	Clark	970-879-3922
Sweitzer Lake	Delta	970-874-4258
Sylvan Lake	Rifle	970-625-1607
Trinidad Lake	Trinidad	719-846-6951
Vega	Collbran	970-487-3407

ADDITIONAL ACTIVITIES AND RESOURCES

Boulder Mountaineer Climbing School, 303-442-8355
Boulder Rock School (Boulder Rock Club), 303-447-2804

American Camping Association (Kid's summer camp), 303-778-8774
Bureau of Land Management, 303-239-3600
Colorado Association of Campgrounds, Cabins & Lodges, 303-499-9343
Colorado Geological Survey, 303-866-2611
National Park Service, 1-800-365-2267
The Colorado Trail (465-mile biking & hiking trail), 303-526-0809
US Forest Service, 303-275-5350 or 1-800-280-2267

WINTER SPORTS

Cross-country Skiing; Dog Sledding; Downhill Skiing; Ice Climbing; Ice Skating; Snowboarding; Snowmobiling; Snowshoeing; Sleigh Rides

> *Recommended Reading:* Colorado Publishers produce excellent books on these subjects, please see these listings in Appendix A: Westcliffe Publishers, Fulcrum Publishing

Colorado is world-famous for its winter sports. Many summer sports have their counterparts in winter (hiking/snowshoeing, rock climbing/ice climbing, in-line skating/ice skating). This allows you, with the proper change of clothing, to enjoy your favorite type of activity year-round.

Cross-country Skiing: It's not unusual to see the city parks full of Cross-country skiers after the first good snowfall of the season. Many are just warming up for serious treks into the backcountry. Cross-country skiing is becoming increasingly popular with many novices heading straight for the woods. This can be very dangerous. Every year skiers die in avalanches usually caused by their own activity and perfect avalanche conditions. Don't get in over your head (literally). Don't let your enthusiasm override your experience.

Colorado Cross-country Ski Association, 970-887-2152
Colorado Avalanche Information Centers: Aspen, 970-920-1664; Colorado Springs, 719-520-0020; Denver, 303-236-9435; Durango, 970-247-8187; Ft. Collins, 970-482-0457; Summit County, 970-668-0600; Vail, 970-827-5687

Downhill Ski Areas and Resorts: You won't have any problem finding complete information about the 24 ski areas in Colorado. Every fall dozens of magazines and directories become available for the new ski season. One of the best sources is Colorado Ski Country USA, 303-837-0793. Many resorts offer special rates, ski schools, and multi-day passes. It can get as confusing as buying discount airline seats so please check with each resort for details. The prices vary at each area.

Ski Area	Reservations	Snow Report
Arapahoe Basin	888-ARAPAHOE	970-468-0718
Aspen Buttermilk	800-262-7736	888-277-3676

156

Aspen Highlands	800-262-7736	888-277-3676
Aspen Mountain	800-262-7736	888-277-3676
Aspen Snowmass	800-598-2004	800-277-3676
Beaver Creek	888-284-0928	888-284-0928
Breckenridge	800-221-1091	970-453-6118
Copper Mountain	970-968-6227	970-968-2100
Crested Butte	800-544-8448	970-349-2323
Eldora	888-2-ELDORA	888-2-ELDORA
Keystone	800-258-9553	800-248-0732
Loveland	800-225-LOVE	303-571-5554
Monarch	888-996-7669	800-228-7943
Powderhorn	800-241-6997	970-268-5700
Purgatory	800-525-0892	970-247-9000
Silvercreek	800-754-7458	800-754-7458
Ski Cooper	800-933-3901	719-486-2277
Steamboat Springs	800-922-2722	970-879-7300
Sunlight	800-221-7098	800-445-7931
Telluride	800-525-3455	970-728-7425
Vail	888-284-1461	888-284-1461
Winter Park	800-977-2754	303-572-SNOW

ADDITIONAL ACTIVITIES AND RESOURCES

Colorado Snowmobile Association, 800-235-4480
Mountain Sports, 303-443-6770
National Weather Service, 303-398-3964
Road Conditions (within 2 hours of Denver), 303-639-1111
Road Conditions (state-wide), 303-639-1234

WATER SPORTS

Boating; Kayaking; River Rafting; Sailing; Scuba Diving; Swimming; Water Skiing; Windsurfing

Recommended Reading: Colorado Publishers produce excellent books on these subjects, please see these listings in Appendix A: Outdoor Books & Maps

My last abode before I left Florida was a classic 38' wooden yacht. While driving to Colorado I thought I would never see another boat, windsurfer, or Jet Ski again. I was very wrong. Colorado has over 150 major lakes and reservoirs that provide the water enthusiast with ample opportunities. When you add some of the best rafting rivers in the country, no one should be left unsatisfied. However, before you rush out to hookup the boat trailer or buy a surplus 2-person survival raft to hit the rapids, be advised that since most boating areas are "controlled" lakes and reservoirs they are subject to many rules, regulations and restrictions. Unless you are a very experienced kayaker or rafter, don't hit the rapids on your own. This can be hazardous to your health. There are numerous outfitters who can provide a fine white-water experience.

Believe it or not, scuba diving is actually quite a popular sport in Colorado. There are many lakes and reservoirs in the state that provide interesting dive experiences. You must be certified to dive but there are several metro area centers that provide the training.

BICYCLING

Mountain Biking; Bicycle Touring; Bicycle Races

Recommended Reading: Colorado Publishers produce excellent books on these subjects, please see these listings in Appendix A: Outdoor Books & Maps, Pruett Publishing

It seems there are as many bicycles in Colorado as there are automobiles. Many two-car garages have the better car in one side and 3-6 bicycles in the other. There are literally thousands of miles of designated bike paths in the state. If you were allowed to camp along the way (which you're not), you could spend an entire week touring the greater Denver metro area without ever leaving the bike paths. Home to some of the most beautiful scenery in the country, Colorado also hosts several of the most grueling cycling events in the world.

Probably the best known annual bicycle tour is the week-long *"Ride the Rockies"* sponsored by the Denver Post. This fully supported ride (the sponsors provide campsites and transport all gear) is very strenuous and many participants (limited to 2,000) spend most of the year training for this one ride. For more information call the Denver Post at 303-820-1338.

The downside to this sport's growing popularity is the inevitable conflict between cyclists and automobiles or hikers vying for the same limited spaces. Many of the state's best hiking trails have recently become two-foot-deep ruts due to overuse by mountain bikes. Collisions and other altercations are becoming almost commonplace. Please follow the "Golden Rule," use common sense, and respect the environment while cycling.

SKY-HIGH ADVENTURE

Ballooning; Flying; Glider Rides; Hang Gliding; Para Gliding; Skydiving

Recommended Reading: Colorado Publishers produce excellent books on these subjects, please see these listings in Appendix A: Fulcrum Publishing

If at times you find yourself in awe at Colorado's natural beauty, you ought to see it from the air (and not from 30,000 feet in route to DIA).

A Balloon Affair   Denver   303-691-3322

A Balloon Safari Company	Denver	303-289-5455
Aero Sports Ballonists	Steamboat Springs	970-879-7433
Golden Wings Hang Gliding	Golden	303-278-7181
Grand Junction Balloon	Grand Junction	970-243-8553
Looney Balloons Inc	Littleton	303-979-9476
Parasoft Inc Paragliding School	Boulder	303-494-2820
Sky Fighters, Inc	Denver	303-790-7375
The Cloud Base (gliding)	Boulder	303-530-2208

WEEKEND GETAWAYS

Bed And Breakfast Accommodations; Cabins, Cottages & Lodges; Scenic Drives; RV Parks; Dude and Guest Ranches

> *Recommended Reading:* Colorado Publishers produce excellent books on these subjects, please see these listings in Appendix A: Fulcrum Publishing, Roberts Rhinehart Publishers, Rocky Mountain Vacation Publishing

In Colorado, almost every portion of the state offers something to do or see that is worth the drive. However, getting up at 4 a.m., driving 2-4 hours to do something and then driving back the same day is not my idea of fun. Neither is sleeping on the hard ground without running water. Fortunately, there are options. In fact, one of the most popular forms of entertainment in Colorado is the weekend getaway. The best book for planning a getaway is *The Colorado Guide* by Fulcrum Publishing. This book lists almost every town and city in Colorado and describes activities, lodging and dining. The other publishers listed above also produce great books for different aspects of weekend getaways.

Bed & Breakfast Accommodations: There are over 350 Bed & Breakfast establishments in Colorado spread out among 119 towns, cities, and villages.

Cabins, Cottages, or Lodges: If a cabin, cottage, or lodge is more your style you can choose from over 230.

RV Parks & Campgrounds: Colorado has 400% more RV Parks and campgrounds in the mountains than any other state in the country.

Dude & Guest Ranches: They say reservations at dude and guest ranches sharply increased with the release of the movie *City Slickers.* If true, that was good news for the 40 or so operating in Colorado.

ADDITIONAL RESOURCES

Association of Historic Hotels of the Rocky Mountain West, 303-546-9040
Bed & Breakfast Innkeepers of Colorado Association, 800-832-6657
Bed & Breakfast Rocky Mountains, 303-860-8145
Colorado Association of Campgrounds, Cabins, and Lodges, 303-499-9343
Colorado Dude & Guest Ranch Association, 970-887-3128 / 970-724-3653
Colorado Hotel and Lodging Association, 303-297-8335

159

Colorado Reservation Service, 800-777-6880
Distinctive Inns of Colorado, 800-777-6880

TOURS

Mine Tours; Winery Tours; Archaeological Tours; Historical Tours; Four-Wheel-Drive Tours

> *Recommended Reading:* Colorado Publishers produce excellent books on these subjects, please see these listings in Appendix A: Johnson Books, Fulcrum Publishing , Preutt Publishing

The word "tour" usually conjures up visions of being herded around with a bunch of strangers on a pre-planned, packaged, and boring walk or drive through an area that you can look at but not touch. This kind of tour is available in Colorado but that is not what this section is about. Since Colorado has such a rich history (both pre- and modern), sites with historical value or interest literally cover the state. If your interest lies in dinosaur fossils, Indian petroglyphs, or still active gold mines, you're in luck.

If on the other hand, you are a bit of a wine lover, the nine or so Colorado wineries always welcome guests for tastings. There is even an annual bicycle tour that can be quite grueling (it's only 30 miles on flat terrain, but it stops at every winery and vineyard along the way).

Ever wonder what the backcountry of Colorado is really like? Many mountain locations offer four-wheel-drive tours that get you back to where even hikers or horses fear to tread.

Colorado Mining Districts: Old mining districts are great places for prospecting, gold panning, ghost towns, and mine tours. The following cities were once active gold and/or silver mining areas: Alma; Aspen; Bonanza; Breckenridge; Boulder County; Central City; Climax; Creede; Crested Butte; Cripple Creek; Empire-Georgetown-Silver Plume; Fairplay; Garfield; Gilman; Idaho Springs; Lake City; La Plata; Leadville; Montezuma; Ouray; Rico; Silver Cliff; Silverthorn; St. Elmo; Summitville; Telluride; Tincup-Pitkin.

WARNING: There are over 23,000 open mine shafts and tunnels in Colorado. Most are unmarked, nearly invisible until it's too late, and some are several hundred feet deep. Use extreme caution while in mining backcountry.

Colorado Wineries and Vineyards: (call for hours and directions)

Carlson Vineyards	Palisade, CO	970-464-5554
Colorado Cellars	Palisade, CO	970-464-7921
Grand River Vineyards	Palisade, CO	970-464-5867
Minturn Cellars	Minturn, CO	970-827-4065
Pikes Peak Vineyards	Colorado Springs, CO	719-576-0075

| Plum Creek Cellars | Palisade, CO | 970-464-7586 |
| Vail Valley Vintners, Ltd | Palisade, CO | 970-464-0559 |

PROFESSIONAL SPORTS

> *Recommended Reading:* Colorado Publishers produce excellent books on these subjects, please see these listings in Appendix A: Westcliffe Publishing, Roberts Rinehart Publishers

I think it must be a state law to be a sports fanatic if you live here. At least in Denver it seems that Professional Sports is the unofficial religion. Key players instantly qualify for sainthood and the best are elevated to demi-god status. When a home team plays well, sports news takes precedent over any national or international event. The good side is, when a team is playing at home it's a perfect time to go shopping or anything else non-sports related. That being said, Denver is one of only ten cities in the U.S. with four professional sports teams. Over 4.5 million fans attended home games during the 1994 baseball, basketball, and football seasons. The Rockies play at the new Coors Field which seats 50,000. The Broncos play at Mile High stadium which seats 75,000 and both the Nuggets and Avalanche use McNichols Sports Arena with 19,000 seats. Plans to build the Pepsi Center have recently been approved. This arena will be located in downtown Denver and accommodate even more sports fans.

Baseball: The Colorado Rockies, Coors Field, 303-762-5437
Basketball: The Denver Nuggets, McNichols Sports Arena, 303-893-3865
Football: The Denver Broncos, Mile-High Stadium, 303-433-7466
Hockey: The Colorado Avalanche, McNichols Sports Arena, 303-893-6700

DOWNTOWN DENVER

Elitch Gardens; Brew-Pubs; Other Activities

When I first arrived in Denver about 10 years ago, the state was in an economic bust, the downtown business district had a high vacancy rate and LoDo (lower downtown) was a collection of abandoned and boarded-up warehouses and was not a safe place after dark. How times change.

Today, 7,000 companies employ over 100,000 people downtown. Many commute to work via mass transportation such as RTD's new light-rail service that transports an average of 14,000 riders a day with 8 stops in the downtown area. RTD also operates 20 daily bus routes from downtown to Denver International Airport. With so many visitor attractions, downtown Denver offers in excess of 4,100 hotel rooms. In 1990, Denver completed its new Colorado Convention Center that has almost 300,000 square feet of exhibit space and hosts large conventions and meetings throughout the year.

161

Once nearly forsaken by full-time residents, downtown now boasts new loft projects that are commanding some of the highest prices in the state. Today the area has roughly 9,000 residents who are literally surrounded by many of the state's largest-drawing attractions and a vibrant nightlife.

The most popular area is LoDo. Literally transformed from skid row to the hottest spot in the state in a matter of a few years, LoDo offers a dazzling array of activities and attractions. LoDo is home to 40 some art galleries and most of Denver's 20 brewpubs that offer a selection of fine, hand-crafted brews and full menus. But if you don't care to dine at a brewpub, over 80 new restaurants have opened in downtown with 30 or so in LoDo. In addition, with the recent opening of Coors Field, sports bars are popping up by the dozens. Any of the "Visitor's Guides" available everywhere contain complete information on what to see and do in LoDo.

Elitch Gardens, the first amusement park in the country to relocate to a downtown area, is now located in the Platte River Valley in close proximity to Coors Field. Open only during the summer, Elitch's has 21 rides including a huge wooden roller coaster which consumed 500,000 board feet of lumber, 14 tons of nails, 32 tons of nuts, washers, and bolts, and 3,450 gallons of paint (just for the first coat). With 6 entertainment stages, 6 restaurants and 84,000 feet of gardens, you can plan on spending an entire day there. For more information call 303-595-4386 or 800-ELITCHS.

LEISURE, FUN & THE UNUSUAL

Concerts; Festivals; Limited-Stakes Gambling; Hot Springs; Narrow-gauge & Scenic Train Rides, Golf, Tennis

Recommended Reading: Colorado Publishers produce excellent books on these subjects, please see these listings in Appendix A: Pokerbook Press, Fulcrum Publishing , Westcliffe Publishers

Concerts and Festivals: I can't even attempt to list all the festivals and concerts that take place in this state every year. They literally number in the hundreds. In addition to the hundreds of annual events, there are probably an equal number of one-time, unique gatherings occurring across the state at any given time. Many annual events, such as the Renaissance Festival in Larkspur or the People's Fair in downtown Denver draw hundreds of thousands. On the other hand, during the summer, it's not uncommon to see a few hundred people sprawled out in a small city park listening to free concerts by a variety of artists. But don't worry about missing anything. There is always a special section in most newspapers highlighting upcoming events for every season.

Limited-Stakes Gambling: In 1991, several historic mining towns decided their economic salvation could be found in gambling. They went through the

162

legal necessities and hence, Black Hawk, Central City, and Cripple Creek have become wall-to-wall casinos. Colorado casinos are limited to slots, blackjack, and several varieties of poker with the maximum bet being $5. However, most allow you to play several hands of blackjack at once and there is currently an effort underway to raise the limit to $25. Driving and parking can be a hassle (especially if you plan to have a cocktail or two), so many casinos and private companies offer shuttle service from many areas including several ski resorts. For more information contact the Black Hawk Gaming Owners Association, 303-420-8583; the Central City Public Information Office, 303-582-1889; or the Cripple Creek Chamber of Commerce, 800-526-8777.

Hot Springs: Long before the advent of hot tubs, the Ute Indians discovered the almost magical powers of the huge hot springs and vapor caves of Glenwood Springs. Today the enormous hot-spring-fed pools are still the major attraction in Glenwood (800-221-0098) but certainly not the only one. Almost all the other activities mentioned thus far in this chapter are available in the area. Other towns with natural hot springs include Alamosa, Buena Vista, Durango, Gunnison, Hot Sulphur Springs, Idaho Springs, Nathrop, Ouray, Pagosa Springs, Ridgway, Salida, and Steamboat Springs. Each town's Chamber of Commerce or Visitor's Center will have additional information.

Narrow Gauge & Scenic Train Rides: The original narrow-gauge railways were built to supply the mines and export their products. Today many of these railways and trains have been restored and offer some of the most spectacular scenery in Colorado. Most run during summer months only so call before making plans:
Buckskin Joe Park and Railway, Canon City, CO., 719-275-5485
Cripple Creek/Victor Narrow Gauge Railroad, 719-689-2640
Cumbres & Toltec Scenic Railroad, Antonito, CO., 719-376-5483
Durango-Silverton Narrow Gauge Railroad, 970-247-2733
Georgetown Loop Railroad, Metro: 670-1686, or 303-569-2403
Manitou and Pikes Peak Cog Railroad, 719-685-5401

Golf & Tennis: Colorado Golf Association, 303-779-4653; Colorado Golf Resort Association, 303-770-0100; Colorado Golf Country USA, 303-688-8262; Colorado Tennis Association, 303-695-4116

THE ARTS & CULTURE
Theater; Opera; Dance; Museums/Planetariums/Zoos

The capital of Florida is Tallahassee, which is not much more than a small cow-town that happens to house the state government. On the other hand, Denver, the capital of Colorado, is also the state's largest city with most of the better locations for the arts & culture. The best are highlighted below.

The Denver Performing Arts Complex: Located in downtown Denver, the "Plex" is the largest performing arts center under one roof in the world. It contains 9 theaters with a total of 9,212 seats. This complex hosts over 1,200 performances a year including many Broadway productions. 303-893-3272.

Denver Art Museum: Newly renovated in 1993, the DAM houses the largest Native American collection in the world. 303-640-2793.

Denver Botanical Gardens: Located in Denver's Capital Hill neighborhood, the DBG is famous for its award-winning Tropical Conservatory with an extensive collection of orchids, numerous water gardens, the Rock Alpine Garden, and a Japanese Garden complete with teahouse. 303-331-4000.

Denver Zoo: Birthplace of the world-famous polar bears "Klondike and Snow," the zoo is also well known for its large, naturalistic habitats including the new Tropical Discovery. This exhibit is a complete indoor rain forest with an amazing diversity of tropical plants and animals. 303-331-4110

Denver Museum of Natural History/ Gates Planetarium/ IMAX Theater: All located in City Park under one roof, this complex has been known to draw immense crowds during the summer months or during the premieres of special exhibits. The Museum of Natural History is the fifth largest in the country and can literally take all day to walk through. Gates Planetarium offers regular laser-light concerts and special events while the IMAX Theater, with its 4 story high screen, is an experience not to be missed. 303-370-6300.

For more information about arts and culture around the state, please call:

Colorado Council on the Arts, 303-894-2617

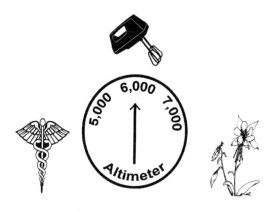

CHAPTER TEN
EIGHT MILES HIGH

HIGH-ALTITUDE LIVING
Health Precautions
Cooking
Gardening

The information in this chapter was compiled from various sources including, but not limited to, government reports and publications (Federal, State, and Local); materials provided by business and civic organizations; and books produced by independent Colorado publishers including:

Crème de Colorado Cookbook, C & C Publications
Colorado Cache Cookbook, C & C Publications
Cooking with Colorado's Greatest Chefs, Westcliffe Publishers, Inc.
The Xeriscape Flower Gardener, Johnson Books

For a complete description of the above books and related titles, please see the Publisher's listing in Appendix A.

Colorado may be many things, but sea level is not one of them. Colorado's highest point is Mt. Elbert at 14,433 feet. The lowest is in the valley created by the Arkansas River at 3,350 feet, with 6,800 feet being the average elevation for the state.

High-altitude living can present unique challenges for the inexperienced lowlander. The air is literally thinner, the atmospheric pressure lower, the sun is a mile or two closer, and the seasonal transitions can be unpredictable. The uninitiated can experience medical maladies, culinary catastrophes, and botanical botcheries. All these, however, can be avoided with a little understanding of how the world works at nosebleed altitudes.

HEALTH PRECAUTIONS

Newcomers to Colorado may experience a variety of medical problems ranging from shortness of breath or a bloody nose to full-blown altitude sickness. To better understand the causes behind these symptoms we need to start with a little basic physics.

Our atmosphere, containing 21% oxygen by volume, has a normal atmospheric pressure of 760 torrs (14.7 pounds per square inch) at sea level. The barometric pressure decreases with an increase in altitude (12.28 lb/sq in. at 5,000 feet; 10.2 lb/sq in. at 10,000). The barometric pressure up to altitudes of approximately 15,000 feet can sustain human life. Keeping in mind the average altitude in Colorado is 6,600 feet, consider that the FAA regulations require airliner cabins to be pressurized to the equivalent of 6,000 feet and that military and private pilots are required to use pressurized oxygen while flying at or above 10,000 feet. Many of Colorado's mountain towns approach this limit.

The human body uses oxygen to cleanse toxins and although muscles can function temporarily without oxygen, a build-up of toxins quickly limits metabolic functions. Oxygen deficiency most directly affects brain and eye tissues, and a decrease in barometric pressure can cause minute blood vessels to swell or rupture. Outlined below are the most common aliments experienced by newcomers and tips on avoidance.

ALTITUDE SICKNESS AND RELATED SYMPTOMS

NOSE-BLEEDS

I was born and raised on the gulf-coast of Florida. Having spent my entire life at sea level, I was perplexed by having unexplained none-bleeds every time I visited my sister in Denver prior to actually moving here. Within hours of leaving the airport, I would begin the ritual of creating crimson Rorschach inkblots on an endless procession of tissues, paper-towels and finally, my newly purchased handkerchiefs. After consulting several experts (bartenders, cab drivers and the like), I determined the nose-bleeds were caused by both a decrease in atmospheric pressure, causing the nasal blood-vessels to swell, and the remarkably low humidity levels of high-altitude. There is not much you can do to prevent this occurrence, although, in most cases the symptoms last only 72 hours or so. However, as we are constantly reminded by the over-the-counter drug companies, "If symptoms persist for more than seven days, consult a physician."

SHORTNESS OF BREATH

During physical exertion at high-altitudes, even the most physically fit athletes experience a degree of breathlessness until acclimatization has occurred. Because the air is thinner here, it contains less oxygen by volume than at sea level. Therefore, even heavy breathing can barely compensate for the lack of oxygen until your body has adjusted. Many professional sports teams arrive in Denver several days before a big game just to allow the players time to acclimatize. Likewise, most seasoned skiers spend a couple of days at mid-altitudes before hitting the 12,000-foot slopes. The best advice is to avoid heavy exertion until you have had time to adjust to new heights.

EYE IRRITATION

Many people experience varying degrees of eye irritation after arriving in Colorado. This is caused by the same factors as nosebleeds. As mentioned above, brain and eye tissue are most quickly effected by a lack of oxygen and the low humidity tends to dry out the sensitive tissues of the eyes. Also, if you happen to be in the Denver Metro area, our infamous "brown cloud" of toxins can aggravate this irritation. The quickest relief comes from lubricating eyedrops.

ALTITUDE SICKNESS

I have met visitors to Colorado who claim to experience altitude sickness as soon as they climb a flight of stairs in Denver (5,280 feet). I also know a few mountain climbers and hikers who can't wait to reach a 14,000-foot peak so they can have a cigarette, seemingly with no ill effects. I'm not sure why some display symptoms in the foothills and others can climb K2 in the Himalayas without oxygen. The one thing I do know is that altitude sickness is most unpleasant and should be taken very seriously.

The condition itself results from a state of acute oxygen deficiency (hypoxia) which can most definitely occur at altitudes above 12,000 - 13,000 feet. Symptoms of hypoxia include mild intoxication and stimulation of the nervous system, followed by progressive loss of attention and judgment. If left untreated, unconsciousness will occur and a prolonged lack of sufficient oxygen may cause permanent brain damage.

For newcomers, a mild case of altitude sickness can be combined with the aforementioned conditions to produce light-headedness, nausea, headache, excessive yawning and overall "I wish I were dead" symptoms. It should be noted the consumption of alcohol at high-altitudes may increase the effects or likelihood of the above. Take it easy the first couple of nights at the ski-lodge and if you think you are experiencing altitude sickness, slow down, descend to lower altitudes and don't be shy about asking for help.

SUNBURN

At higher altitudes, concern also needs to be given to nuclear radiation dangers (sunburn). The earth's atmosphere acts as a filter for the sun's harmful ultra-violet rays. At higher altitudes, the air is actually thinner than at sea level and thus can not screen-out the same amount of radiation. In fact, at 6,000 feet UV rays are approximately 50-60% stronger than at sea level. Simply put, sunburn can occur more quickly and severely at altitude, especially on snow-covered terrain where the sunlight is reflected. Use sunblock during outdoor activities!

HIGH-ALTITUDE COOKING

Without exception, every time my father visits Colorado, whether he is in my kitchen or my sister's kitchen, we can count on the failure of his most prized recipes. Immediately following, we wait for the blame to fall on our "damn ovens" or "!#&*? stoves." Having lived in Florida his entire life and having perfected his recipes through thousands of experiments, my dad refuses to accept the fact that further adjustments are necessary at high-altitude. I must admit it took me six years of living here to figure out how long to properly boil an egg. Besides, my dad can scream at my oven all he wants as long as I finally get one of his homemade cheesecakes!

In addition to the basic physics covered in the previous section, we discover the source of most culinary catastrophes experienced by visitors and residents alike. Remembering the relationship between altitude and air pressure, add the following facts. As air pressure drops, water boils at lower temperatures. At sea level, water boils at 212°F. Each 500-foot increase in altitude causes a drop of approximately 1°F in the boiling point. At very high altitudes, water boils at a relatively low temperature and since heat, not boiling, cooks food, more time is required for food to reach the desired internal cooking temperature. Additionally, water evaporates much more quickly than at sea level. Below is a quick-reference guide for standard adjustments followed by more detailed directions:

Foods cooked by boiling take more time to reach cooking temperature.

Pressure cookers require an adjustment in pressure within the cooker, or a longer period of processing, since they, too, are affected by altitude.

Sea level temperatures for candies and frostings must be lowered as altitude increases to prevent over-concentration of the sugar mixture from excessive evaporation of the water.

Recipes must be adjusted for flour mixtures that contain considerable amounts of sugar and shortening, and are leavened with carbon dioxide gas from baking powder or soda and acid. When air is used for leavening, as in angel cakes, or steam is used, as in popovers, few adjustments are necessary.

Since deep-frying vaporizes the moisture in foods, and liquids vaporize at lower temperatures in higher altitudes, temperatures used in deep-frying should be reduced in proportion to the rise in altitude.

When **baking**, use the following adjustments: Reduce each teaspoon of **baking powder** by 1/4; decrease each cup of **sugar** by 2-3 tablespoons; increase by 3-4 tablespoons each cup of **liquid**; for **fats**, no adjustments are necessary unless substituting, then 1 cup of shortening equals 3/4 cup of butter or oil; **Oven temperature** should be increased by 25°F. Reduce by 25°F when using glass containers; Slightly increase all **cooking times**; and for best results at higher altitudes, use smaller pans and grease and flour or parchment paper, especially for cakes.

RICE, SOUPS AND VEGETABLES

Rice, soups and vegetables all require approximately 1/4 cup more water for each cup used and 10-15 minutes of additional cooking time. Vegetables such as green cabbage, Irish potatoes, parsnips, rutabagas, squash, sweet potatoes and turnips require 4-11% more time at 5,000 feet; 20-25% more time at 7,200 feet; and 55-66 % more time at 10,000 feet. Cauliflower, onions, beets and mature carrots may require at least twice the cooking time at 5,000 feet as at sea level.

High altitudes make little or no difference in temperatures for **baking** vegetables such as squash, potatoes, and sweet potatoes.

Quick cooking conserves flavor and food value in vegetables. Small vegetables may be cooked whole, but larger ones should be cut up for faster cooking. Add vegetables to rapidly boiling water. Bring temperature back to boiling point rapidly and maintain it at this point throughout the cooking period. Better flavor and color will result from pressure cooking instead of long boiling. Cook only until tender to save both minerals and vitamin C. Because minerals and water-soluble vitamins C and B dissolve, the cooking water should be used.

FROZEN VEGETABLES

Frozen vegetables, commercial or home packed, cook faster than similar fresh products. Usually it is sufficient to add only a minute or two to the time designated for sea level cooking. Dense vegetables, such as cauliflower, will require additional cooking time. Keep your own records as to the time required at your altitude. No hard and fast rules can be applied. Peas, snap

169

beans, and mixed vegetables may be cooked without thawing. Solid pack vegetables, such as greens, should be partially thawed before cooking.

MEAT

Meat cooked by simmering or braising requires additional time at higher altitudes. In general, one-fourth more time may be required at 5,000 feet than at sea level. Use the sea level timetable for meats cooked in the oven, because oven temperatures are not affected by altitude change.

EGGS

In boiling eggs at varying altitudes, you must do your own testing. This means timing the eggs and recording the desired results. Try to use the same covered saucepan for cooking eggs and note whether you get the best results from eggs that are at refrigerator or room temperature. The "three-minute" egg may take up to six minutes or longer, according to altitude and cooking conditions. In Denver, I have found it takes exactly eleven minutes after the water comes to a boil to make perfect hard-boiled eggs. The best thing I recommend is a little egg-shaped plastic gizmo you put in with the eggs. It changes color as the eggs go from raw to hard-boiled and has never failed me at any altitude. However, since my 4 year old destroyed mine and I have not been able to find a replacement.

PRESSURE COOKERS

These conveniences may reduce some of the problems of vegetable cookery at high altitude. The temperature of the boiling water is raised because of the pressure built up within the sealed container. The boiling water and steam will cook foods faster than open kettle boiling.

At most altitudes, the cooking time of vegetables in the pressure cooker is no more than 1-2 minutes over sea level timing.

CANNING

Non-acid fruits and vegetables should be processed in a pressure cooker, with an increase of one pound pressure for each 2,000 feet elevation. It is also desirable to increase processing time—by one minute for each 1,000 feet above sea level, if indicated time is 20 minutes or less, and by two minutes per 1,000 feet when sea level requirement is more than 20 minutes.

High-acid fruits and vegetables may be safely canned in a boiling water bath.

FROSTINGS AND CANDIES

Just as water boils at a temperature below 212° F. at the higher altitudes, all other liquids also boil at lower temperatures. Boiling causes loss of moisture through evaporation. The lower the boiling point, the sooner evaporation begins. At high altitudes, when sugar mixtures are cooked at the temperatures suggested in sea-level recipes, the faster loss of water causes the mixture to become too concentrated. Depending on the type of sugar mixture being prepared, the results may be "sugary" (where sugar recrystallizes out), or "hard."

To adjust sugar recipes for altitude, reduce the finished temperature. If you use a candy thermometer, test first the temperature at which water boils. While there will be minor changes from day to day, due to weather conditions, the range is usually slight. At 5,000 feet altitude, water boils at approximately 202° F., ten degrees less than at sea level. Thus, correct the finished temperature for the candy or frosting by subtracting the 10°. Example: If a sea-level recipe for creamy fudge gives a finished temperature for syrup at 238° F., at 5,000 feet the thermometer reading would be 228° F. Cold water tests are reliable when a thermometer is not available

CAKES

At altitudes above 3,500 feet, increase the oven temperature 25°F over the temperature required at sea level. For example, cakes baked at sea level at 350°F should be baked at 375°F at all altitudes over 3,500 feet. The faster baking "sets" the cell framework within the flour mixture and helps to prevent falling.

In high altitudes, flour may become excessively dry unless it is stored in airtight containers. More liquid than the recipe calls for may be necessary to bring a batter or dough to the correct consistency. Some sea-level cakes are delicate and defy adjustment to varying altitudes. In which case, choose a new favorite from altitude tested recipes. Some other recipes are so well balanced that little if any adjustment may be necessary up to 5,000 feet. This is especially true of some of the commercial cake mixes. Keep a written record of any adjustments you make.

Without fat: Air, incorporated in the beaten eggs, is the leavening agent in cakes without fat. The eggs should be beaten less at high altitudes, so less leavening power is given to the batter. In angel food cakes beat the whites just until they form soft peaks; in sponge cakes beat the egg or eggs (yolks) only until they are slightly thickened.

With fat: The emulsified shortening available on the market today gives good results in altitude baking. Because the emulsifier enables the shortening to tolerate a larger amount of liquid, it is preferable for the "speed-mix" cakes with high sugar ratio.

Flour: All-purpose flour is preferable in most recipes. Sift before measuring and make the following adjustments: 3,500 to 5,000 feet add 1 tablespoon; 5,000 to 6,500 add 2 tablespoons; 6,500 to 8,000 feet add 3 tablespoons; and 8,000 feet and over add 4 tablespoons.

Eggs: An additional egg may be added to prevent the cake from being too dry and too tender.

Leavening: All types of baking powders and baking soda are treated alike in reductions for increased altitudes. When both baking powder and soda are used in a recipe, make the suggested adjustments in both ingredients. Accurate measurement of leavening is of increasing importance-as the altitude increases. The leavening adjustments begin with 2,000 feet elevation. The adjustments are: 2,000 to 3,500 feet decrease by 1/4 to 1/3 teaspoon; 3,500 to 5,000 feet decrease by 1/3 to 1/2 teaspoon; 5,000 to 6,500 feet decrease by 1/2 to 2/3 teaspoon; 6,500 to 8,000 feet decrease by 2/3 to 3/4 teaspoon; and 8,000 feet and over decrease by 3/4 teaspoon.

COMMERCIAL CAKE MIXES: Buy only mixes that give directions for adjusting to altitudes, and follow directions given. In most instances, this adjustment comes in the addition of a measured amount of flour to the batter, and in a higher oven temperature. If the resulting cake seems excessively tender, an extra egg added to the batter will strengthen the cell structure and make the cake more easily handled. Bake in pans of the size recommended on the package.

Be sure to store commercial and homemade mixes in airtight containers to avoid excessive loss of moisture.

COOKIES: No adjustments are usually needed unless cookies are rich, full of chocolate, nuts, Snickers ® bars or the like. In this case, reduce the sugar and the baking powder as for a baked good. Baking a sample cookie may prevent ruining an entire batch.

DOUGHNUTS: The sea-level recipe is usually too rich for use at higher elevations. The dough will absorb too much fat and crack during the frying. As in the case of some cakes, it is suggested that, instead of trying to adapt an old favorite recipe to the altitude, you adopt a new favorite that has been developed and tested to conditions.

YEAST BREADS

In short, use less flour per cup of liquid when mixing. Yeast breads rise faster at higher altitude and first rise should not be quite double in size. Final rise should be about 20-30 minutes. Increase oven temperature by 25° and bake for 10-15 less time.

Good basic recipes for yeast breads can be relied on at different altitudes. The fermentation of sugar in the bread is faster and bread may overproof unless it is watched. The general preference seems to be to reduce the proofing time rather than the amount of yeast. One adjustment that applies to all leavened foods is to bake the product "faster" at higher temperatures. At altitudes over 3,500 feet increase the baking temperature 25° over the sea level temperature.

BISCUITS

Any standard recipe can be relied on to give good results at varying altitudes. An additional tablespoon of milk to each cup of flour improves the quality of the product.

MUFFINS

Slightly less sugar can be used than in a standard sea-level recipe. Try reducing sugar by one teaspoon if finished product does not meet your standards.

QUICK BREADS

Where the amount of sugar is low, little adjustment is needed for increased altitude. Slightly more liquid may be desirable if breads seem to dry excessively in baking. Decrease the temperature in proportion to the rise in altitude. It is difficult to give the definite number of degrees because of the variety of foods fried, but a general recommendation is to decrease the temperature two to three degrees for each 1,000 feet elevation. For example, a recipe for doughnuts gives a temperature of 370° F. When frying at 5,000 feet elevation, use a temperature in the range of 350° F. -360° F.

The cookbooks mentioned at the beginning of this chapter are highly recommended. Not only do they contain recipes that are the cream of the crop, all recipes have also been adjusted for the average altitude in Colorado. See Appendix A for complete descriptions and information.

HIGH-ALTITUDE GARDENING

Colorado offers unique challenges and conditions for any type of horticulture (gardening, landscaping, and farming). This is especially true for newcomers to the state who may be from lower altitudes with more predictable weather patterns and seasonal transitions. When first arriving here, many folks jump right into gardening and landscaping without considering the subtle, yet major differences in Colorado's growing conditions. There was a story on the news about the onslaught of irate customers with whom greenhouses and nurseries were dealing. It seems the vast majority of these customers were newcomers who purchased and then planted their gardens in late March or April. And why not? We were experiencing warm days and mild evenings with plenty of rain to boot. Besides, it was officially Spring and they had always planted this time of year. What they didn't expect was a couple of hard freezes in May. These folks were showing up with trunks full of dead plants demanding refunds.

Due to Colorado's altitude, low humidity, intense sunlight, soil conditions and totally unpredictable weather, one would be well advised to do a little research before breaking out the shovels and potting soil. This section, as with most in this book, is intended to provide only the basics, to act as a guide. The end of this chapter contains a list of additional resources where complete information can be obtained. Let's look at some basics for the Rocky Mountain region:

Humidity: In Florida, like many coastal areas, it is not uncommon to have both temperature and humidity in the 90's. There is a vast difference between that and temperatures in the 90's with humidity in the teens. Combined with intense sunlight and prolonged heat waves, the evaporation rate of water is tremendous. It is not uncommon for evaporation rates in parts of Colorado to exceed 50 inches of water per year while receiving only 10-20 inches from precipitation. The end result is increased need for supplemental irrigation. In Denver, the average noon humidity during January is 43% while in July it averages 36%.

Sunlight: Thr effects of sunlight are intensified at higher altitudes. This holds true everywhere. However, because of Colorado's latitude and geography, we also get about 3 additional hours of sunlight per day compared to cloudier regions and on the average have 300 days of sunshine per year. All this combined means many plants that require full sun elsewhere may grow very well in partial shade here.

Growing Seasons: Sheridan, WY. has a frost-free growing season of 123 days (May 21 - Oct 21); Salt Lake City, UT.'s is 202 days (Apr 12 - Nov 1); Denver's is 159 days (May 6 - Oct 12). There are parts of the country where by mid-May you would be almost ready to harvest your first crop of vegetables. If you came from one of those areas it is hard to adjust to having to wait until May 6th or later to even safely plant. Please take note: 159 days is the season for Denver, not Colorado! Because of the great diversity in altitudes and weather conditions, parts of Colorado have longer seasons and many places have much shorter ones. Check with your local experts before planting. If you simply can't wait until mid-May I highly recommend using "walls-of-water." This product is a tee-pee shaped, double-walled, multi-chambered vinyl contraption that you fill with water and place around new plantings. The water traps the heat of sunlight during the day and slowly releases it at night when it gets cold. The manufacturer claims it can jump-start your growing season by six weeks and I have personally had good luck with them. Check with a local garden shop for availability.

Temperature Extremes: Having grown-up in Florida, I was accustomed to very mild temperature fluctuations. The temperature and humidity usually ranged from unbearably hot and sticky to almost unbearably hot and sticky. Allowing for the slight change in seasons, the vegetation in Florida knew what to expect. Not so in Colorado! Temperature fluctuations can be drastic and sudden, regardless of season. During Spring, we can have stretches of hot weather lasting days or weeks immediately followed by a week of snow and hard freezes. In Winter, the temperature can suddenly rise (in a matter of

174

minutes) from below freezing to almost tee-shirt weather due to "Chinook" winds, only to drop again by day's end. This kind of fluctuation is very stressful on many types of plants (not to mention most people). On average, the daily January temperatures in Denver range from 15-42°, while in July they range from 57-88°. These are averages, not examples of the very common extremes experienced.

Micro-Climates: Not only do different weather conditions occur throughout various parts of Colorado, due to everything discussed so far, you can also experience very different growing conditions within the boundaries of your own yard. You can literally have desert-like conditions along a south wall and "Aspen meadow" conditions on the north. The differences between the south and north side of the same house can be equivalent to several thousand feet of mountain elevation change or several thousand miles of latitude change on the plains.

Xeriscape: Xeriscape! Xeriscape! Xeriscape! Simply defined Xeriscape means water-wise gardening. 40-60% percent of clear, cool, drinking water supplied to cities throughout the region is used for landscape irrigation! A Xeriscape approach to landscaping can result in a 50% reduction of needed irrigation. Additional benefits are lower initial cost per square foot and greatly reduced maintenance needs. If done properly, most Xeriscape yards not only save a tremendous amount of water, they also give the yard's owners a lot more time to enjoy other aspects of Colorado's outdoors. *The Xeriscape Flower Gardener,* by Jim Knopf is an excellent resource for learning about all the benefits of this environmentally friendly art.

ADDITIONAL RESOURCES

High-Altitude Recipes

Crème de Colorado Cookbook, C&C Publications
Colorado Cache Cookbook, C&C Publications
Cooking with Colorado's Greatest Chefs, Westcliffe Publishers, Inc.
See Publisher's listing in Appendix A for details

High-Altitude Gardening

The Xeriscape Flower Gardener, A Waterwise Guide for the Rocky Mountain Region, Johnson Books. See Appendix A.
Successful Gardening for Colorado and the *Rocky Mountain Plant Guide,* both available from most nurseries and greenhouses.

Additional information available from:
Colorado Nurserymen's Association, 303-758-6672
Associated Landscape Contractors of Colorado, Inc., 303-757-5611
Colorado Greenhouse Growers, 303-427-8132

Public Xeriscape Demonstration Areas:

City of Arvada Public Works Center, 303-420-0984
Colorado Springs Mesa Treatment Plant, 719-520-0300
Career Enrichment Park, Westminster, CO, 303-428-2600
Denver Water Department, 303-628-6340
Denver Botanical Gardens, 303-331-4000
Douglas County Executive Building, 303-660-7400
Longmont Public Library, 303-651-8360
Oxley Homestead, Golden, CO, 303-526-0284
Fort Collins Xeriscape Demonstration Garden, 970-221-6681

Denver Botanical Gardens: DBG offers numerous classes, instruction, and advice about high-altitude gardening and Xeriscape. In addition, they have a complete library with over a dozen books on Xeriscape and their staff includes botanists, horticulturists, landscapers, and professional gardeners.

WORLDWIDE
MOVING

CHAPTER ELEVEN
SO FAR AWAY

GETTING FROM THERE TO HERE
Moving Tips
Moving With Children
Temporary Housing
Relocation Services

Recommended Sources for Additional Information (See Appendix A):
Moving With Children, Gylantic Publishing Company

I have moved more times than I can remember. What I do remember is swearing to myself (after every move) I would never do it again. I told my wife when we build our dream house and move, we will sell our current home fully furnished with all accessories, and whatever doesn't fit in the cars, will stay.

We've all been there. The endless lists, the sleepless nights (going over the lists), the packing, the loading, the cleaning, the trip, the unloading and unpacking, the utilities, new bank accounts, etc. Unplanned and unprepared, a major move can put the best of us down for the count. Hopefully, this chapter will assist you in making the most of your next move.

MOVING TIPS

Moving across town or across the country can be made easier if you break it down into three phases: The Preparation Phase, The Work Phase, and The Settling-in Phase. Use the tips below to make a checklist for each phase.

THE PREPARATION PHASE

One Month Prior To Moving: Make all reservations and arrangements for truck rentals or moving companies (see moving company tips below). Start acquiring necessary moving supplies such as boxes, tape, labels, etc. If you plan to drive to your new home, plan the travel route. Start a special file to save all moving receipts: many moving costs may be tax deductible. Develop your plan for packing (see Work Phase below). Make sure important records (legal, insurance, and medical) are in a safe and accessible place. Notify the Post Office of your new address.

Two Weeks Prior To Moving: Notify all utility companies of your move and sign up for necessary services at your new location. Completely service your car if it will be used or driven. Start recruiting help for the move (this is the test of true friendship). Confirm all reservations made previously. Confirm payment requirements from any moving companies. Make arrangements to close or transfer all bank accounts.

THE WORK PHASE

Packing: Have all packing supplies in one place (boxes, bubble wrap, marking pens, tape measure, furniture pads, rope, tools and knife, tape and scissors). Label boxes with the contents and the room where they belong in your new home. Number each box and keep a list of the contents. Make sure fragile items are clearly marked. Designate certain boxes or suitcases for personal items you'll need during the move. Keep a medical kit handy.

Cleaning: Cleaning is 90% planning and 10% effort so make a plan! Start with all necessary cleaning supplies so your momentum isn't broken. Do a preliminary job on the bathroom and kitchen, but expect them to be used up until the last time you close the door to your old home. It's easy to be immersed in your work so keep the "Child Safety" rules in mind around cleaning supplies.

THE SETTLING-IN PHASE

Physical: Make sure your new home (especially the bathroom and kitchen) is perfectly clean (you'll never go back and do it right once they are full of stuff). Check-off every numbered box from your list as it comes into the house. The first box in should be your tool kit of unpacking supplies (knife, tape measure, large trash bags, and necessary tools for re-assembly). The second thing in should be a radio or tape player. Get all boxes and used packing out of the house as soon as they are emptied.

Emotional: The following suggestion applies to all phases of moving: without fail, schedule in some time to relax and enjoy yourself (a movie, a bike ride, pizza and wine on the balcony). Allow yourself to grieve the loss of moving (friends, family, favorite places). Look forward to meeting new friends, starting your new job, and finding new favorite places. Accept the fact moving is a major thing. Take it easy, you don't have to adjust to everything at once.

MOVING WITH CHILDREN

If you're a parent you already know children do not think, feel, or react as adults. What may seem like a logical, well-planned, check-listed sequence of events to you may be very traumatic for children. While tending to the million details of a move, it's easy to overlook how it might affect your children. *Moving With Children* is an outstanding book by Gylantic Publishing. It covers every aspect of the moving process in general and offers the following information.

Preparation Phase Stress Factors For Children: The unpredictability of the moving schedule, the presence of strangers in the house, the disruption of familiar family routines and activities, reduced time and attention and possible periods of separation from parents, unaccustomed travel to visit a new neighborhood or community prior to the move and the process of having to break the news and answer questions about the move to friends, classmates, and neighbors.

Work Phase Stress Factors For Children: The disruption of a comfortable family structure, the physical demands of packing and cleaning, the necessity of giving away or leaving behind familiar belongings, physically leaving friends and neighbors, the excitement, disruption and physical labor of moving day and the possible rigors of traveling to a new house.

Settling-In Phase Stress Factors For Children: The possible delay, loss of or damage to possessions during the move, the physical demands of unpacking, storing and decorating, the work of making home comfortable, the re-establishment of familiar family routines and schedules, the absence of a familiar support group, the process of becoming acquainted with a new community and meeting new neighbors.

If ignored or improperly handled the tremendous amount of stress placed on children during a move can result in a wide-range of emotional and physical symptoms. If you are planning a family move and don't have a Ph.D. in child psychology I recommend the book mentioned above.

Moving Company Tips: The Better Business Bureau reports a 38% increase in complaints about moving companies since 1990. Money Magazine offers the following tips on how to protect yourself from scams and incompetence:

Get a binding estimate before the move and make sure the amount is written into the contract. It costs about $3,500 to move the contents of a three-bedroom house to a different state.

Before signing an agreement, inquire about the company with the local BBB and state or local consumer affairs department. The Interstate Commerce Commission allows interstate movers to give you only 60 cents per pound for lost or damaged goods. To cover potential damage, check your existing homeowners or renters policy and buy extra coverage if necessary.

Ask about expected gratuities before hiring and write them into the contract. If your mover demands more money anyway and you're stuck, consider paying but write your protest on the bill as evidence. Specify in the contract that the company will be held responsible for damage to items you packed.

Storage Tips: If you plan to have your possessions in storage for more than a few days, find out how the moving company plans to do this. It is common for companies simply to park the semi-trailer in their lot and leave it until you are ready. In Colorado this can be the wrong thing to do. Due to our intense sunshine, during the summer temperatures inside the trailer can exceed 130 degrees for extended periods. That combined with our low humidity can play havoc with furniture finishes, glue joints, framed art, music collections and the like. During the winter, temperatures inside a trailer can fluctuate 50-80° between day and night. Excessive expanding and contracting can also damage furniture. Find another method of storage if possible or get written guarantees about damage from the companies who will, of course, deny any of the above is true.

TEMPORARY HOUSING/RELOCATION SERVICES

If you find yourself here before your belongings or will have an extended wait while your new home is finished, you will need temporary housing. There are numerous companies in Colorado that specialize in matching people with apartments, condos, or rental homes. Most of their clients are making a permanent move but these companies also work with newcomers who need temporary housing for one month, six months or longer. The best part is, usually there is little or no cost to you because costs are paid by the landlord or management company. If you are not already working through a relocation service, contact one of the companies below:

Relocation Concepts (Individual)   Aurora   303-695-0971
Relocation Resources (Corporate)   Denver   303-297-0500
Colorado Relocations Services   303-971-0971

180

CHAPTER TWELVE
NEW KID IN TOWN

RESOURCES / PHONE LISTS

INDEX OF PHONE LISTS ELSEWHERE IN THIS BOOK

AREA CODES AND PREFIXES

As with many other states, Colorado is rapidly adding new area codes and prefixes. Please consult a US West phone book for current information. All numbers and area codes shown below are current as of October 15, 1997.

FRATERNAL ORGANIZATIONS

Colorado is home many chapters of fraternal organizations. The list below is arranged by organization name first, followed by the city and phone number.

A F & Am Hayden Valley Lodge	Hayden	(970) 276-3433
A F & Am Yampa Lodge	Craig	(970) 824-5882
Ahepa Denver Chapter 145	Denver	(303) 321-5715
Al Kaly Temple	Pueblo	(719) 544-0658
American Legion	Byers	(303) 822-9562
American Legion	Canon City	(719) 275-9919
American Legion	Durango	(970) 247-1590
American Legion	Florence	(719) 784-6125
American Legion	Holyoke	(970) 854-3486
American Legion	Pagosa Springs	(970) 264-4884
Arvada Jaycees	Arvada	(303) 431-5849
Aurora Lodge # 156	Aurora	(303) 366-0402
Beta Theta Pi Fraternity	Golden	(303) 279-3081
Bethany Chapter 148 OES	Nucla	(970) 864-2195
B'nai B'rith Lodge 171	Denver	(303) 393-7358
Boys & Girls Club-Metro Denver	Ward	(303) 443-7394
Brighton K Of C Council	Brighton	(303) 659-0661
Carpenters Union	Denver	(970) 532-3704
Civitan Club Colorado Springs	Colorado Springs	(719) 574-9004
Colorado Masons Benevolent Fnd	Englewood	(303) 290-8544
Colorado Springs Shrine Club	Colorado Springs	(719) 632-3881
Colorado State Grange Schlrshp	Aurora	(303) 752-0406
Delta Chi Fraternity	Greeley	(970) 353-7630
Denver Consistory	Denver	(303) 861-4261
Denver Lodge 5 Af & Am	Denver	(303) 534-0939
Disabled American Veterans	Colorado Springs	(719) 392-7589
Eagle Lodge Inc	Denver	(303) 393-7773
Eagle's Fraternal Order	Denver	(303) 820-2063
Edgewater Lodge Af & Am	Denver	(303) 233-0247
El Jebel Shrine Office	Denver	(303) 455-3470
Elks Lodge	Akron	(970) 345-2294
Elks Lodge	Alamosa	(719) 589-2362
Elks Lodge	Arvada	(303) 424-2278
Elks Lodge	Aspen	(970) 925-3516
Elks Lodge	Aurora	(303) 360-7204
Elks Lodge	Boulder	(303) 442-5003
Elks Lodge	Broomfield	(303) 469-1708

Elks Lodge	Canon City	(719) 275-1880
Elks Lodge	Central City	(303) 582-5181
Elks Lodge	Colorado Springs	(719) 633-5077
Elks Lodge	Cortez	(970) 565-3557
Elks Lodge	Craig	(970) 824-3557
Elks Lodge	Creede	(719) 658-2661
Elks Lodge	Cripple Creek	(719) 689-2625
Elks Lodge	Deer Trail	(303) 769-4480
Elks Lodge	Delta	(970) 874-3624
Elks Lodge	Denver	(303) 455-3557
Elks Lodge	Denver	(303) 238-1307
Elks Lodge	Denver	(303) 296-1006
Elks Lodge	Durango	(970) 247-2296
Elks Lodge	Englewood	(303) 781-0257
Elks Lodge	Evergreen	(303) 674-5591
Elks Lodge	Florence	(719) 784-3892
Elks Lodge	Fort Collins	(970) 493-3777
Elks Lodge	Fort Morgan	(970) 867-6711
Elks Lodge	Glenwood Springs	(970) 945-2286
Elks Lodge	Grand Junction	(970) 243-0675
Elks Lodge	Greeley	(970) 330-5217
Elks Lodge	Gunnison	(970) 641-1527
Elks Lodge	Hotchkiss	(970) 872-3355
Elks Lodge	Idaho Springs	(303) 567-9996
Elks Lodge	La Junta	(719) 384-9161
Elks Lodge	Leadville	(719) 486-0236
Elks Lodge	Littleton	(303) 794-1811
Elks Lodge	Longmont	(303) 776-1055
Elks Lodge	Louisville	(303) 666-8600
Elks Lodge	Monte Vista	(719) 852-2456
Elks Lodge	Montrose	(970) 249-4852
Elks Lodge	Northglenn	(303) 452-1644
Elks Lodge	Ouray	(970) 325-4510
Elks Lodge	Pueblo	(719) 544-5922
Elks Lodge	Rangely	(970) 675-8533
Elks Lodge	Rifle	(970) 625-2195
Elks Lodge	Salida	(719) 539-6976
Elks Lodge	Silverthorne	(970) 468-2561
Elks Lodge	Sterling	(970) 522-0515
Elks Lodge	Telluride	(970) 728-6362
Elks Lodge	Trinidad	(719) 846-2980
Elks Lodge	Victor	(719) 689-2974
Elks Lodge	Walsenburg	(719) 738-1210
Elks Lodge	Westminster	(303) 429-2227
Elks Lodge	Wray	(970) 332-4907
Elks Lodge # 309	Colorado Springs	(719) 633-1727
Elks Lodge 1586	Brighton	(303) 659-2802
Elks Lodge 809	Greeley	(970) 330-3557

Englewood Shrine Club	Englewood	(303) 789-0272
Epsilon Sigma Alpha Intl	Fort Collins	(970) 223-2824
Eureka Lodge Af & Am	Pueblo	(719) 542-9738
Filipino-America Community	Edgewater	(303) 233-6817
Footprinters	Denver	(303) 861-7519
Fraternal Order Of Eagles	Arvada	(303) 433-8035
Fraternal Order Of Eagles	Aspen	(970) 925-9912
Fraternal Order Of Eagles	Aurora	(303) 366-5165
Fraternal Order Of Eagles	Brighton	(303) 659-4973
Fraternal Order Of Eagles	Broomfield	(303) 466-4928
Fraternal Order Of Eagles	Castle Rock	(303) 688-3947
Fraternal Order Of Eagles	Colorado Springs	(719) 632-1934
Fraternal Order Of Eagles	Colorado Springs	(719) 596-2207
Fraternal Order Of Eagles	Commerce City	(303) 288-0861
Fraternal Order Of Eagles	Englewood	(303) 762-9046
Fraternal Order Of Eagles	Englewood	(303) 762-8107
Fraternal Order Of Eagles	Federal Heights	(303) 426-4665
Fraternal Order Of Eagles	Fort Collins	(970) 498-9535
Fraternal Order Of Eagles	Glenwood Springs	(970) 945-5506
Fraternal Order Of Eagles	Grand Junction	(970) 243-6454
Fraternal Order Of Eagles	La Salle	(970) 284-6880
Fraternal Order Of Eagles	Lamar	(719) 336-3780
Fraternal Order Of Eagles	Pueblo	(719) 564-3695
Fraternal Order Of Eagles	Pueblo	(719) 564-5715
Fraternal Order Of Eagles	Walsenburg	(719) 738-1900
Fraternal Order Of Eagles 179	Trinidad	(719) 846-3821
Fraternal Order Of Eagles 3226	Denver	(303) 427-2236
Fraternal Order Of Police	Brighton	(303) 280-1464
Fraternal Order Of Police	Colorado Springs	(719) 591-5591
Fraternal Order Of Police	Denver	(303) 650-1110
Fraternal Order Of Police	Fort Collins	(970) 204-0256
Fraternal Order Of Police	Loveland	(970) 669-3660
Fraternal Order Of Police	Westminster	(303) 280-1464
Friendship Lodge 185 Af & Am	Denver	(303) 934-9730
Garden Home Grange Hall	Denver	(303) 934-1372
George Washington Lodge 161	Englewood	(303) 761-2571
Grand Chapter Of Colorado	Denver	(303) 759-5936
Grand Lodge	Colorado Springs	(719) 471-9587
Grandview Grange	Littleton	(303) 798-7433
Harmony Lodge 61 Af & Am	Denver	(303) 534-9918
Homestead Village	Aurora	(303) 750-9116
Hop Sing Assoc	Denver	(303) 377-2265
Independent Order Of Foresters	Colorado Springs	(719) 531-0304
Independent Order Of Foresters	Lakewood	(303) 988-2242
IOFF	Boulder	(303) 442-5669
IOFF	Grand Junction	(970) 245-9576
IOFF Hall	Cedaredge	(970) 856-7558
IOFF Hall	Delta	(970) 874-4588

184

Jaycee's	Boulder	(303) 443-1030
Knights Of Columbus	Arvada	(303) 423-4603
Knights Of Columbus	Aurora	(303) 366-6314
Knights Of Columbus	Burlington	(719) 346-7600
Knights Of Columbus	Canon City	(719) 275-1412
Knights Of Columbus	Cheyenne Wells	(719) 767-5353
Knights Of Columbus	Colorado Springs	(719) 392-9928
Knights Of Columbus	Colorado Springs	(719) 637-8052
Knights Of Columbus	Commerce City	(303) 287-0945
Knights Of Columbus	Denver	(303) 861-2419
Knights Of Columbus	Denver	(303) 455-6888
Knights Of Columbus	Denver	(303) 288-3272
Knights Of Columbus	Denver	(303) 934-9606
Knights Of Columbus	Englewood	(303) 789-0132
Knights Of Columbus	Federal Heights	(303) 426-9424
Knights Of Columbus	Fort Collins	(970) 484-1881
Knights Of Columbus	Grand Junction	(970) 242-9746
Knights Of Columbus	Greeley	(970) 352-9774
Knights Of Columbus	La Junta	(719) 384-2120
Knights Of Columbus	Lakewood	(303) 238-8740
Knights Of Columbus	Lamar	(719) 336-3591
Knights Of Columbus	Northglenn	(303) 460-8407
Knights Of Columbus	Pueblo	(719) 564-9620
Knights Of Columbus	Sterling	(970) 522-0857
Knights Of Columbus	Trinidad	(719) 846-0450
Knights Of Pythias Inc	Denver	(303) 458-9083
Knights Of Pythias Inc	Denver	(303) 936-9771
Lambda Chi Alpha	Fort Collins	(970) 482-4096
Loyal Order Of Moose	Aurora	(303) 366-2061
Loyal Order Of Moose	Canon City	(719) 275-1790
Loyal Order Of Moose	Colorado Springs	(719) 632-2914
Loyal Order Of Moose	Denver	(303) 936-6869
Loyal Order Of Moose	Evans	(970) 339-5715
Loyal Order Of Moose	Fort Collins	(970) 493-3056
Loyal Order Of Moose	Grand Junction	(970) 242-4754
Loyal Order Of Moose	Longmont	(303) 776-4911
Loyal Order Of Moose	Loveland	(970) 667-2525
Loyal Order Of Moose	Northglenn	(303) 457-3391
Loyal Order Of Moose	Nucla	(970) 864-7610
Loyal Order Of Moose	Pierce	(970) 834-0960
Mac Bean Clan	Lakewood	(303) 233-6002
Masonic Lodge	Akron	(970) 345-6522
Masonic Lodge	Alamosa	(719) 589-2361
Masonic Lodge	Arvada	(303) 424-9941
Masonic Lodge	Boulder	(303) 449-2711
Masonic Lodge	Brighton	(303) 659-3484
Masonic Lodge	Brush	(970) 842-2503
Masonic Lodge	Canon City	(719) 275-3818

185

Masonic Lodge	Castle Rock	(303) 688-4131
Masonic Lodge	Cedaredge	(970) 856-3062
Masonic Lodge	Central City	(303) 582-5525
Masonic Lodge	Colorado Springs	(719) 632-8994
Masonic Lodge	Colorado Springs	(719) 635-1174
Masonic Lodge	Del Norte	(719) 657-3635
Masonic Lodge	Denver	(303) 393-7825
Masonic Lodge	Denver	(303) 778-1039
Masonic Lodge	Denver	(303) 778-9787
Masonic Lodge	Denver	(303) 534-7424
Masonic Lodge	Denver	(303) 377-7645
Masonic Lodge	Durango	(970) 259-5416
Masonic Lodge	Englewood	(303) 789-9805
Masonic Lodge	Estes Park	(970) 586-8097
Masonic Lodge	Fort Collins	(970) 493-0888
Masonic Lodge	Fort Morgan	(970) 867-7534
Masonic Lodge	Georgetown	(303) 569-2811
Masonic Lodge	Glenwood Springs	(970) 945-5013
Masonic Lodge	Golden	(303) 279-9902
Masonic Lodge	Grand Junction	(970) 242-0120
Masonic Lodge	Greeley	(970) 353-1776
Masonic Lodge	Gunnison	(970) 641-1406
Masonic Lodge	Holyoke	(970) 854-3518
Masonic Lodge	Hotchkiss	(970) 872-3384
Masonic Lodge	Idaho Springs	(303) 567-2811
Masonic Lodge	La Junta	(719) 384-2271
Masonic Lodge	Lafayette	(303) 665-6876
Masonic Lodge	Lamar	(719) 336-5331
Masonic Lodge	Littleton	(303) 794-1771
Masonic Lodge	Longmont	(303) 776-3515
Masonic Lodge	Mancos	(970) 533-7721
Masonic Lodge	Manitou Springs	(719) 685-5304
Masonic Lodge	Monte Vista	(719) 852-3913
Masonic Lodge	Montrose	(970) 249-3943
Masonic Lodge	Monument	(719) 488-3785
Masonic Lodge	Pueblo	(719) 544-1056
Masonic Lodge	Rocky Ford	(719) 254-3861
Masonic Lodge	Salida	(719) 539-2708
Masonic Lodge	Springfield	(719) 523-6531
Masonic Lodge	Steamboat Spgs	(970) 879-0062
Masonic Lodge	Sterling	(970) 522-2366
Masonic Lodge	Woodland Park	(719) 687-2732
Masonic Lodge	Wray	(970) 332-4939
Montezuma Lodge	Dolores	(970) 882-7945
NCO Assn	Aurora	(303) 364-3077
NCOA	Colorado Springs	(719) 576-0757
NCOA	Colorado Springs	(719) 596-3088
Odd Fellows 13	Golden	(303) 279-1272

Odd Fellows 145	Arvada	(303) 424-5815
Odd Fellows 25	Edgewater	(303) 233-0372
Odd Fellows 48	Durango	(970) 247-8420
Odd Fellows Grand Lodge	Canon City	(719) 275-1606
Odd Fellows Hall	Canon City	(719) 275-9853
Odd Fellows Hall	Fort Lupton	(303) 857-2970
Odd Fellows Hall	Greeley	(970) 353-0061
Odd Fellows Hall	Sterling	(970) 522-3028
Odd Fellows Hall Ioof	Colorado Springs	(719) 633-4838
Odd Fellows Hall Ioof	Colorado Springs	(719) 633-2002
Odd Fellows Lodge	Longmont	(303) 776-4588
Odd Fellows Lodge	Loveland	(970) 667-4584
Odd Fellows Union Lodge 1	Arvada	(303) 427-0412
Phi Delta Theta Fraternity	Fort Collins	(970) 493-7511
Phi Kappa Tau Fraternity	Fort Collins	(970) 484-8266
Pueblo Shrine Club	Pueblo West	(719) 547-3184
Rebekah Lodge	Craig	(970) 824-4829
Retired Enlisted Assn	Colorado Springs	(719) 596-0927
Rose Hill Grange	Commerce City	(303) 288-9803
Rosicrucian Order Amorc	Edgewater	(303) 985-8602
Schlaraffia Denvera	Denver	(303) 455-1783
Scottish Rite Bodies Aas	Grand Junction	(970) 245-2277
Scottish Rite Temple	Pueblo	(719) 544-5697
Silver State Lodge 95 Af & Am	Pueblo	(719) 545-1412
Sons Of Norway	Denver	(303) 232-1700
Sons Of Norway Fjellheim Lodge	Colorado Springs	(719) 574-3717
South Denver Lodge 93	Denver	(303) 777-9809
Spmdtu	Antonito	(719) 376-5470
Union Lodge 7 Af & Am	Denver	(303) 534-5051
Veterans Of Foreign Wars	Broomfield	(303) 460-9557
Veterans Of Foreign Wars	Colorado Springs	(719) 632-9874
Veterans Of Foreign Wars	Colorado Springs	(719) 632-2776
Veterans Of Foreign Wars	Craig	(970) 824-7145
Veterans Of Foreign Wars	Grand Junction	(970) 242-9940
Veterans Of Foreign Wars	Las Animas	(719) 456-2822
Veterans Of Foreign Wars	Ordway	(719) 267-4735
Veterans Of Foreign Wars	Platteville	(970) 785-9989
Westminster Grange Hall	Westminster	(303) 428-3191
Westminster Lodge 176	Westminster	(303) 429-9895

DAILY / WEEKLY NEWSPAPERS

When my wife and I were looking for property in Colorado we would always pick up a copy of the local paper. This offers the opportunity to get a feel for the area. Many of these companies will be happy to mail you a copy of their most recent publication. While I have tried to be as thorough as possible, there are several publications (bargain classifieds, thrifty shopping guides, etc.) that are not shown here.

Akron News Reporter	Akron	(970) 345-2296
Valley Courier	Alamosa	(719) 589-2553
Allenspark Wind	Allenspark	(303) 747-0232
Arvada Sentinel Newspaper	Arvada	(303) 425-8755
Olde Towner Newspaper	Arvada	(303) 423-5306
Aspen Daily News	Aspen	(970) 925-2220
Aspen Times	Aspen	(970) 925-3414
Korean Post	Aurora	(303) 366-6006
Korean Times	Aurora	(303) 367-5900
Vail Daily Ltd	Avon	(970) 949-0555
Vail Trial	Avon	(970) 949-4004
Vail Valley Times	Avon	(970) 949-4402
Fairplay Flume	Bailey	(303) 838-2108
Park County Republican	Bailey	(303) 838-4423
Park County Republican Flume	Bailey	(719) 836-2820
Mountain Patriot	Basalt	(970) 927-2495
Pine River Times Inc	Bayfield	(970) 884-2331
Berthoud Recorder Newspaper	Berthoud	(970) 532-3715
Boulder County Business Report	Boulder	(303) 440-4952
Boulder County Kids Newspaper	Boulder	(303) 939-8767
Boulder Weekly	Boulder	(303) 494-5511
Daily Camera	Boulder	(303) 442-1202
Rocky Mountain News	Boulder	(303) 442-8729
Summit Comic News	Breckenridge	(970) 547-0025
Brush News Tribune	Brush	(970) 842-5516
Cattle Country News	Brush	(970) 842-5071
Chaffee County Times	Buena Vista	(719) 395-8621
Burlington Record	Burlington	(719) 346-5381
Ranchland News	Calhan	(719) 347-2366
Daily Record & Marketplace	Canon City	(719) 275-7565
Valley Journal Inc	Carbondale	(970) 963-3211
Castle Rock Chronicle	Castle Rock	(303) 660-8034
Douglas County News-Press	Castle Rock	(303) 688-3128
Douglas County Trail	Castle Rock	(303) 660-2360
Mountain Valley News	Cedaredge	(970) 856-7499
Greenhorn Valley News Inc	Colorado City	(719) 676-3304
Cheyenne Edition	Colorado Springs	(719) 578-5112
Colorado Springs Bus Journal	Colorado Springs	(719) 634-5905
Denver Post	Colorado Springs	(719) 578-0994
Falcon Flyer	Colorado Springs	(719) 634-1593
Gazette Telegraph	Colorado Springs	(719) 632-5511
Independent News Weekly	Colorado Springs	(719) 577-4543
Commerce City Beacon	Commerce City	(303) 289-4600
Commerce City Express	Commerce City	(303) 288-7987
Aspen Park News & Candy Co	Conifer	(303) 838-3806

Cortez Sentinel	Cortez	(970) 565-8574
Montezuma Valley Journal	Cortez	(970) 565-8527
Northwest Colorado Daily Press	Craig	(970) 824-7031
Crested Butte Chronicle	Crested Butte	(970) 349-6114
Tri-County Tribune	Deer Trail	(303) 769-4646
Del Norte Prospector	Del Norte	(719) 657-2211
Delta County Independent	Delta	(970) 874-4421
Colorado Real Estate Journal	Denver	(303) 623-1148
Denver Business Journal	Denver	(303) 837-3500
Denver Post	Denver	(303) 820-1010
Denver Weekly News	Denver	(303) 292-5158
Newspapers & Technology	Denver	(303) 575-9595
Northern Miner	Denver	(303) 863-8600
Rocky Mountain News	Denver	(303) 892-5000
Wall Street Journal	Denver	(303) 778-6615
Westword Newspaper	Denver	(303) 296-7744
Woman's Business News	Denver	(303) 756-0780
Dolores Star	Dolores	(970) 882-4486
Dove Creek Press	Dove Creek	(970) 677-2214
Denver Post	Durango	(970) 259-4165
Four Corners Weekly	Durango	(970) 385-6963
Kiowa County Press	Eads	(719) 438-5352
Eagle Valley Enterprise	Eagle	(970) 328-6656
North Weld Herald Newspaper	Eaton	(970) 454-3466
Estes Park Trail Gazette	Estes Park	(970) 586-3356
Canyon Courier	Evergreen	(303) 674-5534
Colorado Serenity	Evergreen	(303) 670-5448
Flagler News	Flagler	(719) 765-4466
Florence Citizen Inc	Florence	(719) 784-6383
Rocky Mountain News	Fort Collins	(970) 484-5678
Rocky Mountain News	Fort Morgan	(970) 867-1713
El Paso County News	Fountain	(719) 382-5611
Fountain Valley News	Fountain	(719) 382-5611
Fowler Tribune	Fowler	(719) 263-5311
Summit Daily News	Frisco	(970) 668-0750
Daily Sentinel	Glenwood Springs	(970) 945-7439
Glenwood Post	Glenwood Springs	(970) 945-8515
New York Times Co	Glenwood Springs	(970) 945-8920
Rocky Mountain News	Glenwood Springs	(970) 945-8920
Golden Transcript	Golden	(303) 279-5541
Daily Tribune	Granby	(970) 887-3334
Grand Lake Prospector	Granby	(970) 887-3334
Daily Sentinel	Grand Junction	(970) 242-5050
Grand Valley Business Times	Grand Junction	(970) 241-0177
Greeley Tribune	Greeley	(970) 352-0211
Rocky Mountain News	Greeley	(970) 353-0160
Gunnison Times	Gunnison	(970) 349-6124
Gunnison-Country Times	Gunnison	(970) 641-1414

Haxtun Herald	Haxtun	(970) 774-6118
Highlander	Highlands Ranch	(303) 791-1172
Holyoke Enterprise	Holyoke	(970) 854-2811
Clear Creek Courant	Idaho Springs	(303) 567-4491
Mountain Messenger	Idaho Springs	(303) 567-9623
Johnstown Breeze	Johnstown	(970) 587-4525
Julesburg Advocate	Julesburg	(970) 474-3388
Middle Park Times	Kremmling	(970) 724-3350
Conejos County Citizen	La Jara	(719) 274-4192
Arkansas Valley Journal	La Junta	(719) 384-8121
La Junta Tribune-Democrat	La Junta	(719) 384-4475
Lafayette News	Lafayette	(303) 665-6515
Louisville Times	Lafayette	(303) 666-6576
Lake City Silver World	Lake City	(970) 944-2515
Lamar Daily News	Lamar	(719) 336-2266
North Forty News	Laporte	(970) 221-0213
Herald Democrat	Leadville	(719) 486-0641
Englewood Herald	Littleton	(303) 794-7877
Highlands Ranch Herald	Littleton	(303) 794-7877
Littleton Independent	Littleton	(303) 794-7877
Daily Times	Longmont	(303) 444-3636
Longmont Daily Times	Longmont	(303) 776-2244
Loveland Daily Reporter-Herald	Loveland	(970) 669-5050
Rocky Mountain News Agency	Loveland	(970) 667-3416
Old Lyons Recorder	Lyons	(303) 823-6625
Mancos Times Tribune	Mancos	(970) 533-7766
Journal Newspapers	Manitou Springs	(719) 685-9201
Pikes Peak Journal	Manitou Springs	(719) 685-9201
Meeker Herald	Meeker	(970) 878-4017
Monte Vista Journal	Monte Vista	(719) 852-3531
Daily Press	Montrose	(970) 249-3444
Daily Sentinel News Bureau	Montrose	(970) 249-5573
Tri-Lakes Times	Monument	(719) 488-9362
Tribune	Monument	(719) 481-3423
Mountain Ear	Nederland	(303) 258-7075
San Miguel County Post	Norwood	(970) 327-4094
Ouray County Newspapers	Ouray	(970) 325-4412
Pagosa Springs Sun	Pagosa Springs	(970) 264-2101
Palisade Tribune	Palisade	(970) 464-5614
High Country News	Paonia	(970) 527-4898
North Fork Times	Paonia	(970) 527-4339
Weekly News Chronicle	Parker	(303) 841-5497
Chieftain & Star Journal	Pueblo	(719) 544-3520
Colorado Tribune	Pueblo	(719) 561-4008
Pueblo Business Journal Inc	Pueblo	(719) 542-3616
Pueblo West Horizon	Pueblo	(719) 544-3834
Pueblo West View	Pueblo West	(719) 547-9606
Rangely Times	Rangely	(970) 675-5033

Citizen Telegram	Rifle	(970) 625-3245
Daily Gazette	Rocky Ford	(719) 254-3351
Saguache Crescent	Saguache	(719) 655-2620
Mountain Mail Newspaper	Salida	(719) 539-6691
Costilla County Free Press	San Luis	(719) 672-3764
Silverton Standard Newspaper	Silverton	(970) 387-5477
Ranchland News	Simla	(719) 541-2288
Snowmass Sun	Snowmass Village	(970) 923-5829
Baca Weekly	Springfield	(719) 523-6600
Plainsman-Herald	Springfield	(719) 523-6254
Steamboat Springs Review	Steamboat Springs	(970) 879-7074
Journal Advocate	Sterling	(970) 522-1990
South Platte Sentinel	Sterling	(970) 522-8148
Eastern Colorado News	Strasburg	(303) 622-4417
Stratton Spotlight	Stratton	(719) 348-5913
Telluride Daily Planet	Telluride	(970) 728-9788
Telluride Times Journal	Telluride	(970) 728-4301
Jackson County Star	Walden	(970) 723-4404
Huerfano World	Walsenburg	(719) 738-1720
Wet Mountain Tribune	Westcliffe	(719) 783-2361
Metro North Newspaper	Westminster	(303) 426-6000
Northglenn-Thornton Sentinel	Westminster	(303) 426-6000
Wiggins Courier	Wiggins	(970) 483-7460
High Mountain Sun	Woodland Park	(719) 687-0803
Ute Pass Courier	Woodland Park	(719) 687-3006
Wray Gazette Inc	Wray	(970) 332-4846
Yuma Pioneer	Yuma	(970) 848-2174

EMPLOYMENT AGENCIES

Mountain Temp Service	Aspen	(970) 920-3686
A-Affordable Employment	Aurora	(303) 341-1133
Career 2000 Inc	Aurora	(303) 696-2000
Express Temporary Service	Aurora	(303) 361-6894
Labor Ready Inc	Aurora	(303) 739-0509
Stand-By Personnel	Aurora	(303) 363-8200
Star Personnel Service	Aurora	(303) 695-1161
U S Job Service	Aurora	(303) 344-0097
Western Temporary Service	Aurora	(303) 745-9494
Accountability	Boulder	(303) 444-3811
Adia Personnel Service	Boulder	(303) 442-2420
Bolder Temporaries Inc	Boulder	(303) 444-1445
First Choice Personnel Network	Boulder	(303) 444-7939
Front Range Personnel	Boulder	(303) 443-4730
Interim Personnel	Boulder	(303) 442-8677
Mountain States Personnel	Boulder	(303) 444-5770
National Career Search Inc	Boulder	(303) 440-5110
Norrell Temporary Service	Boulder	(303) 440-6119
Robert Half Intl	Boulder	(303) 444-1313

Staff Mark	Boulder	(303) 444-4558
Staffing Solutions	Boulder	(303) 443-1700
Tad Temporaries	Boulder	(303) 447-8114
Western Staff Service	Boulder	(303) 444-5982
High Country Temps Inc	Breckenridge	(970) 453-4740
Core Staff Staffing Service	Broomfield	(303) 425-6646
Douglas County Temp Service	Castle Rock	(303) 688-6795
Miller-Denver	Castle Rock	(303) 688-6630
Accel	Colorado Springs	(719) 574-4200
Accounting Solutions Inc	Colorado Springs	(719) 531-6600
Add Staff Inc	Colorado Springs	(719) 528-8888
Adia Personnel Service	Colorado Springs	(719) 591-7000
Adia Personnel Service	Colorado Springs	(719) 532-9000
Apple One Employment Service	Colorado Springs	(719) 599-4100
Ewing Technical Design Inc	Colorado Springs	(719) 633-8777
Express Personnel Service	Colorado Springs	(719) 520-9100
G T Employment Service	Colorado Springs	(719) 380-8998
Geo Search Inc	Colorado Springs	(719) 260-7087
Interim Personnel	Colorado Springs	(719) 636-1606
Job Search	Colorado Springs	(719) 475-9755
Jobnet Of Colorado Springs	Colorado Springs	(719) 260-7279
Labor Finders Of Colorado Inc	Colorado Springs	(719) 630-1982
Labor Ready Inc	Colorado Springs	(719) 632-1883
Med-Temp	Colorado Springs	(719) 578-5819
Need A Nurse Or Nanny	Colorado Springs	(719) 633-1088
Spencer Services	Colorado Springs	(719) 522-1077
Staffing Solutions	Colorado Springs	(719) 599-7400
Stand By Personnel	Colorado Springs	(719) 520-0205
Volt Services Group	Colorado Springs	(719) 471-0858
Labor Finders Of Colorado Inc	Commerce City	(303) 289-1417
Wise Resources	Conifer	(303) 838-8222
Absolute Employment Service	Denver	(303) 839-5700
Access Recruitment	Denver	(303) 534-1333
Accountability	Denver	(303) 297-2929
Accountants & Bookkeepers	Denver	(303) 297-2020
Accountants On Call	Denver	(303) 571-1110
Accounting Solutions Inc	Denver	(303) 534-1950
Act One Personnel Service	Denver	(303) 756-7200
Adia Personnel Service	Denver	(303) 399-7706
Bader & Co	Denver	(303) 572-6028
Bank Temps Inc	Denver	(303) 861-4115
Blackstone Group	Denver	(303) 796-7500
Careers Limited	Denver	(303) 832-5200
Claims Overload Systems	Denver	(303) 388-7960
Colorado Assn-Personnel	Denver	(303) 320-3727
Colorado Women's Employment	Denver	(303) 892-8444
Colorado Womens Employment	Denver	(303) 892-8375
Connection Point Recruiters	Denver	(303) 796-9114

Corestaff Staffing Service	Denver	(303) 825-1500
Daniels & Patterson Corp	Denver	(303) 830-1230
Data Processing	Denver	(303) 297-2020
Employment Connection	Denver	(303) 756-1316
Event Pro-Staff Service	Denver	(303) 458-8826
Executemps Inc	Denver	(303) 758-9353
First Choice Nannies Inc	Denver	(303) 368-0299
First Choice Personnel	Denver	(303) 297-2020
Ford Personnel Inc	Denver	(303) 322-2317
Genesis Jobs Inc	Denver	(303) 860-8904
Goodwin Personnel Inc	Denver	(303) 759-8367
H-R Employment Service	Denver	(303) 294-0148
Hospital Shared Service	Denver	(303) 871-7080
Hospitality Personnel Service	Denver	(303) 830-6868
Hunter Group	Denver	(303) 295-0732
Interim Legal Personnel	Denver	(303) 446-2412
Interim Personnel	Denver	(303) 758-8677
J Calloway & Assoc	Denver	(303) 759-2262
J Kent & Assoc Inc	Denver	(303) 777-7734
J L Mark Assoc	Denver	(303) 292-0360
Job Store	Denver	(303) 757-7801
Job Store Staffing	Denver	(303) 757-7686
Jobnet Inc	Denver	(303) 755-1650
Jobs For Industry	Denver	(303) 831-0048
Margaret Hook's Personnel Inc	Denver	(303) 770-2100
Mathews & Ball Inc	Denver	(303) 759-8130
Mile High Employment	Denver	(303) 650-0332
Nesco Service Co	Denver	(303) 757-7737
Noonan Temporary Service Inc	Denver	(303) 753-9630
Officeteam	Denver	(303) 296-2020
Pavlakis Realty	Denver	(303) 757-6441
Phillips Temps	Denver	(303) 893-1850
Police Officer Selection Service	Denver	(303) 777-5322
Preferred Leads Inc	Denver	(303) 782-5447
Printers Personnel	Denver	(303) 399-9495
Quik Temps Inc	Denver	(303) 825-8367
Real Estate Personnel	Denver	(303) 832-2380
Rent-A-Mom Of Colorado	Denver	(303) 322-1399
Resources In Food	Denver	(303) 863-7858
Robert Half Intl	Denver	(303) 296-1010
Rocky Mountain Recruiters Inc	Denver	(303) 296-2000
Roth Young Personnel Service	Denver	(303) 755-5440
Scheer & Assoc	Denver	(303) 757-7357
Senior Skills	Denver	(303) 756-4440
Snap Temporary & Permanent	Denver	(303) 329-6693
Snelling Personnel Service	Denver	(303) 534-3581
Stand-By Personnel	Denver	(303) 399-9522
Summit Staffing Inc	Denver	(303) 575-9210

Summit Staffing Temporary	Denver	(303) 427-7937
Sunny Side Inc/Temp Side	Denver	(303) 320-5361
Talent Tree Staffing Service	Denver	(303) 296-1700
Team Personnel	Denver	(303) 388-8326
Tempforce	Denver	(303) 831-1096
Temporaries Inc	Denver	(303) 893-0411
Today's Temporary Inc	Denver	(303) 294-0055
Unique Talent	Denver	(303) 937-9104
Urban League Of Metro Denver	Denver	(303) 388-5861
Volt Temporary Service	Denver	(303) 373-5525
Volt Temporary Service	Denver	(303) 298-7555
Employ Mint	Durango	(970) 259-1940
Access Personnel Service	Englewood	(303) 534-3535
Career Search	Englewood	(303) 790-1119
Casey Services	Englewood	(303) 721-9211
Cma Group	Englewood	(303) 779-8890
Command Staffing Inc	Englewood	(303) 444-0700
Dennison Associates Inc	Englewood	(303) 741-5850
Denver Temporary Service	Englewood	(303) 694-6661
Dunn & Nelson	Englewood	(303) 694-1998
Edp Recruiting Service Inc	Englewood	(303) 694-2222
Eleventh Hour Inc	Englewood	(303) 220-5300
Eleventh Hour Personnel	Englewood	(303) 220-8892
G T Employment Service	Englewood	(303) 796-8367
Healthcare Recruiters Intl	Englewood	(303) 779-8570
J Kinney & Assoc Corp Inc	Englewood	(303) 220-7337
Labor Finders Of Colorado Inc	Englewood	(303) 781-6655
Labor Ready Inc	Englewood	(303) 722-0318
Mac Temps	Englewood	(303) 721-6360
Medical Personnel Resources	Englewood	(303) 762-0806
National Executive Resources	Englewood	(303) 721-7672
Office Placement Service	Englewood	(303) 973-9333
Peakload Temporary Service	Englewood	(303) 629-1953
Personnel Plus	Englewood	(303) 694-6233
Placement Professionals Inc	Englewood	(303) 721-8308
Printers Personnel	Englewood	(303) 788-1319
Pro Staff Personnel Service	Englewood	(303) 793-3888
Remedy Intelligent Staffing	Englewood	(303) 770-9675
Resumes On-Line	Englewood	(303) 781-0055
Robert Half Intl	Englewood	(303) 694-9111
Sales Consultants	Englewood	(303) 752-2550
Snelling Personnel Service	Englewood	(303) 779-3060
Source Finance	Englewood	(303) 773-3799
Stand-By Personnel	Englewood	(303) 761-0105
Talent Tree Staffing Service	Englewood	(303) 643-3439
Talent Tree Staffing Service	Englewood	(303) 694-4522
Tempstaff Inc	Englewood	(303) 220-1094
Triad Consultants	Englewood	(303) 220-8516

Trish & Assoc	Englewood	(303) 989-8900
United Personnel Of Colorado	Englewood	(303) 741-6983
Volt Temporary Service	Englewood	(303) 721-8400
Western Temporary Service	Englewood	(303) 741-3140
Wow Employment Inc	Evergreen	(303) 674-5504
Adia Personnel Service	Fort Collins	(970) 204-4801
Career Connections	Fort Collins	(970) 221-3511
Colorado Division-Employment	Fort Collins	(970) 223-2470
Express Temporary Service	Fort Collins	(970) 226-4300
Fits Temporary Service	Fort Collins	(970) 225-0085
Mountain States Personnel	Fort Collins	(970) 484-5590
Olsten Staffing Service	Fort Collins	(970) 221-2633
Western Staff Service	Fort Collins	(970) 223-3434
Technology Transition Support	Golden	(303) 277-0400
Mesa Employment	Grand Junction	(970) 245-6372
Quick Temps Inc	Grand Junction	(970) 241-6007
Resource Centers Jobs Program	Grand Junction	(970) 243-0190
Western Temporary Service	Grand Junction	(970) 243-6505
Labor Finders Of Colorado Inc	Lakewood	(303) 238-4120
Labor Ready Inc	Lakewood	(303) 274-1466
Office Placement Service	Lakewood	(303) 421-4930
Roegand Co	Lakewood	(303) 986-1112
SOS Technical Service	Lakewood	(303) 989-0625
Insurance Professional	Littleton	(303) 470-7811
Professional Search Placement	Littleton	(303) 779-8004
Recruiting Resources	Littleton	(303) 797-2575
Search Network	Littleton	(303) 932-1024
Snelling Personnel Service	Littleton	(303) 794-4331
Teddy Bear Care	Littleton	(303) 795-5691
Apple One Employment Service	Longmont	(303) 682-0200
Aspen Temporaries Inc	Longmont	(303) 776-9661
Dunhill Personnel System	Longmont	(303) 444-5531
Express Personnel Service	Longmont	(303) 772-7201
Dunn & Nelson Inc	Northglenn	(303) 494-0604
G T Employment Service	Northglenn	(303) 451-5602
Staffing Solutions	Northglenn	(303) 457-0900
Express Personnel Service	Pueblo	(719) 545-9120
Interim Personnel	Pueblo	(719) 544-8955
Kelly Services	Pueblo	(719) 545-9300
Western Temporary Service	Pueblo	(719) 543-8196
Pro Staff Personnel Service	Westminster	(303) 426-6726
Stand-By Personnel	Westminster	(303) 427-5151
Tec Consults Inc	Westminster	(303) 426-6242
Western Temporary Service	Westminster	(303) 657-5990
Automotive Personnel	Wheat Ridge	(303) 420-8852
Career Forum Inc	Wheat Ridge	(303) 425-8721
Colorado Technical Staffing	Wheat Ridge	(303) 421-9735
Pro Staff Personnel Service	Wheat Ridge	(303) 456-1638

TELEVISION STATIONS

KRMT	Arvada	(303) 423-4141
Aspen Channel	Aspen	(970) 925-9579
Aspen Snowmass Video Magazine	Aspen	(970) 920-9292
Aspen Video Guide-Channel 11	Aspen	(970) 925-2251
ESPN	Aspen	(970) 925-2251
Grass Roots Community Tv-12	Aspen	(970) 925-8000
Pro Video	Aspen	(970) 925-5050
CTVA	Aurora	(303) 671-0938
KACT	Aurora	(303) 340-2260
Universal Broadcasting	Aurora	(303) 671-9722
Vail Resorts Inc	Avon	(970) 476-5601
Vail Valley Community Tv	Avon	(970) 949-5657
News 4 Boulder Valley Bureau	Boulder	(303) 442-4244
Vacation Channel	Breckenridge	(970) 453-0230
JTV	Broomfield	(303) 465-2364
Community News Svc	Colorado Springs	(719) 520-5000
K 38 CUTV	Colorado Springs	(719) 637-1138
KKTV	Colorado Springs	(719) 634-2844
KMGH	Colorado Springs	(719) 633-7777
KOAA	Colorado Springs	(719) 632-5030
KRDO	Colorado Springs	(719) 632-1515
KXRM	Colorado Springs	(719) 596-2100
TV 43	Colorado Springs	(719) 574-7777
Bill Engler Six News-Sports	Craig	(970) 824-7265
Crested Butte TV Inc	Crested Butte	(970) 349-7528
Five Points Media Ctr Corp	Denver	(303) 295-1357
KBDI Public Tv-12	Denver	(303) 296-1212
KCEC	Denver	(303) 832-0050
KCNC	Denver	(303) 861-4444
KDVR	Denver	(303) 595-3131
KMGH	Denver	(303) 832-7777
KRMA	Denver	(303) 892-6666
KTVJ TV	Denver	(303) 832-1414
KUBD TV 59	Denver	(303) 751-5959
News Hour With Jim Gehrer	Denver	(303) 455-8222
KREZ	Durango	(970) 259-6666
KWHD-TV	Elizabeth	(303) 646-0870
ESPN	Englewood	(303) 740-8940
Jones Intercable Inc	Englewood	(303) 792-3111
KTVD	Englewood	(303) 792-2020
KWGN	Englewood	(303) 740-2222
KWHD	Englewood	(303) 773-9953
Nostalgia Network Inc	Englewood	(303) 694-1811
Tele-Communications Inc	Englewood	(303) 267-5500

Time Warner Cable	Englewood	(303) 799-1200
Channel 8 Estes Park	Estes Park	(970) 586-6045
Translator Service	Estes Park	(970) 586-2959
Fort Collins Evening News	Fort Collins	(970) 493-1600
KCNC	Fort Collins	(970) 244-4444
KUSA	Fort Collins	(970) 484-5332
Optical Audio Productions	Fort Collins	(970) 484-5535
TCI	Fort Collins	(970) 493-7400
News 4 Mountain Bureau	Frisco	(970) 668-0444
KUSA West Slope Bureau	Glenwood Springs	(970) 945-9999
KJCT TV	Grand Junction	(970) 245-8880
KREX	Grand Junction	(970) 242-5000
KRMJ TV	Grand Junction	(970) 245-1818
Gussinson County Metro Recren	Gunnison	(970) 641-9148
TV 20 Elk Mountain Television	Gunnison	(970) 641-1271
Mountain View Engineering	Leadville	(719) 486-2085
Channel 3-The Longmont Channel	Longmont	(303) 776-1424
KREY	Montrose	(970) 249-9601
Professional Antenna Tower Svc	Montrose	(970) 249-5926
Mountain Channel	Pine	(303) 838-9815
KDJ 24 TV	Pueblo	(719) 542-4277
KKTV	Pueblo	(719) 542-6247
KOAA	Pueblo	(719) 544-5781
KRDO	Pueblo	(719) 543-0013
KTSC	Pueblo	(719) 528-5050
KTSC-TV	Pueblo	(719) 543-8800
KTVS	Sterling	(970) 522-2729
TCTV Telluride Community TV	Telluride	(970) 728-3838
KVBA TV 8	Vail	(970) 479-0800
Trinity Broadcasting Of Denver	Westminster	(303) 650-5515
CNN	Woody Creek	(970) 925-2251

INTERNET SERVICE

America Net Com	Arvada	(303) 940-8357
Internet Publications-America	Arvada	(303) 423-8711
Meeting Places Inc	Aurora	(303) 341-0009
Colorado Internet	Boulder	(303) 443-3786
ABS Internet & Cad	Colorado Springs	(719) 579-6423
Berkeley Software Design	Colorado Springs	(719) 593-9445
Colorado Internet Connection	Colorado Springs	(719) 574-8924
Colorado Software Solutions	Colorado Springs	(719) 473-2800
Computer Labs Inc	Colorado Springs	(719) 590-4125
Cyber Help Inc	Colorado Springs	(719) 634-2771
Horizon Interactive Inc	Colorado Springs	(719) 593-7377
Inovatec Inc	Colorado Springs	(719) 596-9360
Marketwise Data Svc	Colorado Springs	(719) 579-0993
Netgrafx	Colorado Springs	(719) 380-0400
Northstar Software	Colorado Springs	(719) 520-9321

Old Colorado City Comms Co	Colorado Springs	(719) 632-4848
Pegasus Learning Co	Colorado Springs	(719) 634-4969
Rocky Mountain Internet Inc	Colorado Springs	(719) 576-6845
Web Post	Colorado Springs	(719) 520-9395
XLN Cafe On-Line	Colorado Springs	(719) 447-9566
Business Technology Consultant	Denver	(303) 639-6010
Colorado Legal Network Inc	Denver	(303) 436-9500
Colorado Supernet Inc	Denver	(303) 296-8202
Evergreen Internet Inc	Denver	(303) 370-6800
Information Exchange	Denver	(303) 296-6245
Internet Store	Denver	(303) 592-9747
LDR	Denver	(303) 393-7300
Majordomo's Inc	Denver	(303) 830-0442
On Point Communications	Denver	(303) 321-8302
Online Systems Svc Inc	Denver	(303) 296-9200
Onramp Communications	Denver	(303) 534-3131
Roecker Design Group Inc	Denver	(303) 455-4800
Uncover Co	Denver	(303) 758-3030
Worldnet Marketing Inc	Denver	(303) 292-3004
Hartman's Mercantile	Durango	(970) 247-5589
Digital Page	Englewood	(303) 799-7919
Leader Group Inc	Englewood	(303) 773-9700
Yellow Net Of The Rockies	Englewood	(303) 761-3161
Acxes Com	Evergreen	(303) 674-4620
Actnet	Fort Collins	(970) 490-1849
Cullerton Consulting	Fort Collins	(970) 493-2101
EZ Link Internet Access	Fort Collins	(970) 482-0807
Fort Net Communications	Fort Collins	(970) 416-6565
Fortnet	Fort Collins	(970) 224-5991
Front Range Internet Inc	Fort Collins	(970) 224-3668
Info Vision Inc	Fort Collins	(970) 224-4441
Page Plus	Fort Collins	(970) 484-1933
Pointclick Internet Svc	Fort Collins	(970) 498-9871
Theory Y Productions	Fort Collins	(970) 493-1728
Verinet Communications	Fort Collins	(970) 416-9152
Dash	Foxton	(303) 674-9784
Knight Web Technologies Inc	Golden	(303) 279-6204
Advanced Internet Designs	Grand Junction	(970) 245-8460
Omni Investigations & Training	Grand Junction	(970) 242-4323
Online Colorado	Grand Junction	(970) 241-8643
Rural Net	Grand Junction	(970) 256-7344
Sportsmans Dream	Grand Junction	(970) 241-8643
Western Internet Connections	Grand Junction	(970) 523-5188
Clark & Thompson Online Svc	Greeley	(970) 353-8126
Internet Communications Corp	Greenwood Village	(303) 770-7600
Computer Store	Gunnison	(970) 641-0555
A Better Video By J Gaudio Co	Littleton	(303) 933-4496
Abwam Inc	Littleton	(303) 730-1414

Yellow Net Corp	Littleton	(303) 797-7676
Online Marketing Network	Loveland	(970) 593-9311
Rocky Mountain Internet	Loveland	(970) 663-1038
Great Western Electronic Rent	Montrose	(970) 249-2166
Montrose Internet	Montrose	(970) 249-9722
Best Buy's Computers	Pueblo	(719) 545-0977
Rocky Mountain Internet	Pueblo	(719) 542-4745
Ad Tech On Line Advertising	Pueblo West	(719) 547-4274
Independence Network Corp	Ridgway	(970) 626-5399
Premier Systems	Yuma	(970) 848-0475

STORAGE FACILITIES

The phone numbers shown below represent a small potion of storage facilities available in the major cities of Colorado. With respect to space allotted, this list has been condensed greatly. Please consult your local Yellow Pages for a complete list.

Aspen Mini Storage	Aspen	(970) 920-3333
Aspen Secure Storage	Aspen	(970) 920-4298
Aspen Self Storage Warehouses	Aspen	(970) 925-8333
Columbine Moving & Storage	Aspen	(970) 925-2201
A An A Moving & Storage	Aurora	(303) 364-4275
A-Aaakey Mini Storage	Aurora	(303) 755-8111
Abco Mini Storage	Aurora	(303) 341-0277
Affordable Moving & Storage	Aurora	(303) 693-7077
All American Moving Service	Aurora	(303) 373-5101
Altura Self Storage	Aurora	(303) 343-4020
Aurora Mini-Storage	Aurora	(303) 343-3389
Chambers East Mini-Storage	Aurora	(303) 340-4144
Harbor Plaza Mini & Outdoor	Aurora	(303) 690-2759
Lock-Ur-Own Storage Inc	Aurora	(303) 364-6032
Public Storage	Aurora	(303) 690-3031
Security Self Storage	Aurora	(303) 338-0800
Self Storage	Aurora	(303) 344-2429
U S Storage Inc	Aurora	(303) 341-0122
U-Haul Co	Aurora	(303) 340-3070
U-Stor	Aurora	(303) 340-2121
West Evans Mini-Storage	Aurora	(303) 755-0913
Wolf's Mini Storage	Aurora	(303) 341-0223
A Ace Self Storage	Boulder	(303) 444-7870
Arapahoe Self Storage	Boulder	(303) 449-5851
BMM Self Storage	Boulder	(303) 449-6770
Boulder Bins	Boulder	(303) 443-2002
Boulder SSI Storage Center	Boulder	(303) 449-6597
City Moving & Storage Inc	Boulder	(303) 447-2440
North Broadway Self Storage	Boulder	(303) 449-6900
Secur Care Self Storage	Boulder	(303) 444-7867
Storage Containers	Boulder	(303) 938-8286

Western Disposal Service	Boulder	(303) 444-2037
Breckenridge Mini Storage	Breckenridge	(970) 453-6669
Arrow Mini Storage	Castle Rock	(303) 688-7417
Castle Rock Mini-Storage Inc	Castle Rock	(303) 681-2131
Castle Rock RV& Boat Storage	Castle Rock	(303) 688-4280
Haulaway Storage Containers	Castle Rock	(303) 688-0344
Jerry Street Self Storage	Castle Rock	(303) 688-0693
Park Street Storage	Castle Rock	(303) 688-2242
Triple N	Castle Rock	(303) 688-9757
8th Street Self Storage	Colorado Springs	(719) 633-1820
A A Self Service Storage	Colorado Springs	(719) 475-2032
A Better Self Storage	Colorado Springs	(719) 471-8800
A Low Cost Self Storage	Colorado Springs	(719) 574-2065
A-1 Self Storage Warehouses	Colorado Springs	(719) 591-8900
AAA Self-Store-All Warehouse	Colorado Springs	(719) 392-5954
Able Movers Inc	Colorado Springs	(719) 591-9330
Academy Moving	Colorado Springs	(719) 531-7553
Academy Place Storage	Colorado Springs	(719) 574-7111
Academy South Mini-Storage	Colorado Springs	(719) 391-0222
Agape Moving & Storage	Colorado Springs	(719) 596-6300
All American Moving Service	Colorado Springs	(719) 390-8080
Amick North American	Colorado Springs	(719) 597-8850
Arrow Moving & Storage Co	Colorado Springs	(719) 390-5439
Astro/Securcare Self Storage	Colorado Springs	(719) 390-4677
Astrozon Self Storage	Colorado Springs	(719) 390-4288
Austin Bluffs East Self Stge	Colorado Springs	(719) 572-9100
Bekins Moving & Storage	Colorado Springs	(719) 520-5700
Centennial Blvd Self Storage	Colorado Springs	(719) 260-0055
Central Self-Storage	Colorado Springs	(719) 591-1957
Chapel Hills Self Storage	Colorado Springs	(719) 590-7135
City Center Self Storage	Colorado Springs	(719) 633-1331
Colorado Springs Moving Inc	Colorado Springs	(719) 636-8987
Commercial Self Storage	Colorado Springs	(719) 535-2782
Downtown Mini Warehouse	Colorado Springs	(719) 630-1575
El Paso Mini Storage	Colorado Springs	(719) 635-3405
Goeson Moving & Storage	Colorado Springs	(719) 596-3306
Interstate Secure Storage	Colorado Springs	(719) 633-0222
Knob Hill Storage	Colorado Springs	(719) 630-1575
Mobile Mini Storage	Colorado Springs	(719) 390-7316
Mobile Mini-Warehousing	Colorado Springs	(719) 390-1900
Motor City Mini-Storage	Colorado Springs	(719) 633-6952
North Nevada Self Storage	Colorado Springs	(719) 633-8923
Northside U-Store-It	Colorado Springs	(719) 635-0488
Old Mill Self Storage	Colorado Springs	(719) 634-6332
Peak View Self Storage	Colorado Springs	(719) 473-7445
Pikes Peak Moving & Storage	Colorado Springs	(719) 475-2806
Public Storage	Colorado Springs	(719) 598-8485
Rampart Self-Storage	Colorado Springs	(719) 592-0662

Rite Place Self Storage	Colorado Springs	(719) 633-7652
Rockrimmon Self Storage	Colorado Springs	(719) 532-1880
Rocky Mt Moving And Storage	Colorado Springs	(719) 634-0908
Self Storage	Colorado Springs	(719) 599-8717
Storage Group	Colorado Springs	(719) 573-0142
Storage Trust	Colorado Springs	(719) 570-1300
Stor-N-Lok	Colorado Springs	(719) 576-0800
Stx Truck & Equipment Sales	Colorado Springs	(719) 599-3575
Sun Self Storage	Colorado Springs	(719) 633-6058
U-Haul Co	Colorado Springs	(719) 574-6500
Westwind Storage	Colorado Springs	(719) 447-0452
S Platte Canyon Storage	Columbine Valley	(303) 932-9311
64th & Clay Storage	Denver	(303) 427-6123
70th & Washington Mini-Park	Denver	(303) 288-1111
A & R Transfer Co	Denver	(303) 320-9092
A A Wholesale Outside Storage	Denver	(303) 295-1313
A Bargain Evans/Holly Storage	Denver	(303) 756-4154
A Better Self Storage	Denver	(303) 337-2064
A Business Storage Inc	Denver	(303) 893-1414
A Designed Moving Co	Denver	(303) 296-3447
Able Movers Inc	Denver	(303) 333-1090
Adams County Self Storage	Denver	(303) 477-3844
Alameda Storage	Denver	(303) 363-0939
All American Mini Storage Inc	Denver	(303) 573-6464
American Worldwide Intl	Denver	(303) 371-4003
Amick North American	Denver	(303) 333-8212
Atlantic North American	Denver	(303) 373-5383
Benedict Warehouse & Transfer	Denver	(303) 292-5077
Berkeley Moving & Storage Co	Denver	(303) 399-1815
Big City Storage	Denver	(303) 573-3863
Buehler Moving & Storage	Denver	(303) 388-4000
Certified Discount Mini Storage	Denver	(303) 295-0450
Complete Container Service	Denver	(303) 428-6800
Cowen Moving & Storage	Denver	(303) 433-0264
Devonshire Mini Warehouse	Denver	(303) 288-1119
Downtown Denver Storage Inc	Denver	(303) 298-0176
Downtown Self Storage	Denver	(303) 292-9816
Fort-U Store It	Denver	(303) 337-4044
Iliff Mini Storage	Denver	(303) 755-8222
Indoor Storage Center	Denver	(303) 295-2446
Kangaroo Self-Store-It	Denver	(303) 286-1232
Lakewood Self Storage	Denver	(303) 989-6330
Lowell Mini Storage	Denver	(303) 657-3661
Mini U-Storage	Denver	(303) 337-3945
Movemasters	Denver	(303) 777-2290
Nationwide Inc	Denver	(303) 296-2933
Nationwide Self Storage	Denver	(303) 751-9702
Northridge Storage	Denver	(303) 428-0128

Private Self Storage	Denver	(303) 426-0584
Public Storage	Denver	(303) 936-9404
Santa Fe Record Storage	Denver	(303) 534-8342
Secure Self Storage	Denver	(303) 751-1726
Shurgard Storage Center	Denver	(303) 469-1147
Storage Center	Denver	(303) 477-5998
U-Haul Co	Denver	(303) 534-6072
USA Central Denver	Denver	(303) 333-5741
U-Stor	Denver	(303) 761-2277
U-Stor-All	Denver	(303) 722-0370
Wagner Rents	Denver	(303) 433-2727
West Evans Mini-Storage	Denver	(303) 922-1555
A Discount Storage	Englewood	(303) 761-1099
Almost Anything Stored	Englewood	(303) 761-5511
Arapahoe & Holly Self Storage	Englewood	(303) 694-9400
Self Storage	Englewood	(303) 789-9585
Warehouse Mini-Storage	Englewood	(303) 781-5110
Evergreen Business Center	Evergreen	(303) 674-6012
Floyd Hill Mini Storage	Evergreen	(303) 670-5019
Mountain Mini Storage Inc	Evergreen	(303) 674-8400
Old Mine Mini Storage	Evergreen	(303) 674-6431
A Big A Self Storage	Fort Collins	(970) 224-2424
A Low Cost Self Storage	Fort Collins	(970) 223-1443
A Plus Mini's Self Storage	Fort Collins	(970) 226-5625
A-1 U Store-It Warehouses	Fort Collins	(970) 493-8313
ABC Storage	Fort Collins	(970) 482-9921
All Seasons Storage	Fort Collins	(970) 484-5898
All Storage-Mini Self Storage	Fort Collins	(970) 484-2090
Colonial Self Storage Co	Fort Collins	(970) 482-0894
Dandelion Moving & Storage	Fort Collins	(970) 484-1717
G & P Mini-Storage	Fort Collins	(970) 493-6277
Maxi-Storage	Fort Collins	(970) 226-6800
Rite Place Self Storage	Fort Collins	(970) 484-3769
U Stuff It	Fort Collins	(970) 493-3895
Nationwide Self Storage	Golden	(303) 277-1658
Shut & Lock Self Storage	Golden	(303) 233-5627
Public Storage	Littleton	(303) 797-1449
Self Storage	Littleton	(303) 798-8078

APPENDIX A
RECOMMENDED READING FROM
COLORADO PUBLISHERS

The following Colorado publishers contributed materials for this book. Many have numerous titles about different aspects of Colorado and therefore have their own catalogs. Please check with your favorite bookstore for the titles or you can order directly from the publisher. Please note the prices indicated below may have changed since this publication and **do not** include shipping & handling which varies with each order. Please contact the publisher for details before ordering. All books listed are paperback unless otherwise noted.

Bradford Publishing (Free Catalog Available)
1743 Wazee Street, Denver, CO 80202, 303-292-2590
Colorado Child Support Handbook, $21.95
Colorado Revised Statutes 1997 Vehicles and Traffic, $12.95
Friendly Divorce Guidebook for Colorado, 2nd Edition, $26.50
Landlord & Tenant Guide to Colorado Evictions, $18.50
Winning Big in Colorado Small Claims Court, $17.95
1998-1999 Catalog of Legal Forms (over 1000 pre-printed legal forms), free

C & C Publications, The Junior League of Denver, Inc.
6300 East Yale Avenue, Suite 110, Denver, CO 80222, 303-782-9244
Colorado Cache Cookbook, $15.95
Crème de Colorado Cookbook, Hardbound, $19.95

Communications Creativity (Free Catalog Available)
PO Box 909, 425 Cedar Street, Buena Vista, CO 81211, 800-331-8355
Big Ideas for Small Service Businesses: How to Successfully Advertise,
    Publicize, and Maximize Your Business or Professional Practice, $15.95
Country Bound: Trade Your Business Suit Blues for Blue Jean Dreams, 2nd
    Edition, $19.95
Discover the Good Life In Rural America: The City Slicker's Guide to Buying
    Country Real Estate Without Losing Your Shirt, $12.95

Gylantic Publishing Company
PO Box 2792, Littleton, CO 80161-2792, 303-797-6093
Moving With Children: A Parent's Guide To Moving With Children, $12.95
Many other self-help/recovery titles.

Fulcrum Publishing (Free Catalog Available)
350 Indiana Street, Golden, CO 80401, 800-992-2908
Ancient Walls: Indian Ruins of the Southwest, full color, $19.95
Colorado's Fourteeners: From Hikes to Climbs, $16.95
Rocky Mountain National Park: Classic Hikes & Climbs, $14.95
Rocky Mountain Skiing, $21.95
Rocky Mountain Walks, $15.95
Seasonal Guide to the Natural Year, $15.95
The Colorado Guide, 4th Edition, $19.95 (Highly Recommended)

Ice Castle Editions
PO Box 280166, Lakewood, CO 80228-0116, 303-988-6424
Leadville's Ice Palace, A Colossus in the Colorado Rockies, $16.95

Johnson Books (Free Catalog Available)
1880 South 57th Court, Boulder, CO 80301, 800-258-5830
A Roadside Guide To Rocky Mountain National Park, $12.95
Roadside History of Colorado, Revised Edition, $13.95
Tales, Trails and Tommyknockers: Stories From Colorado's Past, $8.95
The Archaeology of Colorado, $19.00
The Four Corners Anasazi: A Guide to Archaeological Sites, $17.95
The Xeriscape Flower Gardener for the Rocky Mountain Region, $16.95
Many, many other Colorado titles!

League of Women Voters of Colorado
1410 Grant Street #B-204, Denver, CO 80203, 303-863-0437
Colorado: The State We're In, 1995 Revised Edition, $5.00

Magnolia Street Press
2600 Magnolia, Denver, CO 80207, 303-322-2822
Colorado Private Elementary and Secondary Schools, 1997-98, $11.50
The Guide to Metro Denver Public Schools, 1997-98 Edition, $14.50

Outdoor Books & Maps
PO Box 417, Denver, CO 80201, 1-800-352-5342
Best of Northern Colorado Hiking Trails, $12.95
Colorado Lakes & Reservoirs Fishing & Boating Guide, 6th Edition, $12.95
The Best of Colorado Biking Trails, 2nd Edition, $9.95
The Complete Colorado Campground Guide, 4th Edition, $12.95

Pokerbook Press
PO Box 17851, Boulder, CO 80308, 303-665-9008
Poker, Hold 'Em, Book One, $8.95 / Intermediate, $8.95
Poker, 101 Ways to Win, $17.95

Pruett Publishing Company (Free Catalog Available)
2928 Pearl Street, Boulder, CO 80301, 800-247-8224
A Climbing Guide to Colorado's Fourteeners, 3rd Edition, $16.95
A Colorado History, 7th Edition, $25.00
Making Tracks: An Introduction to Cross-Country Skiing, $14.95
Rocky Mountain Wineries: A Travel Guide to the Wayside Vineyards, $16.95
Many, many other similar Colorado titles!

Roberts Rinehart Publishers (Free Catalog Available)
5455 Spine Road, Mezzannine West, Boulder, CO 80301, 800-352-1985
Absolutely Every Bed & Breakfast in Colorado, 4th Edition, $16.95
Alpine Flower Finder: Wildflowers Found Above Treeline, $5.95
In The Shadow of the Rockies: An Outsider's Look Inside a New Major
League Baseball Team, Hardbound, 21.95
Chronicles of Colorado, $14.95
Colorado's Backyard Wildlife, $10.95
Handbook of Rocky Mountain Plants, 4th Edition, $19.95
Rocky Mountain National Park Natural History Handbook, $12.95
Rocky Mountain Safari: A Wildlife Discovery Guide, full color, $9.95
Many, many other Colorado/nature titles including several for children!

Rocky Mountain Vacation Publishing
5101 Pennsylvania Ave., Suite #5, Boulder, CO 80303-2799, 800-886-9343
Colorado Cabins, Lodges and Country B & B's, $17.95
Colorado RV Parks: A Pictorial Guide, $9.50

University Press of Colorado (Free Catalog Available)
PO Box 849, Niwot, CO 80544, 800-268-6044
Colorado: A History in Photographs, Hardbound, $29.95
Colorado: A History of The Centennial State, 3rd Edition, $27.50
Denver: Mining Camp to Metropolis, $27.50
Exploring Colorado State Parks, $19.95
Rocky Mountain Flora, $20.00
The Colorado General Assembly, Hardbound, $29.95
Many, many other similar Colorado titles available!

Westcliffe Publishers (Free Catalog Available)
PO Box 1261, Englewood, CO 80150-1261, 800-523-3692
Colorado Hut to Hut: A Guide to Skiing and Biking Colorado's Backcountry,
    full color, $24.95
Cooking with Colorado's Greatest Chefs, hardbound, full color, $35.00
Explore Colorado, full color, $19.95
Guide to Colorado Wildflowers, Volumes I & II, full color, $24.95 each
Places around the Bases: A Historic Tour of the Coors Field Neighborhood,
    $16.95
The Colorado Trail: The Official Guidebook, full color, $22.50
The Complete Guide to Colorado's Wilderness Areas, full color, $24.95
Many, many other Colorado titles and full color calendars!

APPENDIX B
MAPS
COLORADO COUNTIES

COLORADO SUB-STATE REGIONS

COLORADO NATIONAL FOREST

© Copyright 1995, Outdoor Books and Maps, Denver, CO.

COLORADO STATE PARKS

DENVER INTERNATIONAL AIRPORT

"Denver's airport is an invaluable asset to the city, the region and the nation's air system. Its outstanding capabilities are now evident to travelers and businesses. Continued strong growth in the city's economy has generated stronger businesses and more passengers. The success of DIA is driving nearby development and helping to create jobs. As DIA grows, so will opportunities."

Wellington Webb, Mayor of Denver

Denver International Airport moves people and cargo more efficiently than any other major airport. DIA passenger and cargo traffic robustly increased in 1996 as airlines and passengers discovered how well Denver's airport works. The high-performance airfield elevated Denver to one of the very best airports for on-time arrivals and fewest delays.

DIA's operational excellence has also helped create a fertile environment for surrounding business development. Plans for the airline-related business and long-term commercial development became reality in 1996 and as the area around Denver International Airport is experiencing potent growth.

Location: 23 miles northeast of downtown Denver

Size: 34,000 acres; 53 square miles

Average number of passengers per day: 88,000

Number of airlines: 21

Major/national
America West
American
Continental
Delta
Frontier
Midwest Express
Northwest
Reno
Sun Country
Trans World
United
USAir
Vanguard

Foreign flag
Air Canada
Martinair Holland
Mexicana de Aviacion

Regional/Commuter
Aspen Mountain Air
Air Wisconsin (United Express)
Great Lakes Aviation (United Express)
Maverick Airways
Mesa (United Express)

Average number of daily flights: 1,100

Runways: five; each 12,000 feet long

Concourses: three airside concourses – A, B, and C

Gates: 94 (including access gates to commuter facilities)

Terminal building: Elray B. Jeppesen Terminal (dual-sided)

Elevation: 5,431 feet

Number of parking spaces: More than 13,000 in two parking garages adjacent to terminal; 6,400 additional long-term economy spaces available in lots next to garages; 3,600 spaces in overflow lots.

DIA has great parking options. Shuttle parking is only $4 per day and Economy Parking is only $5 per day. Curbside Valet Parking is also available at Terminal Passenger Pick-Up, Level 4. There is a 70 minute grace period offered for terminal parking, 71-120 minutes is $4 and a maximum of $10 for each 24 hour period for extended terminal parking.

Parking for the disabled is available on all levels of the Terminal Parking Garage (excluding Level 3) and in the Long Term (Economy) Parking lots.

Parking Information: General parking information menu and suggestion line, please call (303) 342-4096.

Vehicle Assistance: Emergency car starts, tire inflations, lock outs, lost vehicles and more than 30-day stays. 24 hours a day/ 7 days a week, please call (303) 342-4650.

RTD SKYRIDE

Skyride busses operate between DIA and metro Denver park-n-Rides. They generally run between 4:00 a.m. – midnight. Route and schedule information is available by calling (303) 299-6000.

FUN FACTS ABOUT DIA

- 2.5 million cubic yards of concrete were used to construct five runways, taxiways and aprons.

- DIA has 1,200 flight or baggage information display monitors.

- A quarry in Marble, Colorado, supplied the white marble used on areas of the terminal walls. This stone is from the same quarry that supplied marble for the Tomb of the Unknown Soldier and the Lincoln Memorial.

- The total area of DIA is 53 square miles, twice the size of Manhattan Island, New York, and larger than the city boundary of Boston, Miami or San Francisco

- DIA has a fiber optic communications spine with 5,300 miles of cable. That is enough cable to run from New York City to Buenos Aires, Argentina. That length is longer than the River Nile. Its 11,365 miles of copper cable would be enough to run from Los Angeles to Paris and back.

RTD

The Regional Transportation District is a public agency created in 1969 by the Colorado General assembly to develop, operate and maintain a mass transportation system for the benefit of the people in RTD's six county service area. The service area includes all of Boulder, Denver and Jefferson counties and parts of Adams, Arapahoe and Douglas counties. A 15-member board of directors elected for four-year terms governs the District.

- Service area population: 2.1 million

- Cities and towns served: 41

- Square miles in service area: 2,406

- Bus stops: 9,708

- Park-n-Ride facilities: 59

- Light Rail Service: 17 vehicles, 5.3 miles of track, 15 stations

- Total number of routes: 166

    Local – 52

    Express – 48

    Regional – 20

    Limited – 12

    Boulder City Local – 11

    Boulder City Limited 3

    Longmont City Local- 8

    SkyRide - 5

    Miscellaneous – 7 (Mall Shuttle, Light Rail, Goodwill, etc.)

For more information, please call (303) 299-6000.

DEPENDABLE LEGAL FORMS FROM BRADFORD PUBLISHING

Bank and Loan Forms
659 Residential Loan Application
    Uniform Commercial Code Forms
    Promissory Notes

Court Forms
    Dissolution of Marriage Kits
    Child Support Forms
    Wage Assignment Forms
    Simplified Civil Procedure Forms (County Court)
    Eviction Forms (Unlawful Detainer)
    Adoptee Search Forms
    Change of Name Forms
    Colorado Probate Forms
    Power of Attorney Forms
    Will Forms, Will Supplies and Books
    Bankruptcy Forms

Real Estate Forms
    Sales Contracts
    Listing Contracts
    Leasing Contracts
    Lead Paint Disclosure Forms

Real Property Forms
    Leases and Rental Forms
    Lien Forms
    Eviction Forms
    Deeds of Trust
    Quitclaim Deeds
    Warranty Deeds

Automobile Forms
50A   Application for Title
50E   Application for Duplicate Title

50F   Verification of Vehicle Identification Number
910B   Bill of Sale, Motor Vehicle
910P   Power of Attorney, Motor Vehicle
911   Odometer Mileage Certificate
915   Chattel Mortgage, Motor Vehicle

Bills of Sale
Leases
Mobile Home Forms
Powers of Attorney

Complete Incorporation Kits
Corporation and Partnership Forms
Secretary of State Filing Forms
Stock Certificates

A complete catalog of books and over 1000 pre-printed legal forms is available from Bradford Publishing, 1743 Wazee Street, Denver, Colorado 80202, (303) 292-2500.

BIBLIOGRAPHY

1993 Local Government Financial Compendium, Colorado Division of Local Government, 1995

1994 Annual Report, Colorado Department of Revenue, 1994

1994-1995 Colorado Education and Library Directory, Colorado Department of Education, 1994

1994-95 Tuition and Fee Report, Colorado Commission on Higher Education, 1994

1994/95 Official Denver Visitors Guide, Denver Convention & Visitors Bureau, 1994

A Climbing Guide to Colorado's Fourteeners, Third Edition, Walter Borneman & Lyndon Lampert, Pruett Publishing, Boulder, CO, 1994

A Colorado History, Seventh Edition, Ubbelohde/Benson/Smith, Pruett Publishing, Boulder, CO, 1995

A Roadside Guide to Rocky Mountain National Park, B. Willard & S. Foster, Johnson Books, Boulder, Co, 1990

Absolutely Every Bed & Breakfast in Colorado, Third Edition, Toni Knapp, Travis Ilse Publishers, Niwot CO, 1994

Ancient Walls, Indian Ruins of the Southwest, Chuck Place, Fulcrum Publishing, Golden, CO, 1992

Best of Northern Colorado Hiking Trails, Jack O. Olofson, Outdoor Books & Maps, Denver, CO, 1995

Big Ideas for Small Service Businesses, Marilyn & Tom Ross, Communication Creativity, Buena Vista, CO, 1994

Bike With a View, Mark Dowling, Concepts in Writing, Denver, CO, 1994

Colorado: A History of the Centennial State, 3rd Edition, Abbott/Leonard/McComb, University Press of Colorado, Niwot, CO, 1994

Colorado's Fourteeners, From Hikes to Climbs, Gerry Roach, Fulcrum Publishing, Golden, CO, 1992

Colorado at a Glance, Department of Local Affairs, 1994

Colorado Business Start-Up Kit, Colorado Business Assistance Center,

Colorado Cabins, Cottages & Lodges, Hilton and Jenny Fitt-Peaster, Rocky Mountian Vacation Publishing, Boulder, CO, 1993

Colorado Cache Cookbook, The Junior League of Denver, Inc., C & C Publications, Denver, CO, 1978

Colorado Child Support Handbook, Charles P. Brackney, Bradford Publishing, Denver, CO, 1997

Colorado Cycling Guide, Jean and Hartley Alley, Pruett Publishing, Boulder, CO, 1990*Colorado Department of Regulatory Agencies,* Department of Regulatory Agencies, 1993

Colorado Driver's License Handbook, Colorado Department of Motor Vehicles, 1995

Colorado Fact Booklet, Department of Local Affairs

Colorado Factbook, Vol. V, No. 1, Pyramid Publications, 1994

Colorado Hut to Hut, Brian Litz, Westcliffe Publishers, Englewood, CO, 1992

Colorado Lakes & Reservoirs, Jack O. Olofson, Outdoor Books & Maps, Denver, CO, 1994

Colorado Occupational Employment Outlook 1994-1999, Colorado Department of Labor and Employment, 1994

Colorado Private Elementary and Secondary Schools, 1995-96, Margorie Hicks, Magnolia Street Press, 1995

Colorado Revised Statutes 1997, Vehicles and Traffic, Bradford Publishing, Denver, CO, 1997

Colorado RV Parks, Hilton and Jenny Fitt-Peaster, Rocky Mountian Vacation Publishing, Boulder, CO, 1995

Colorado Ski Country USA, Ski Guide 1997/98, Colorado Ski Country USA, 1997

Colorado, The State We're In, League of Women Voters of Colorado, 1995

Country Bound, Trade Your Business Suit Blues for Blue Jean Dreams, Marilyn and Tom Ross, Communication Creativity, Buena Vista, CO, 1992

Crème de Colorado Cookbook, The Junior League of Denver, Inc., C & C Publications, Denver, CO, 1987

Denver, Mining Camps to Metropolis, S. Leonard & T. Noel, University Press of CO, Niwot, CO, 1990

Discover the Good Life in Rural America, Bob Bone, Communication Creativity, Buena Vista, CO, 1994

Exploring Colorado State Parks, Martin Kleinsorge, University Press of CO, Niwot, CO, 1992

Friendly Divorce Guidebook for Colorado, 2nd Edition, M. Hauer, J.D. and S.W. Whicher, Bradford Publishing, Denver, CO, 1997

Get Out of Town, A Comprehensive Guide to Outdoor Activities in the Boulder Area, M. Harding & F. Snalam, All Points Publishing, Boulder, CO, 1994

Governor's Advocate Corps. A Citizen's Handbook to Colorado State Departments, Governor's Advocate Corps, 1995

Handbook of Rocky Mountain Plants, Ruth Ashton Nelson, Roberts Rhinehart Pubs, Niwot, CO, 1992

Landlord & Tenant Guide to Colorado Evictions, Victor M. Grimm, Esq., Bradford Publishing, Denver, CO, 1995

Leadville's Ice Palace, Darlene Weir, Ice Castle Productions, Lakewood, CO, 1994

Mountain Bike Rides in The Colorado Front Range, William L. Stoehr, Pruett Publishing, Boulder, CO, 1988

Moving With Children: A Parent's Guide to Moving with Children, T. Olkowski & L. Parker, Gylantic Publishing, Littleton, CO, 1993

Newcomers' Packet, Colorado Department of Education, 1995

Places Around The Bases, Diane Bakke and Jackie Davis, Westcliffe Publishers, Englewood, CO, 1995

Reports from the Colorado Economic and Demographic Information System, Colorado Division of Local Government, 1995

Roadside History of Colorado, James McTighe, Johnson Books, Boulder, CO, 1984

Rocky Mountain National Park Classic Hikes & Climbs, Gerry Roach, Fulcrum Publishing, Golden, CO, 1988

Rocky Mountain National Park Natural History Handbook, John C. Emerick, Roberts Rhinehart Pubs, Niwot, CO, 1995

Rocky Mountain Safari: A Wildlife Discovery Guide, Cathy and Gordon Illg, Roberts Rhinehart Pubs, Niwot, CO, 1994

Rocky Mountain Skiing, Claire Walter, Fulcrum Publishing, Golden, CO, 1992

Rocky Mountain Walks, Gary Ferguson, Fulcrum Publishing, Golden, CO, 1993

Rocky Mountain Wineries, L. Collison & B. Russell, Pruett Publishing, Boulder, CO, 1994

Seasonal Guide to The Natural Year, Ben Guterson, Fulcrum Publishing, Golden, CO, 1994

State Report Card 1994, Colorado Department of Education, 1994

Tales, Trails and Tommyknockers, Myriam Friggens, Johnson Books, Boulder, CO, 1979

The Archaeology of Colorado, E. Steve Cassells, Johnson Books, Boulder, CO, 1983

The Best of Colorado Biking Trails, Jack O. Olofson, Outdoor Books & Maps, Denver, CO, 1994

The Colorado General Assembly, John A. Straayer, University Press of Colorado, Niwot, CO, 1990

The Colorado Guide, 4th Edition, B. Caughey & D. Winstanley, Fulcrum Publishing, Golden, CO, 1997

The Colorado Trail, Randy Jacobs, Westcliffe Publishers, Englewood, CO, 1994

The Complete Colorado Campgroud Guide, Jack O. Olofson, Outdoor Books & Maps, Denver, CO, 1992

The Complete Guide to Colorado's Wilderness Areas, John Fielder & Mark Pearson, Westcliffe Publishers, Englewood, CO, 1994

The Entrepreneur's Resource for Success, The Colorado Small Business Development Center

The Four Corners Anasazi, Rose Houk, San Juan National Forest Association, 1994

The Guide to Metro Denver Public Schools, 1995-96 Edition, Margorie Hicks, Magnolia Street Press, 1995

The Mountain Bike Guide to Summit County, Colorado, Laura Rossetter, Sage Creek Press, Silverthorne, CO, 1993

The Mover's Guide, Targeted Marketing Solutions, Inc, 1993

The Practical Steps to Successful Business Ownership, U.S. Small Business Administration, 1995

The Xeriscape Flower Gardener for the Rocky Mountain Region, Jim Knopf, Johnson Books, Boulder, CO, 1991

US West Guide to Home Office Success, US West, 1995

Winning Big in Colorado Small Claims Court, Charles P. Brackney, Bradford Publishing, Denver, CO, 1996

INDEX

ORDER FORM

COLORADO: A Newcomer's and Resident's Manual

If you can't find this book in your favorite bookstore it can be ordered directly from the publisher for **$14.95** per copy plus tax and shipping & handling as indicated below:

If shipped within Colorado add the following sales tax:

Denver – 7.3%, Six County RTD – 3.8%, or State – 3%

Shipping: $4.50 for one book and $1.00 for each additional.

ORDERS ONLY Call:

Denver Area: 303-292-2500
National: 800-446-2831
FAX: 303-298-5014

(Call between 8 a.m. - 5 p.m. Mountain Time, FAX 24 hrs day)

Please send me _____ copies of **COLORADO: A Newcomer's Manual.**

_____ X $14.95   = _____
_____ X _____   = _____   Colorado resident tax per book
Shipping Charges   = _____
Total enclosed   = _____

_____ Check/money order enclosed

Charge my _____ VISA _____ MasterCard

Name _____ Phone (___) _____

Organization _____

Address _____

City/State/Zip _____

Card# _____ Exp _____

Signature _____

Bradford Publishing Company
1743 Wazee St
Denver, CO 80202